THE CLASSICS OF WESTERN SPIRITUALITY
A Library of the Great Spiritual Masters

President and Publisher
Kevin A. Lynch, C.S.P.

EDITORIAL BOARD

JOHN CASSIAN
CONFERENCES

TRANSLATION AND PREFACE BY
COLM LUIBHEID

INTRODUCTION BY
OWEN CHADWICK

PAULIST PRESS
NEW YORK • MAHWAH

Cover Art:
KEVIN F. NOVACK, C.S.P. is a free-lance artist who is a member of the pastoral team at
the St. Thomas More Newman Center, Ohio State University.

Library of Congress
Catalog Card Number: 85-80344

ISBN: 0-8091-2694-X (paper)

Published by Paulist Press
997 Macarthur Boulevard
Mahwah, New Jersey 07430

Printed and bound in the
United States of America

CONTENTS

Translator of this Volume

COLM LUIBHEID was born in 1936 in Dublin, Ireland. He received his B.A. and M.A. at University College, Dublin, and in 1961 he was awarded a Ph.D. in Classics at Princeton University.

Since 1961 he has been a member of the teaching staff at University College, Galway. He has translated the John Climacus and Pseudo-Dionysius volumes in this series.

Author of the Introduction

OWEN CHADWICK is the Regius Professor-Emeritus of Modern History, Cambridge University. His many distinguished works on the history of the Church include *Catholicism and History* (1978), *The Popes and European Revolution* (1981), *The Reformation* (1964), and *John Cassian* (2nd ed., 1968).

Foreword

John Cassian wrote twenty-four Conferences, but inescapable reasons of space demanded that only nine of these could be selected to appear in the present volume. Selection implies omission, and since omission is the parent of regret it is only to be expected that someone who cares for the achievement of Cassian will be moved to protest at what has been left out; but my hope is that the nine texts will at least give a sense both of what the man was trying to do and of the subtle range of his concerns.

The translation is based on the text prepared for *Sources Chrétiennes* by Dom E. Pichery.

I would like to express by gratitude to John Farina of the Paulist Press, who has proved to be a most helpful, kind, and encouraging editor. And in this, as in so many other enterprises, a special word of thanks goes, as ever, to my wife, Pat.

Colm Luibheid

PREFACE

Even by the standards of the twentieth century, John Cassian was a man who had journeyed far. Born in what is now Rumania, he traveled to the Holy Land, then throughout Egypt, thereafter to Constantinople and Rome, and by the time of his death, around the year 435, he had moved to the south of Gaul. His travels brought him into contact with men and women of numerous backgrounds and circumstances. It was an era in which for Christians a multiplicity of experiments had revealed the possibilities and indeed the limitations of monastic life. It was a time of passionate doctrinal involvement, with all the great questions concerning the relationships first within the Trinity and then between the human and divine natures of Christ coming under increasingly rigorous scrutiny. It was a season of councils, of controversy, and, for men such as John Chrysostom, of high tragedy. It was a period when the old and the new, the traditional and the innovative, surfaced in myriad and sometimes bewildering combinations.

Much of all this came to be reflected in the writings that bear the name of John Cassian, in the *Institutes* and in the *Conferences.*[1] True, he was a monk writing for monks. But in a more profound and timeless way he was a salient example of the problem faced by any Christian who is somehow obliged to reconcile an admired past with the needs and the burdens of his own day. His commitment was to the life of the spirit, and this within the perspectives of the later fourth century and the first third of the fifth century, but his reflections, his concerns, his

---

1. Among numerous recent discussions of the life and work of John Cassian the following should be specially noted: Owen Chadwick, *John Cassian*, 2d ed. (Cambridge, 1968); and Philip Rousseau, *Ascetics, Authority and the Church* (Oxford, 1978). The latter has a very useful bibliography.

efforts to speak words of weight and value mark him at once as a writer entitled to the respect of any age, including our own.

For in his way John Cassian is someone responding as he can to the old problem of what to make of the life one has. And that problem in its turn rests on the deeper one of making sense of whatever reality we have happened to meet. Is reality any deeper than the farthest reach of our own perceptive capacities? Is this—what we encounter—all of it? The old question refuses to go away. It nags and worries. It surfaces in a sick man amid the fading of things. It presses on the spectator of a dead child. Can this be all of it?

Of course not, says a teacher in the jauntier, more confident times when the well-turned proposition compels assent, when the expert marshaling of words seems enough to guarantee the existence of awesome and accessible domains of transcendence.

Indeed this is all there is, says an assertive poet, writing over four centuries before Cassian and claiming that craven, degenerate superstition has managed to poison the wells of living by means of its assertion that there exists another domain over and beyond our own, where the dead are brought to be forever tormented.[2]

More quietly, more humbly, others see in a chunky rock, in the recurring flavors of a type of wine the only tokens of reliable, dependable reality.[3] To believe in anything more is to take too great a chance.

But the willingness to take just such a chance is surely a mark of the Christian. A creature of the day and of circumstance, the Christian nevertheless claims, at times weakly, at times with powerful courage, that God does indeed exist, that there is somewhere an enduring and timeless domain where the burdened heart may aspire to find ease. The Christian has in him the capacity to hope for better things. After all, he has much to remember, words, for instance, such as the following: "You come out of the things below: I come from the things above. You come out of this world; I do not come out of this world. I have told you that you will die amid your own wrong turnings. For if you do not have trust in the fact that I am the One, you will die amid your own wrong turnings."[4]

John Cassian was one of those who, taking such words to heart,

---

2. Lucretius, *De Rerum Natura, passim,* but note especially Book 3, lines 37FF.
3. Thus cf. the poems "Sandstone Keepsake" and "Sloe Gin" in Seamus Heaney, *Station Island* (London and Boston, 1984).
4. Jn 8:23–24.

worked to move as far as possible from the "things below" and to embrace a style of living that would give access to "the things above." The example of the pioneers of monasticism was there to guide him and to encourage him. There was more. John Cassian did not believe that always and without exception the life of the monk was played out, as it were, in the anterooms of eternity, that a man had to await death before he could come directly into the presence of his Maker. Like Augustine, he was convinced that even amid the trappings of earthliness there could occur, did occur, direct one-to-one encounters with God.[5]

> To gaze with utterly purified eyes on the divinity is possible—but only to those who rise above lowly and earthly works and thoughts and who retreat with Him into the high mountain of solitude. When they are freed from the tumult of worldly ideas and passions, when they are liberated from the confused melee of all the vices, when they have reached the sublime heights of utterly pure faith and of preeminent virtue, the divinity makes known to them the glory of Christ's face and reveals the sight of its splendors to those worthy to look upon it with the clarified eye of the spirit.[6]

Here indeed was the goal. This was what the monastic effort was all about. The ruthless, self-disciplined introspection, the fasting, the vigils, the meditations on Scripture, the urge to pray without ceasing— these were the shaping ingredients of a dynamism whose longed-for and promised outcome was the direct encounter with God, briefly within time and forever beyond the writ of mortality.

Hence the consuming need to get the life-style right. Hence the passionate analysis—reflected in Cassian's writings—of all the complex details of spirituality. Which was the most productive route for a man or woman to take? The eremitic? The cenobitic? A way reflecting the best of each? And who would decide? For the endless debate and discussion did not and could not take place in a vacuum.

By the time Cassian came to write his books, he had moved to Gaul, where he came face to face with the fact that the cenobitic life was becoming more common than the eremitic route, which had been taken by those first great figures of the Egyptian movement whom he so ardently venerated—hence an uncertainty that some modern schol-

---

5. For a celebrated attempt to express the nature of such a one-to-one encounter, cf. Augustine, *Confessions* 9.10.25.

6. *Conferences* 10.6.

ars have claimed to detect in his work. The problem essentially is whether in his view a spiritual life passed in isolation is superior to one lived in community. At times it looks as if Cassian considers the solitary, eremitic way to represent a higher and superior activity.[7] Actually he distinguishes in the *Conferences* between a life-style and a disposition of spirit, between milieu and mind. It is a distinction that corresponds to the immediate aim of the monk—*puritas cordis*, "cleanness of heart"—and his ultimate objective of reaching the kingdom of God.[8] Each goal has to be attained, though with the former required to precede the latter. Each goal demands the achievement of certain practical steps, which the accumulated experiences of the Egyptian desert had sought to identify in as precise a form as possible. Whether one is an anchorite or a cenobite it is, at the end, an individual, not an entire community, who wins through to the kingdom. And because this is so and because Cassian was caught between, on the one hand, his deep admiration of the great Egyptian fathers and, on the other, his task of providing guidance for the increasing numbers who sought to live communally as monks and nuns, there is nothing too surprising in the fact that sometimes, hankering back to the giants of the past, he seems to set a higher value on the solitary life while at other times he thinks of the cenobitic and the eremitic ways as stages or aspects of the life of the individual.

In any case the situation he encountered in Gaul presented him with the classic problem of having to accommodate a revered tradition to human needs for which that tradition had made inadequate provision. The essence of his difficulty can be stated simply enough. There was on one side the shining example of those great and rare men who had completely withdrawn from Egyptian society and who had manifestly attained the summits of personal holiness. But on the other side there was the bitter truth of human frailty, which ensured that most of those embarking on a religious life would require the continuous guidance not of their own increasingly enlightened consciences but rather of concerned yet impartial mentors. Indeed if there is one figure who evokes the constant denunciations of Cassian, it is the monk who takes himself for a teacher. The history of the desert, as Cassian tirelessly proclaims, was filled with examples of men who would listen to none but themselves and whose lives had moved inexorably into spiritual disaster.

---

7. *Conferences* First Preface, 4.
8. *Conferences* 1, *passim*, but especially section 4.

PREFACE

This high road to catastrophe was taken especially by those un-tutored and undirected men in whom a sense of proportion, the capacity for introspection, and a close understanding of the processes of self-delusion had faltered or vanished. As a terrible, paradigmatic example, Cassian relates the story of Hero,[9] a man who lived a solitary and penitential life for over half a century. He fasted strictly, even amid the jubilation of Easter Sunday. He refused all contact with fellow ascetics. He thrust away any occasion where the advice, the encouragement, and the insights of others might have been available to him. Year after year he followed his lonely way until, in a mood of subtle and potent hubris, he became convinced at last that the unrelieved rigor of his self-imposed burdens had not only made him spiritually perfect but had even earned him a dispensation from the laws of nature and of earthliness. And to prove the truth of his conviction he leapt off the edge of a rocky pit. He was dead two days later.[10]

It is a story set down with horror by Cassian, and the purpose of the telling comes as part of the repeated insistence on the need of all but the very few to be open to the guidance and the directives and the insights of others. For without such guidance the monk runs the continuous risk of losing whatever feeling he has for the way things are.

Hence the lengthy reflections embodied in the *Conferences*. It is not dry and finicky detail that really concerns John Cassian. If he deals at length with topics ranging from the pitfalls risked by the soul to the question of how much solid food a monk should consume every day, the reason lies in his heartfelt awareness of the sheer difficulty that may beset the journey to the kingdom of God. If his memory is continually haunted by the great solitary heroes of the Egyptian desert, his practical unillusioned intellect knows that any advice he proffers now, in the closing years of his own pilgrimage, must be grounded in a deep feeling for the extent to which Christian men and women need each other's help and guidance. This is one reason why the *Conferences* can be taken to be not only a source of invaluable historical material and an authoritative view of early monasticism but also a sort of parable, an extended metaphor of the complexity awaiting anyone who seeks to pursue the life of the spirit.

---

9. *Conferences* 2.5.

10. An eerily similar situation is described in the section on Mount Athos in the novel *Report to Greco* by Nikos Kazantzakis. The pilgrim sees on the shore of an inlet the bones of anchorites who, convinced that they had become angels, had leapt from their cells in the cliff face.

Owen Chadwick

INTRODUCTION

To the inhabitants of the Mediterranean world during the later fourth century A.D., the world seemed to be in decline. The frontiers were under threat, the countryside insecure, the taxation system unjust, government not respected. The Roman Empire was falling to pieces and no one could conceive what other kind of world there could be. The circumstances of daily life forced men and women to ask where they could find not only physical safety but hope in circumstances that looked so menacing. And in the East of the empire, in Egypt and Syria, they found a movement that began to draw recruits, and was soon to be one of the main social forces within the eastern provinces of the empire: the monks and nuns and hermits. But it was not only in the East. Saint Augustine wrote a famous book to persuade that secular Rome with its prosperity was not a necessary sign of God's favor or God's will, and that men and women were to seek another kingdom more lasting, the kingdom of God.

John Cassian (born about 365, died about 435) was a contemporary of Saint Augustine in western Europe. He founded a house for monks in Marseilles and another house for nuns. He also had much influence over various hermits or hermit communities that populated the islands or the woods of Provence.

Unlike Saint Augustine, he had long experience of the East. He knew both Greek and Latin, probably Latin more intimately than Greek, for he wrote an excellent Latin style and probably came from one of the Latin-speaking communities of what is now Romania. Then he spent time as a young monk in a monastery at Bethlehem near the cave of the Nativity, and later sat for several years at the feet of the famous leaders of the movement in Egypt. He sat humbly at the feet of the great masters of Egyptian spirituality, but not so humbly that he did not retain a critical and analytical mind. We know of this process

1

of criticism and analysis only from his written work, later by a quarter of a century. But the nature of the written work proves that even while he was in Egypt he began to sift and weigh the various ideals of the monastic life that he found presented to him by his masters. Probably the process of sifting was at first half-conscious. But he meditated on it over the years, dismissed some suggestions and developed others, revered Egypt and its spirituality but certainly not everything he found there, and started to create out of the diversity of Egyptian ideas a coherent scheme of spirituality, a scheme that was still Egyptian—still permeated through and through with the Egyptian ethos and atmosphere—and yet was a harmony in its main lines. This is not to say that he did not sometimes contradict himself. Sometimes he confused the reader and confuses him to this day.

He wrote *Institutes*, a book for beginners in the monastic life or for those planning to found monasteries; then the *Conferences*, a study of the Egyptian ideal of the monk, his greatest and most influential book; and finally a work on the incarnation to counter the doctrines attributed to Nestorius the Patriarch of Constantinople. He was still alive about A.D. 432 but we do not hear of him thereafter.

Cassian never lost the feeling of humility, or of debt to his masters. The teaching of the Egyptians was like an ocean that has no visible horizon and that no single mind can hope to plumb or encompass. He felt that in venturing out into this ocean with his sounding lead, his private boat was very small. Sometimes he thought of this body of thought not as an ocean but as a deep mine. Occasionally he wondered whether the ideal is so high that it must always remain an ideal to pursue rather than a way of life to be followed successfully. It might have been expected that this sense of reverence and gratitude would have made him uncritical, like a widow writing an obituary notice of a beloved husband. But this is one of the most interesting features of Cassian's mind. Despite the reverence and gratitude, it is a critical mind. Despite the sense of the loftiness of the moral ideal, is a main conviction that this ideal can indeed be practiced—with certain things wisely changed, according to the temperature or the food supply or the physical environment—in the circumstances of western Europe. The disciple needs common sense, moderation (*discretion* as Cassian praised the virtue), perseverance, patience, and willingness to endure; but then the soul will find that the way of life to God, so far from being inaccessible to weak men and women, is strengthening and happy.

A part of this feeling of the unplumbed depths of the realm of moral life and spirituality that is to be investigated is the conviction of *reserve*, as a later age would have called it though Cassian did not. No one can understand these matters by a pure act of the intellect. It needs moral growth, or at least a desire for moral growth, to understand the way of moral growth. Therefore a master of the spiritual life cannot hope to do any good by casting his insights at people who are not prepared to receive them. Cassian even had a feeling that if a master or director of souls tried to put what he knew in front of people not capable of understanding what he was talking about, God could make that master inarticulate and incapable of coherent explanation, so that the truth should not be corrupted or misunderstood. At base this quest is not an intellectual one, though the intelligence must guide. He is also conscious that truth is not won in a moment. It is given in meditation or digestion or rumination. You read, for example, a piece of Scripture; you learn it with the head; you see what it means, externally; you say prayers about it; and then one night a few nights later you wake up and realize that it has a very profound meaning for you, of which you had not been conscious in your waking hours. It is a sudden realization, as though a heavy sleeper is woken by a light (*Conference* 14.10). This feeling is very strong in Cassian. The truths with which he wishes to deal are never shallow. They are, so to speak, apprehended by being, that is, by the best and most profound soul of humanity, which rather grows into apprehensions than sees them instantly, even though the final conviction comes with the force of a sudden light.

No one who reads Cassian for long can doubt that this is a prayerful and pious mind indeed, but must see that it has other qualities. It is a powerful mind, integrated and constructive. This is one of the leading Fathers of the ancient Church, though too long unrecognized as such except by Benedictine monks.

Among the various theories put forward in Egypt was that of an intellectual school that based itself in part on the tradition of Greek thought that went back to Plato. The soul seeks the ultimate unity or oneness of the world, which is conceived variously as a spiritual or an intellectual entity. The soul seeks this One, which is permanence, unity, foundation of the universe, Being beyond all being, ultimate Mind. Its method of seeking is to strip itself of all distractions that turn the attention to anything lower in the scale of value, that is, everything not the One. Some of these distractions are mere distractions of the mind, as when a child's attention is distracted by a toy in a shop window. But other distractions are moral, that is, the instincts of fallen humanity turn the mind to a scale of values far lower—to food, or to sex, or to gain in property, or to eminent position, or to respect by one's fellows and colleagues, or to mere comfort, or, lastly, to mere boredom with the quest after the things of the spirit.

This tradition of thought was the school of a Greek minority among the monks of Egypt. It was known as Origenist, because Origen of Alexandria was the Christian thinker who interpreted Plato's thought into a Christian language and a Christian moral context. Its leading man in Egypt, while Cassian resided there, was Evagrius of Pontus. We possess many of the works of Evagrius. Therefore we can see that in broad lines Cassian's work followed the system of spirituality the Origenist Evagrius suggested. It laid stress on the union of mind with ultimate Mind by contemplation. This purity of contemplation was achieved through passionlessness, because passion of every sort distracts the soul. Therefore it is achieved through a moral growth that depends on self-discipline and self-denial. Though this Origenist system was mystical—one to One, mind to Mind by immediate apprehension—it had also the mental aspect, the philosophical aspect, descended from Plato himself. It thought almost as much of mental processes as of moral growth.

Evagrius of Pontus talked much of pure prayer. He gave it a philosophical slant. He talked of knowing God as Three-in-One. The God to which he aspired was rather like Plato's One or Essence. But he was a systematizer. He already started to bring order into the various monkish ideas of prayer and the moral life, which were diverse among the various cells and communities of the Egypt and Syria of the fourth century. His philosophical language made him suspect to many of his contemporaries—mostly to those who could not understand him, but also to some who could. When Cassian wanted to mention him, he did not think it prudent to mention his name. But Evagrius was a thinker, and for all his unusual language a very Christian thinker. All over the East they might suspect his name, but they struggled to keep his works in their libraries, cautiously, under the name of other authors. They wanted to be able to profit from his ideas.

Cassian inherited this Origenist system. Perhaps he even had to flee from Egypt when the Origenists were driven out in a political storm in A.D. 399. Nevertheless he sat lightly to the Origenist ideas. His phrase for passionlessness is "purity of heart," a positive phrase destined to be far more satisfactory in the history of Christian spirituality,

4

and having the merit of being a phrase from the gospel. But in certain other ways his way of putting things was not a mere translation of an Origenist system. For all his long and at times involved Latin paragraphs, he liked to be simpler. He had a strong desire for the practical. He never lost sight of the moral end, as distinct from the mental end. Occasionally he hinted at a doubt of too much philosophy when it is applied to these moral matters. He allows the phrase "Christian philosophy" as a way of describing the spirituality of the monks. But he did not like the quiet peace of the hermitage to be troubled by an excess of philosophical thinking. That is a way of distracting the mind even if it does not do worse, for example, to push the mind toward error in religion or to make the mind feel proud of its cleverness.

The intention of the twenty-four Conferences (attributed to fifteen Egyptian Fathers) was to show the Egyptian way of life to the monks of Provence; perhaps also, though far less certainly, to the nuns of Provence. The Egyptian way, or rather ways, of life had an ordered intention. Cassian needed to make his version of it more ordered than the original. You aim to know God. You must go into a community. Then you will live with others who have the same intention and the same aspiration. Over years in that community you must learn to practice prayer, and the moral life that is necessary to prayer—continence, poverty, obedience. Then, when you are set in your ways of prayer and habits of conduct, you may pass further out into solitude away from the habitations of man. You may occupy a hermitage. There the silence and the remoteness allow you to listen more continuously to the Word of God and to come into His presence. But this hermitage must not be withdrawn totally. For withdrawal into total solitude was found to lead to moral collapse, mental eccentricity, even to madness. The hermit was one of a company of hermits, who lived under a common discipline with a superior; who said their allotted psalms, each in his cell, at common times each day; who met on Sundays at least, sometimes on Saturdays as well, for common worship and a common meal and a discussion of the spiritual life.

Egypt, or Cassian's version of Egypt, condemned (1) anyone who tried to be a hermit without first being trained in a community, (2) anyone who tried to be a hermit in such total withdrawal that he could not even receive the sacrament on feast days of the Church, (3) anyone who was a solitary in the sense of having no body of rules that he needed to try to keep, and (4) anyone who made up rules for himself that were not derived from the generally accepted rules, believed to stem from the experience of earlier fathers and their wise judgment. The word *sarabite* was used to describe persons in these categories.

Therefore Cassian's work had two intentions, and the two intentions were mixed as ideas occurred to him. He wanted to point toward the highest modes of prayer, and that meant keeping in his eye the solitary in his hermitage. And he wanted to show the community of monks how to be a good and harmonious community. The intentions were mixed because the two ways of life were divided by no clear line. The hermit in his loose hermit congregation also needed the virtues of a community. Some monks in a community with a rigidly common life, where every hour of the day was mapped into work or worship or food or sleep, could aspire toward modes of contemplation and unceasing prayer as high as the hermit in his solitude. Cassian's books on how to pray well are as useful to the monk or the nun as to the hermit. His books on how to live well in society are almost as useful to the hermit as to the monk or to the nun.

For example: Conferences 16 and 17 have nothing to do with prayer—at first sight hardly anything to do with the spiritual life. But they deal in awkward questions for any community dedicated to virtue. Conference 17 is the problem of the "white lie." Truth is virtue; everyone ought to speak the truth all the time. Yet no community can exist as a community if all its members speak the truth all the time. To avert quarrels, truth must be compromised. Mere courtesy at times demands the silence that may leave the wrong impression and is intended to leave the wrong impression. Humility may demand the wrong answer to a question whether you have done a great deal, perhaps whether you have worked a miracle. Brotherly love may demand the wrong answer to a question when the true answer would be calamitous for another brother's reputation and so hurt the community as well as its individual member. Cassian's monastery worried over the problem. Was absolute truth so absolute that it took precedence over all other forms of charity? Cassian laid it down that it is very bad to say what is untrue. Nevertheless it is sometimes the least of evils to say or imply what is not true. A lie is like hellebore. It is poison to the healthy, a medicine only to a patient at death's door. "If speaking the truth causes grievous crisis, we cannot but resort in desperation to what is not true; but only in such a way that our conscience bites us as we do it" (*Conference* 17.17). Though unchallengeable in reason, this teaching was later a ground for one of the criticisms lodged against Cassian as an unsound teacher.

INTRODUCTION

Conference 16 touched a still more important aspect of community life: friendship. Later guides were not fond of the idea that one monk should have a special friendship with another monk. They were afraid of cliques inside the monastery, or of monks feeling an out-group excluded from the in-group, or of a loyalty that was not a loyalty to the whole house. Charity encompasses all in its embrace, all alike.

Cassian was not of this opinion. Personal friendships are inevitable and natural. They will not last if they rest on superficial resemblances of character or a temporary endeavor in a common task. They will last only if they rest on common moral qualities. If they so rest, they are infinitely precious, *amicitiae pretiosissimae*. Cassian had experience on which he could draw. He studied in the Bethlehem monastery with his older friend Germanus. With Germanus he sat at the feet of the holy men of Egypt. He owed, or felt that he owed, a lasting debt to a close personal friendship with Germanus, and this friendship rested on a common moral aim.

Yet a community of men may easily quarrel, and a monastery is not exempt. People who have sacrificed their all to join may still quarrel over the use of a pen. More lastingly, they may quarrel over a difference of opinion about principle or policy. Everyone must remember that the mind is not infallible, and that the cleverer or more learned person does not always see so straight as the slower and less informed. Then, ways of healing a quarrel can bring new quarrels. Someone hits you on the cheek. You turn the other cheek ostentatiously, and plead the authority of the Lord—but the Lord's authority is always for forgiveness and healing. Someone offends you and you go away, pointedly, to say your prayers, or go away and fast pointedly and outrageously—and the Lord's authority is for settling the quarrel directly. Someone offends and your face is studiedly impassive, far more irritating than an angry reply. False patience is worse than retort.

No one will mistake the common sense, and indeed the sensibility. Cassian might not always be right. But he was an ethical guide of rare quality, especially for that date and age and place. He can be long, and repetitive. On occasion he can be boring. He spends more time than is reasonable on sexuality. Mostly he does not bore. Ethical behavior is never the most lively of subjects. Sometimes Cassian would have done well to be more laconic. But often he fascinates on subjects not naturally fascinating. He knew a lot. He knew a lot about the ancient world. He knew of the sexual experience of eunuchs and of boys before puberty—probably this knowledge came from pastoral care in the city of Con-

7

stantinople, where for a few years he was a cleric. Despite the belief in the necessity of celibacy for the monks, he had no suspicion of coitus; it is a natural part of the life of the laity, a necessity of humankind.

Cassian had no "double standard" of ethics. That is, he nowhere suggested that the layperson in the world was a being of a moral status inferior to that of the monk. At that date the monk was rarely in holy orders. The world of that falling generation might look up to the monks as those who responded to a higher moral demand. Cassian and his contemporaries said or implied that it was easier to find God, or easier to seek God, in retirement from the world. But good men and women in civil society have their place. The Church is one but its members have various vocations, and each individual has different gifts and diverse aptitudes. "There are plenty of roads to God," wrote Cassian (*Conference* 14.6). Let every person try to pursue the chosen profession faithfully and there is a chance of perfection.

Circulating among the stories of the Egyptian desert were several anecdotes to prove the point. Cassian took one story and adapted it.

A farm laborer who passed in his carriage of harvest cured a lunatic of a demon whom the holy abba John was not able to exorcise. John was astounded that a man dressed in workers' clothes could do what he could not, and began to inquire. He found that the laborer was married; that before his day's work, and after it, he stepped into a church to thank God for his daily bread; that he always gave God a tithe of his produce; and that he took care not to allow his cattle to damage his neighbor's field. John could hardly think that these virtues were extraordinary enough to warrant such extraordinary power. He decided that a virtue still hidden must exist. Finally he discovered that the laborer had intended to be a monk, but the authority of his parents persuaded him to marry, and he had treated his wife as a sister without anyone else knowing.

The story illustrated the importance of the self-sacrifice of a continent man. But it also illustrated the sanctity of the laborer working within the world. It is evident that though the laborer was in the world, the virtue he practiced was monastic.

From its earliest moments, the monastic movement was conscious that its way of life was a way of "perfection." This phrase implied a criticism of the way of life of those in secular business. This criticism was more implied than explicit; for a constant theme was the contrast between the holy laborer in this world and the bad monk in his cloister.

INTRODUCTION

"The soul in this world who is full of gentleness is worth more than a monk full of passion and anger," Evagrius had written; or again, "The person in this world who ministers to the sick is worth more than the hermit who has no care for his neighbor" (*Sentences*, nos. 34 and 78). Abba Silvanus in Egypt said flatly, "In the last judgment many monks will go to heaven and many seculars will go to paradise" (*Vitae Patrum* 5, 3, 15).

Many such anecdotes from the desert nevertheless left monasticism secure in its preeminence as a way to perfection. The seculars who are holier than the monks are always monks in their hearts. The seculars are rare and exceptional, the monks are normal.

In Cassian's generation many of the laity repudiated the doctrine that the monk's life is of superior moral quality. But within the movement everyone accepted that in the gospel Christ preached a perfection and that the way of the monks either is, or is nearest to, that way. Cassian shared this conviction. His history of the primitive Church thought that those early times were fervent; and the monks tried to maintain that primitive fervor into a generation where so many of the lukewarm infected the Church. But he more than once accepted that all good professions of life are God-given and in them any man or woman might be saved, and therefore might approach "perfection."

But is this perfection ever perfect in this life? He thinks not. First, some kinds of perfection are not compatible with other kinds of perfection. It is a perfection of the gospel to take no thought for the morrow. To fulfill this doctrine perfectly is possible only for the monk in a community. The secular, or the hermit, needs to think about the next meal. Peace of heart is perfection. But this is possible only for the solitary. No one therefore can be perfect in all ways of life. Perfection is "partial perfection"; Cassian used the Greek word *merike*, a "part thing," to describe it. There is not one state of perfection but several states, according as a particular way of life makes it possible. This enables Cassian to see perfection as possible for those in the world. Normally Cassian thought of the absence of anxiety as a sign of virtue. But he could recognize, in another and ministerial way of life, that anxiety in the care of all the churches was a way of perfection (*Conference* 23.2).

In this book of translations appears Conference 11, with the title "On Perfection." It is a beautiful and moving Conference on the motive for right conduct; how the motive must rise, from acts out of fear of punishment or of hell, or out of acts performed in hope of gain or of heaven, to acts done because the act is right, and right is right; as a son starts obeying his father out of discipline and ends by obeying his father out of love.

And in the course of that exposition we read (12): "It was not at all possible to propose to all together the same crown of perfection, since everyone does not have the same virtue, the same disposition of will, or the same zeal. Hence the Word of God lays down the *different degrees and the different measures of perfection.*" He can even say that we "mount" from one kind, or one rung in the ladder, of perfection to another. The Savior says that in His Father's house are many mansions.

The idea of perfection rested on a difficult series of texts. In the mood of the fourth century, with its social division between clergy and laity, and its deeper social division between secular and monk, any thinker could easily go astray, in the sense of depriving ordinary men and women of any chance of perfection. Cassian's stature rested in part on his attitudes here. His mind never for an instant associated perfection with outward acts, observation of rules, and so on. The only perfection that mattered was inward, a state of the soul. Adalbert de Vogüé called Cassian "the grand theorist of the idea of perfection" (in *Dizionario di Istituti di Perfezione* 6 (1980): 1454). The hermit or the monk, the cleric or the layman or laywoman, the end of their perfection is in all cases charity, Saint Paul's charity of 1 Corinthians 13. It is as though perfection were full of movement, a direction toward, a loving aspiration after God, which cannot be precisely defined in terms of a state at any separated moment, but is a loving response to the love of God.

The twenty-third Conference, not translated in this volume, is odd despite some rare passages of high prose. The latest Conferences among the twenty-four are marked by a new tone, suggesting that at least they are very late work. There may have been tampering with the text by another hand or hands after Cassian's death. But this Conference is Cassianic in tone and theme. Part of the oddity arises simply from the subject, the need to confute people who argued that a saint can be sinless in this life. For Cassian these relative perfections are not at all the same as sinlessness. Abba Theonas took Saint Paul's text "I do not the good that I would" and argued that it must apply to saints like Saint Paul and not to sinners, that is, it applies to the "perfect." Since perfection consists in contemplation, a loving attention to God, and since the mortal creature is always bound to fail in the light of the Creator's glory, no absolute perfection can exist in this world for anyone. The vision of God is given from time to time. No one here can make it permanent.

INTRODUCTION

So Cassian sang one of his last and fairest songs, on the true penitence of the saint.

I

The core of Cassian's book, and the core of his spirituality, lies in the two Conferences on Prayer (9 and 10) and the one after them (11) on perfection.

The end of the monk is continual prayer. For this he went into solitude. This is the purpose of his cell. The aim is the constant direction of the mind toward God, undistracted by thoughts or by passions. Therefore the quest for purity of heart is necessary to a right prayer. The possession of purity of heart is necessary to perfect prayer. The worst obstacle to prayer is sin. The next is worry or anxiety about the material circumstances of life—sex, food, money, irritations with colleagues, levity. The next obstacle is pride; humility is an opening of the heart. The next obstacle is what we carry in the mind into our time of prayer. The mind cannot stop thinking about what just happened or what happened yesterday. Into a moment of prayer comes laughter at a joke of the previous hour. Therefore the time before set times of prayer must also be prayerful. The man who is not prayerful as he goes about his daily life will be less prayerful when he gets on his knees. And no one can be prayerful during his daily life unless he is in the quest for purity of heart. To reach toward heights of prayer, the soul needs an underlying tranquility during the times when it is not praying formally.

The next point is that every individual prays in a different way. And every individual may pray in different ways at different moments. No one will pray the same when driven by violent temptation as when in a marvelous feeling of unity with God. Ups and downs, hither and thither. Health, or temperament, or suggestion from outside—every sort of circumstance can affect the nature or form of the prayer. What is certain is that, within these differences of mood or form, prayer will contain certain attitudes or aspirations.

It will contain resolution, even if that is wordless—a wish to be something, even a vow to be something.

It will contain penitence.

It will contain intercession, for you cannot pray without remembering need in other people, whether you remember only the people within your affections or whether you reach outward toward the world and its peace, its kings and its governments.

INTRODUCTION

It will contain thankfulness. To pray is to be in the presence of God. To be in the presence of God is to be aware, wordlessly or not, of His goodness to humanity.

No individual will at any one moment combine penitence and resolution and intercession and gratitude. Different times, different content of prayer. But no one will pray without these four elements appearing, each of them often.

And yet moments can come when all four of these constituents seem to be present—almost, one may say, at a flash. The soul is then like a flame of fire leaping outward in every direction; and it seems not so much to be praying as to be a vehicle through which the Holy Spirit of God is praying. In this highest state of prayer, the diversities are swallowed up into a unity that is the direct and loving confrontation of the soul with its God. This confrontation Cassian describes variously. It is vision. It is contemplation. It is "familiar" like a son with his father. It has a sense of God as sovereign. It has a trust in providence. It has a strong hope in forgiveness. It is lambent, like a tongue of flame. It is not articulate, that is, it is a wordless prayer, and a prayer conscious of the inadequate nature of words. But it may issue in a cry of the heart that can be heard. Or it might issue in tears.

These are moments that come, not a state. They may spring suddenly out of the verse of a psalm as the psalter is recited. Sometimes it is the beauty of a reader that sparks the flame. Sometimes the words of a sermon by a holy man; sometimes a death; sometimes the sudden conviction of sin.

This *wordlessness* excludes the thought of the Bible or its texts. The confrontation of the soul with God is so immediate that words are out of place and insufficient. This applies to biblical words as to any other words. But in Cassian's view all this is undergirded by scriptural texts. The prayerful soul needs feeding. The best food is reading the Bible and meditating on the Bible. "Souls that have made progress toward God . . . never stop nourishing themselves with this food" (*Conference* 10.11). For Cassian all the Bible, Old Testament or Apocrypha or New Testament, was this nourishment. It was all "gospel." At one point, when he called one of the lesser texts of the Old Testament "gospel," more than one copyist could not bear the "error" and corrected it as he copied (see *Conference* 1.19). Cassian was well aware that Israelite morality was imperfect; that the years of the Old Testament were a time of ignorance; and that today we have a better moral understanding (because the "light of the gospel shines so bright," *evangelio coruscante* [*Con-*

ference 17.18]). But all was God's Word. All was nourishment to the soul.

For purposes of prayer, the special book of the Bible was the psalter. For it was written as a book of prayers. It is full of aspiration, penitence, resolution. "When souls in prayer say the psalms, they say them not as though they were some prophet's poetry, but as though they made them up for themselves" (*Conference* 10.11). The psalmist's prayer becomes the Christian soul's own prayer. The words are applied personally. There is a feeling of assurance that the words apply and are meant to apply to the self. The mind feels as though the idea came out of it fresh and original, and was not taken over from anyone else's idea. The meaning is clear to the soul without analysis of the grammar. For such a soul, Scripture is a limpid stream of refreshment that ceaselessly renews the heart and brings the mind before its Maker.

Cassian made a discovery: that through continual repetition an evocative verse usually remains evocative. Centuries later a Russian pilgrim wrote a book of devotion that became famous as *The Way of a Pilgrim* (ed. R. M. French, 1930). The pilgrim described how at every step of his way, and when he was at the roadside, and when he rested at night, he would say to himself, over and over again, the versicle *Lord Jesus Christ have mercy upon me*. At first he found it difficult to keep up, but slowly it became easier and finally the versicle became a steady rhythm, accompanying all that he did. This was his means to a continual recollection. In the eastern churches this formula of repetition had a tradition centuries old. The ideas of prayer were known as *hesychast*, the ideas of the men of quiet. The same idea, or a similar one, was to appear in the West with the rosary, where someone repeats the same sequence of prayers at each sequence of beads. The first rosaries were not known for some eight centuries after Cassian's death.

In the history of Christian devotion, Cassian was the first to articulate this practice fully. Naturally, he chose a verse from the psalms, "Come to my help, O God; Lord, hurry to my rescue (Ps 69.2). The long section of chapter 10 of the tenth Conference is one of the most beautiful passages of all Christian writing during more than a thousand years of religious devotion. The verse, he says, has penitence. It is a cry to God for protection. It is watchfulness against temptation. It is trust in God's care. Against the demons he thinks it an impregnable fortress. It is proven armor. No one who uses it can despair. In every sort of temptation, you should run to it. In the moments of fruition go to it likewise. "I feel that my spirit has once more found a sense of direction, that my thinking has grown purposeful, that because of a visit of the Holy Spirit my heart is unspeakably glad and my mind ecstatic. Here is a great overflow of spiritual thoughts, thanks to a sudden illumination and to the coming of the Savior. The holiest ideas, hitherto concealed from me, have been revealed to me"—if the moment of fruition is to be longer than a moment, go to this verse. ". . . I have been made whole by the consolation of the Lord, . . . I have been encouraged by His coming, . . . I feel myself guarded by countless thousands of angels, . . . I have the daring to seek out and call to battle those whom I once feared more than death"—then fly to this verse that the moment be longer than a moment. "It should precede all your thoughts as you keep vigil. It should take you over as you rise from your bed and go to kneel. After this it should accompany you in all your works and deeds. It should be at your side at all times . . . you will think upon it 'as you sit at home or walk along your way' (Dt 6:7), as you sleep or when you get up"—write it "in the inner sanctum of your heart."

It will be seen that this little religious text is not the highest moment of prayer, for that moment is wordless. The text is a constant inciter, provoker, reminder toward the highest experience of prayer.

The centuries did not quite bear out the trust Cassian put in this practice of repetition. The Greek directors of souls grew circumspect. They saw that some people found it monotonous, and at last a boring obstacle to real prayer, a trap instead of an open door. In one monastery of Mount Athos, the abbot would allow only a very select group to practice this way of prayer. Cassian had not the same doubt, or the length of experience. Yet he admitted that he personally could not be content with a single unvarying verse. His mind craved variety. He needed the whole body of Scripture, and would let it speak to him or in him as he found it. He has a half implication that the educated need more variety than the uneducated. But he wanted to show that illiterate souls are as capable of God's highest way as the literate. They need only to know one verse of the psalter.

To gain this scriptural undergirding of the life of prayer, Cassian taught that it is good to memorize passages of Scripture. Then the texts will recur to the mind, again and again. They will recur at times when the soul can hardly think about them because occupied with business, or under temptation. And at other times they will recur—most fruitfully perhaps during the silent hours of the night—and then they will be understood and will feel like an illumination.

Just as Cassian had a view of the holy life as an illimitable depth into which the soul penetrates little by little, so he had a sense of the Bible as a book with obvious meanings, but behind the literal sense a series of deeper truths, which will be more and more understood by the soul as it advances morally. "As we strive with constant repetition to commit these readings to memory, we have not the time to understand them because our minds have been occupied. But later when we are free from the attractions of all that we do and see and, especially, when we are quietly meditating during the hours of darkness, we think them over and we understand them more clearly" (*Conference* 14.10).

As was his way, Cassian was more moderate than his masters in all this doctrine of prayer. Evagrius was insistent that pure prayer must be without any images or ideas, even ideas of God. For an idea is a thought *about*, and pure prayer is immediacy and cannot be *about*. At base Cassian agreed with this. But Evagrius spent time putting it into striking epigrams:

> Prayer is the suppression of every concept.
> Blessed is the mind which has acquired a total absence of
> form at the moment of prayer.
> If a vision of God or Christ or the angels comes at the
> moment of prayer, it can only be a device of the devil;
> especially the devil of vanity, who is trying to ruin pure
> prayer.

Such utterances were more striking than helpful. Cassian agreed with the doctrine but put it plainly, modestly, unpretentiously. He did not labor it.

Or again: Evagrius had poetic words on the light the soul will see as it finds God. This meditation on light, or poetry about light, or love of light as the essence of God, was to be of high importance in the Eastern tradition. Eventually it produced a magnificent light-mysticism, but it was not without its dangers. You do not see things lit by the light. You see light itself. Cassian told of the light. It is flame. It is illumination. It is darting. It is unearthly. But he lays no stress on its nature.

Into the context of unceasing prayer came the daily worship of the soul at set times. The Bible gave the Christians a problem, or, rather, a contradiction fertile of much good in the life of the spirit. It suggested prayer "seven times a day." It also said "Pray without ceasing." How did prayer at set times fit into continuous prayer?

To pray seven times, even eight, was fulfilled in monasteries by the structure of the daily offices, every third hour from matins and prime to compline. This was the common prayer of the monastery, and of the groups of hermitages as the hermits, though solitary, said their portion of psalms at times agreed in the hermit community. Corporate prayer could more easily grow to be an empty noise, an outward ritual, than internal private prayer. Internal private prayer could, more easily than corporate public prayer, become no prayer at all. Therefore the quest for prayer without ceasing meant that they tried to see the regular monastic offices as moments in a general and continuous mood of prayerfulness.

From the earliest times of monasteries, these offices of corporate prayer were of obligation. They derived from the set prayers of holy people attached to ordinary congregations in the days before the flight to the monastery. But the movement into solitude gave them new standing and developed their form. It added to the psalmody and the reading of Scripture further items, like hymns or even addresses ("conferences").

But the heads of monasteries, no doubt with reason and after painful experience, did not trust all their monks to live a dedicated life of prayer. They were soon aware that a fully prayerful life is achieved by an elite. Therefore they began to compel their men to more and more corporate prayer. They realized that the general exhortation to private prayer was too vague and too easily disregarded. The length of the offices grew, the number of psalms multiplied, the time spent in church doubled.

Cassian tried to hamper this development. He did not believe in forcing people to an excess of corporate worship. He preferred to put a brake on the number of psalms said together. His experience led him to be very sensitive to the dangers of monotony and boredom and at last even nausea, the affliction or sin that the desert called *accidie*. As he wanted to stop the masochist-monk from maltreating the body, and kept advocating discretion and its accompanying moderation, so he wanted the corporate office, even if frequent, to be of a restrained length. He was always aware of the prayer of the secret heart as taking precedence over the prayer of the lips, even though the ordered forms of worship evoked the sweet prayer of the heart. Perhaps he suffered an illusion, if it was an illusion, that the administrators of monasteries did not share. In this matter he was not an elitist. He did not believe that high states of prayer were the privilege of specially select souls.

INTRODUCTION

Anyone may and can go that way—so he thought. It was a faith that the experience of the abbots failed to confirm.

Cassian's criticism of an excess of corporate worship had small effect, at first, on posterity. In France monks took little notice. They went on multiplying the number of psalms to be said in church. Two makers of rules—the unknown called the Master, and his heir, Saint Benedict—were to save the situation. They laid down sensible restrictions, more or less as Cassian would have preferred. With Benedict's Rule the practice of corporate worship in Western monasteries became manageable, if at times only just manageable. Cassian would have greatly approved if he could have seen Benedict's day. He would not have approved if he had seen what some Benedictines made of Benedict—especially the long and elaborate services designed by Cluny, apparently with the mistaken object of achieving the maximum amount or prayerfulness in the day by that method.

By that time other considerations entered. If a monastery was to survive, its men must cultivate the fields. If they were always in church saying psalms, they would starve. Saint Benedict, when he made the daily offices tolerable in length, magnified their importance in the monastic life above the importance given to them by Cassian. For Benedict they had become *opus Dei*—the work of God, the essential duty of the monk, over which nothing else could be given priority. It was a lowlier ideal; if these men are not saying prayers regularly, why are they there at all? But if the ideal was less exalted, it was still deeply religious. Its object was still the same as Cassian's, to get true prayer instead of formality of prayer, and through true prayer to find oneness with God.

Cassian's union between unceasing prayer at all times and set prayer at set times failed on the weakness of human nature. French monks attempted a new and fascinating way of reconciling the two ideals. Since worship was now, dominantly, corporate worship rather than individual prayer, a plan was made for unceasing corporate worship by rotation. Groups of monks would take it in turn to keep psalmody going in church, for twenty-four hours a day. A hundred years after Cassian, in A.D. 515, King Sigismund of Burgundy repented of the foul murder of a son. At Agaune near the Saint Bernard pass, he founded a monastery of "perpetual chants," and this mode of unceasing prayer came to be called *laus perennis*, perpetual praise. It was a noble ideal. But it was a long way from Cassian's ideal, and it is not mere speculation to think that he would disapprove. It was a contradiction of his outlook. For him unceasing prayer was unceasing in the individual. It consisted in a prayerfulness that lay under all an individual's life. It might be helped by corporate prayer but did not depend on it, and was itself a background to the highest corporate prayer.

We can be almost sure that he did not approve of the monastery of perpetual praise by rotation. For Sigismund of Burgundy was not the first. In Cassian's lifetime an institution like Agaune was founded in Constantinople. There its monks gained the name "the Sleepless." They were soon accused of the type of heresy over prayer that was attributed to the homilies circulating under the name of Macarius of Egypt, and were expelled from the city. When they were expelled, Cassian had perhaps just left Constantinople for Rome. He must have known about the Sleepless. Some years after his death they were after all accepted in the East as a good way of devotion. Though he must have known about them, he did not mention them. They were not his ideal. Their ideal fulfilled neither his ideal of unceasing prayer nor his idea of the purpose of corporate worship.

In Spain of the seventh century there appeared a new and less satisfactory method of attempting unceasing prayer. Instead of making the services longer they made them more numerous, until they reached fifteen during the day. But nearly everything about the Spanish rule where this was decreed would have displeased Cassian. He would have thought that it lacked the moderation that was the essence of the virtue of discretion. He would have said, perhaps, that the corporate saying of psalms, which began as a way to feed prayer, ended by destroying most possibilities of private prayer.

Cassian accepted and used corporate prayer. But he was a man of private prayer. It was the difference between one whose highest priority was the silence of solitude and those whose highest priority was the life of the cenobium or corporate community. The six monastic centuries that succeeded Cassian were centuries of corporate prayer—in the West, much less in the East; for there are some respects in which Cassian, though a westerner, would have felt more at home with the heirs of Egypt among the Eastern churches. At least, the sources for the six Western centuries show little sign of reflection on private prayer and much concern with the regularity of corporate worship.

Despite Cassian, the West was never to have its "Jesus prayer," the repeated and repeated formula, like the East. One might have expected the marvelous paragraphs of Cassian's Conference to have influenced Western devotion permanently. And they did, but in an unexpected way, and it was a way that Cassian may not have intended. Few later Western men of prayer would use Cassian's verse "Come to my help, O God," in the way of a repeated formula. Instead, the text was taken into the offices of corporate worship as a starting versicle and response. This was a symbol of the change, after Cassian's death. The Western monks attended less than Cassian to private secret prayer, and more than Cassian to public corporate worship.

Nevertheless, we must not exaggerate. We see Cassian's ideas changing under the influence of abbot-administrators. Those abbots sometimes dealt with less-than-satisfactory subjects. But all the Middle Ages inherited Cassian's basic ideal. It was enshrined within the Benedictine structure of simplicity. The purity of prayer—that is, its undistracted quality; its "dartlike" quality, short, even sudden, ejaculatory; its frequency, not dependent on church moments, but evoked at any moment of private life—these were Cassianic qualities of prayer, and all the better monks of the Middle Ages still looked to them. Cassianic also is the medieval idea of fusion, or interpenetration, between corporate psalmody and private aspiration; prayerfulness enriching worship in church, worship in church lending a structure and a series of ordered moments to prayerfulness.

Later monasticism found a beautiful phrase to express the idea: *semper in ore psalmus, semper in corde Christus*—always a psalm on the lips, always Christ in the heart. Saint Benedict, when writing a rule of simplicity, and sharing the ideals of Cassian, found another beautiful phrase to describe what vocal prayer needed: "So to say the psalms [at the daily office] that our heart is in harmony with the words on our lips" (Rule of Saint Benedict 19.6). On this difficult point—the relationship between the apostolic prayer that is unceasing and the set times of public prayer—posterity has seen Cassian as the person with the clearest eye and most balanced judgment in all the formative centuries of monasticism.

Entangled within the difficulty was the need for daily work. If a monk prayed too many hours, he starved. If he worked in the fields too many hours, he might as well be a farmer and not a monk. During Cassian's lifetime the monks in Carthage (North Africa) were disturbed by some of their members who refused to work in the fields because they wanted to dedicate all their time to "things of the spirit."

Cassian had no particular problem over this antithesis between enough time for work and enough time for prayer. The prayerful soul easily prays at work. Regular work, even monotonous work, may be good, is sure to be good, for the prayerful spirit. (See chapter 14 of Conference 10 in this translation, by way of example.) But, he saw, work brings anxiety. Anxiety is the death of prayer. Therefore the hours of work, and the load of work, must be enough and not to excess. Bodies need daily food. They have other needs that are unavoidable, like housing or clothing. Anything beyond what is needed is to be suspect: "For example, when a single coin would meet the necessities of our bodies we choose in our effort and in our work to earn two or even three. Similarly with a couple of tunics. It is sufficient to have one for the night and one for the day, but we try to have three or four. One or two cells would be enough to live in, but wishing as the world does for possessions, to have more and more, we build four or five cells" (*Conference* 9.5). The nature of his teaching on prayer is not to find a contrast between the hours of labor and the hours of devotion unless the hours of labor are such as to become distracting.

Into this attitude to work came his fear of monotony. Idleness is the mother of *accidie*. Someone thinks he will do nothing but pray and what happens is that he does nothing; after a time he is bored beyond measure. Cassian much disliked people who said that they were too spiritual to work. Honest labor is part of the self-denial of a Christian. He liked to quote a proverb of the Egyptians: "A monk who works is tempted only by one devil. A monk who idles is tempted by a host of devils" (*Institutes* 10.23). Even if the circumstances are such that there is no need to work hard, because food is easy of access and very cheap, you should still work. For work is part of the Christian life, and the Christian life is the field of prayerfulness.

In a movement of the common man like the sweep into the desert of A.D. 300 to 400, there must appear at times wildness and fanaticism, as is always the case with popular religious movements. Amid the fervor of spirits, to keep a level head was no common undertaking. Some thought that to hurt the body was holiness; some, that total solitude would bring heaven upon earth; some, that eating nothing for too long was the way to be spiritual. The guides of the monks needed sanity and judgment. Cassian kept evoking *discretion*. He wanted people to fast. He spent a lot of words in showing them not to fast to excess and why. He wanted them to spend time at their psalms. He did not want them to spend so much time at their psalms that they neglected their duty. His Conference on discretion shows him the wisest of all the guides who presented this Egyptian tradition to posterity.

INTRODUCTION

Part of fanaticism was miracle-hunting. A people's wonder was easily evoked by the marvelous and easily credited. Miracle-workers won crowds of followers. Cassian did not doubt that miracles happen. Sometimes they are evidence of holiness. But he was very sober. Miracles are not to be looked for. They are not to be trusted in. Live a godly life and if a miracle were to happen, you may thank God and do your best to hide what happened. You are never to admire men who put themselves forward as miracle-workers or healers or exorcists. Only admire them for charity. See if they love. Cassian recorded some marvels, but his object was to show how they arose out of compassion, how the aim was not ostentation but charity. True men of God reject honor paid to them when miracles happen. Humility and charity are always necessary. Miracles are not always necessary. They are not even good for everyone. Most of the Middle Ages, especially the popular Middle Ages, took very little notice of this wisdom.

Fanaticism could merge into a mood better and higher, yet a mood with danger. The disciples of Evagrius talked of a mystical Oneness through prayer. Therefore some extremists would lay such stress on the mystical experiences of prayer as to despise the ordinary sacraments of the Church, or the prosaic life of a Christian congregation. In the Egyptian desert circulated a body of writings under the name of Macarius that were a poetic penetration of experience in prayer, but with too little prose, too little earth, too ardent a rhetoric of prayer. These Macarian homilies were to have a far-flung influence on the spirituality of the Eastern Church, which provided it structure wherein they might be understood without danger. They needed a prosaic context if they were to be fruitful and not productive of fanaticism. A French scholar talked of a "holy anarchy" that wanted to sacrifice everything to prayer. Cassian's discretion was typical of the steady attempt to give spirituality a stable base, and not to let it soar so high that it lost touch with real men and women.

In English devotion a parallel was made by the "Centuries of Meditations" by Thomas Traherne, of the later seventeenth century. Here are wonderful and soaring poetic aspirations after a mystical unity with God in Nature. Yet the reader has to keep kicking himself to remind himself that he is living on the ground. Cassian might have enjoyed reading Traherne, but it was not his type of spirituality.

Now here is a curious thing about Cassian, and some of his contemporaries in the early history of spirituality. They were resolute to keep the monastic communities within the authentic Christian tradition, that is, within the sacraments and the daily life of the Church. But in Cassian's lifetime the devotion of the common people grew very attached to cult objects. In the congregation they thought about saints, and relics, and images, and icons, and dust from saints' tombs, and methods to secure the power of the dead saints, and outward rituals effective with saints. And when we consider Cassian's Conferences in this light, we find—nothing. An entire range of a common people's superstition is missing from his outlook, more absent than in his contemporary Saint Augustine. Discretion was partly the taking of a moderate road between extremes. And partly it was seeing straight, to the essence of the Christian life instead of its periphery.

There is a question now of education, and learning. To his idea of prayer, meditation on the Scripture was indispensable. His talk of the necessary link between meditation and prayer was not his own invention. It was a fundamental attitude in Egypt. It is found in all the spirituality of the early monks, whether in East or West.

The attitude shows that even then a majority of monks were (more or less) literate. Unlike other writers of that age, Cassian troubled himself about the way in which men who could not read could nevertheless link meditation on Scripture with prayer. But the idea ran through all the monastic movement. It was as essential a part of the tradition as celibacy. The meditation was felt to be not only a door opening toward God, but a door opening toward the knowledge of the self, an objective light in which the shadows of the self were seen in their true colors.

This was not precisely *study* of the Bible, if by that word is meant a critical or historical analysis. It contained memorization of texts. But it was more than memorization, for it contained a search for meaning— that is, what it meant obviously for the characters in the Bible; then what it meant for the soul that reads; and finally what it meant for the Church of all time. The study was rather devotional than critical. It was intended more to touch the heart than to inform the head. But it intended also to inform the mind. It could throw up constant problems of interpretation that could be handled only with such elementary tools of exegesis as were then available. Part of the purpose of Cassian's Conferences was to help minds over certain hard passages that they found in their biblical reading and that caused them difficulty. Such difficulties might arise from contemporary events, in that world of barbarian invasion and public insecurity. For example, in the sixth Conference Cassian set out to explain, obviously in reply to troubled questioners, why God allowed holy monks in the wilderness to be murdered by bandits.

Unlike the forms of set prayer, biblical meditation need not be short. It was much nearer to that prayerfulness which could make a background to daily life and work. The memorized text could spring into the mind as the foot dug the spade, or the hands wove the osiers into a basket, or the pen copied the letters of a manuscript. Biblical meditation was not precisely of a set time, in Cassian, for in a manner it might be of any time. As the later Latin tag put it, *totus in lectione totus in oratione*, the whole man in reading, the whole man in praying. Only the makers of rules like Saint Benedict saw that most monks, most people, needed a set time for reading if they were to read.

Cassian's attitude to this meditation was more devotional than some of his successors could quite like. Even in Cassian there exist two elements: (1) memorizing texts; letting them bring light to the soul as and when God allows; ruminating with an open-minded piety; feeding on them so that they lead the mind into prayer and eventually (if He wills it) into an immediacy with God where the words of the text have fallen into oblivion; and (2) the intellectual tradition of scholarship, whereby the student meditates on the meaning of the texts with all the equipment of reason, knowledge, and learning that may be at his disposal.

Cassian allowed the second; and almost entirely advocated the first. But the first was very free. The mind ranged, as it was led; disciplined by the will to avoid (so far as it was possible) distractions, but open to whatever might come from God, and therefore with a sense of freedom. It fed on the text and then let happen what might happen. It was not studying a word of man but listening to a Word of God. If then the freedom brought distraction, or even temptation—if the memory obtruded with a recollection of evil, or of what was worldly, or of what was full of anxiety—the mind turned back to the text, revived its attention, meditated, and again was free to listen.

Was boredom a danger here, as with repetitions of prayer? That was not the impression Cassian gave. Nor was it the impression given by many of the better guides who followed him. Engaged thus with texts, the mind has not to go slogging on over times of monotony. The freedom opens it to what is inspiring, and therefore sweet to the soul. In Cassian we do not hear of minds grinding on bravely in darkness, or of minds summoning all their resources to carry on grimly in the midst of an intellectual desert. The work needs diligence, even hard work, certainly determination and endurance. But this is the Word of God. It brings light; not all the time, not even most of the time; but in darts and illuminations; at unexpected moments; and the moments are so precious that they cast their brilliance over the entire process of meditation. We have heard the texts a thousand times. In the presence of God they can always, though suddenly, become new.

Cassian had something more anti-intellectual than some of his successors. He allowed that a mind could and should study, in the academic sense of study. But he was afraid of it, at least in the young. Academic study, at least in the young, easily led to pride in knowledge, or to a vanity that made a young man speak too quickly in some conference of his elders, and show off his information or his logic. If a young man is to study, Cassian believed, he should keep silent about what he thinks he has acquired. In later centuries Cassian would have resisted premature publication of results in print.

Yet the historian looks back on the long centuries of Benedictine learning, and is grateful for the folios of scholarship that the heirs of Cassian and Benedict gave to the world. The anti-intellectual slant in Cassian was sustained in some spirituality of both East and West. Mercifully for the world and even for the monks, it failed to deter scholarship. Scholars came into monasteries and became professed monks. They brought in their equipment, and did their thing, with the approval and encouragement of enlightened abbots. From time to time the needs of the Church clamored for scholarship. Even bishops might encourage young monks to do what they could with their "leisure" to help. The very nature of monasteries meant that they must throw up scholars; much later, eminent scientists. Cassian's anti-intellectual slant was more put aside than submerged.

But his words were still heard: that moral character is needed for a rightful study of religious truth; that the pride or vanity of scholarship is a corruption of study; that the purpose of meditation on the Bible is to listen. And it must always be remembered that part of Cassian's intellectualism contained a profound truth, not so commonly found among the elite of the early monks: that the illiterate is as capable of penetrating the deepest truths as is the mind of encyclopedic learning.

In his own person Cassian understood this difficulty for the scholar. He was well educated. He knew Latin literature, probably some Greek literature. He looked back with gratitude on the tutor of his youth. He loved poetry, and the legends of the ancient world. He knew some history. When he came into a monastery he lost none of these happy memories of literature. It bothered him that in the middle of a time of prayer some non-Christian song, or non-Christian myth, or history of a battle, perhaps an Aeneid or an Iliad, should poke its way into his mind. His answer was not sublimation, or gratitude for literature as one of God's gifts. He wanted to expel such thoughts. The mind must turn from a non-Christian subject to the most Christian of subjects, namely the Bible. He could drive out the battles of the Iliad by thinking about the battles of the Book of Judges.

The link between religion and literature was a problem of the distant future and never entered his view. That link was soon to be illustrated, without the slightest sign of incongruity or awkwardness, by an Englishman who was the first of the scholar-monks of Western history—the Venerable Bede.

II

Behind all this struggle after God—within all this struggle to be aware of Presence, contemplate Him, be one with Him—lies God's own hand. Here an argument over theology broke in on the ethics. This argument hurt Cassian's reputation. And that probably diminished his influence more than anything else that he wrote.

You aim at knowing God. Therefore you aim at purity of heart. But to become pure in heart, you need to grow in moral decision. You need to put aside passion, and strengthen your power to resist temptation. This is a ladder toward God up which the soul fancies that it climbs. Some later writers on spirituality called it openly by the name *ladder*, "the ladder of perfection." In some Protestant spiritualities, which suspected the word ladder, the word *fight* took its place:

Let not fears your course impede,
Great your strength, if great your need.
Let your drooping hearts be glad;
  March, in heavenly armour clad;
  Fight, nor think the battle long,

    Soon shall victory wake your song.

    Onward then in battle move;
    More than conquerors ye shall prove;
    Though opposed by many a foe,
    Christian soldiers, onward go!

INTRODUCTION

Cassian would not have approved of this Protestant hymn, on religious grounds. He might have forgiven the author for his extreme youth. The course of the soul is indeed impeded by fears. Its needs are great. It must try to raise the drooping heart. It must fight, and it is opposed by many a foe. But Cassian did not share this optimism. The battle is likely to be long. Victory is not likely to wake your song *soon*. You will do very well if you conquer, and you are not at all likely to become *more than conquerors*. The soul faces a fight, or a climb, and is ill-equipped for the struggle. In Cassian's ideas the demons are far more powerful, persistent, and plausible than ever they were to that hymnwriter.

Therefore the soul is always at the mercy of God. It is helpless without His help. Man is free to choose. You must exercise your moral judgment. You must try. You must discipline yourself. But still the soul is helpless without God. The grace of God must help you to begin, continue, and end. Purity of heart is a gift, not an achievement. Still, you must try.

Cassian's contemporary Saint Augustine said more. So overwhelming is the grace of God, so puny and tainted the endeavors of humanity, that all was of God. If God called, the soul cannot repel. If He decides to save, the soul will be saved. He will choose whom He will save. He will bring them to Himself. He will keep them in His protection. He will bring them to heaven infallibly.

The doctrine had nobility. The best divines of the Middle Ages, all the divines of the Reformation, were to rest on this doctrine of Saint Augustine. It was or seemed to be the only way to safeguard the all-power of God and the nothingness of fallen man. Through this doctrine Martin Luther found himself.

The doctrine also had a hardness. The hardness was partly of expression and partly also in its doctrine of God toward those whom He does not choose. But Cassian disliked the doctrine on another ground—the ethical ground. A human being has moral freedom. Resistance to God is possible. Humanity needs God's grace and against the demons needs it desperately. The soul is not compelled to accept what He offers freely.

The atmosphere of Cassian's struggle for purity of heart is not at all like the atmosphere of Saint Augustine. The strength of the Augustinian doctrine lay in freeing the heart from scruples and an excess of introspection and a timidity about faith; and in freeing the heart it made faith an assured trust in God's mercy. "Rest in me and I *will* do it" is a tougher, perhaps a more inspiring faith than "rest in me, and I will help you, so that we shall do it together." But Cassian much preferred this second doctrine of faith. You have moral freedom. You have to recognize that you have moral freedom. You have to recognize that you are under a responsibility to choose the right. Yet you are still helpless without God's grace.

But—is the soul totally helpless? The prodigal son was sick of the husks the swine ate, and turned homeward. And while he was still a great way off, his father saw him and ran to meet him. Are there cases—perhaps rare cases—where the first tiny initiative comes from the soul turning back because sick of husks, and then God comes with his saving grace to help?

To this question Cassian answered *yes*. There are cases—they may be very rare cases—where the soul makes the first little turn. Might the thief on the cross be one such? And because Cassian answered yes to this question, he almost destroyed his reputation as a theologian.

For if Cassian is right, said the critics, we are not helpless without God. Cassian may say that we are helpless. He cannot mean it.

We need not enter this controversy of the centuries. It will be sufficient to say here: (1) No one can doubt that Cassian disapproved of the doctrine of Saint Augustine. He thought it rigid. He thought parts of it untrue. He wrote one Conference, the thirteenth, to confute Saint Augustine. (2) No one can doubt that Cassian was a deeply Christian moralist and never for an instant supposed that a soul could ascend any ladder, or fight any fight, without God pouring in His grace. (3) If Cassian's formula for reconciling freedom with grace may cause doubt to anyone who thinks hard on these matters, no one who reads him with attention and sympathy will fail to admire his endeavor to reconcile the maximum sense of moral freedom and moral responsibility with the maximum sense of dependence on God.

III

Here is a "holy anarchy"—a freedom of the soul to listen to God. But humanity is humanity, and cannot exist in groups without being organized. If it goes solitary (totally) it goes eccentric or worse. If it is not to go solitary, it cannot dispense with administrators.

Cassian's whole outlook is of the soul moving toward the freedom of private prayer, in listening to its Maker and being conscious of the indwelling Lord. But, being a sensible man, and possessing the virtue of discretion, he knew that a community needed organizing: a constitution. He was not very concerned about it. His genius, or vocation, was not that of an administrator.

Since the work of Saint Benedict, the word *monastery* has been inseparable from the idea of a written monastic rule that binds all. Cassian did not yet organize a rule, nor even have the idea of a written rule.

Under God the soul is free. But it will not be truly free unless it follows the hard-won experience of the Fathers. This experience includes instruction, living in a community and keeping its institutes. Therefore although the idea of a rule (in the later sense) was not quite present in Cassian, or at least was far from prominent; although he talked of obedience but seldom of the person to whom obedience is due; although he never talked of any constitutional process of creating an office to which obedience might be owed—though in these senses the soul is free, he knew that the soul needs to be self-disciplined and part of self-discipline is common or community discipline. The atmosphere of Cassian is not one of legal obedience to legally appointed authority. It is one of discipleship to a wise and holy master and therefore acceptance of his advice.

But the monastery had to live, and could not live without rules, or customs which had the force of rules. Since the community was in intention very biblical, every rule or custom was held up against the Bible, or justified by texts from the Bible, or tested by appeal to the Bible. Despite all this, there was not such a thing as a "monastic rule" in the later sense of that phrase. When Saint Augustine wrote a piece on regulating the monastery, he called it "booklet" or "pamphlet." About the same time, Rufinus translated the practical advice of Saint Basil of Caesarea in Asia Minor, and called Basil's rules "institutes," but inside the translation he often used "rule." Saint Jerome (if it was he) translated the Rule of the Egyptian Saint Pachomius and called it by that name. One text of Cassian (*Conferences* 20.2) talked of "the rule of the monastery"; but this comes in a passage that on other grounds is suspect for the possibility of tampering with the text; and if it is Cassian's own, was certainly a production from late in his life. The "rule" was not his usual word. When he wanted to describe the practical arrangements for a common life he called them "institutes"; and he gives the impression that these are rather customs found valuable than any fixed or legal structure for a community. In his book of the *Institutes* he never used the word "rule," in Saint Benedict's sense. If he used it, he meant either the generally accepted customs of the whole monastic movement, or a particular custom, like the measure of psalmody, the extent of fasting. This showed Cassian getting near to his successor Benedict. Though he had not yet the concept of a written rule, he was approaching it.

The rules that were created after his time were diverse, indeed extraordinarily, puzzlingly diverse. Some were very long; some absurdly short; some made provision for all sorts of eventualities, some left nearly everything to the judgment of the superior of the community; some were written down but never put into practice; some are cold law, others are full of warm exhortation, as though the author is a preacher rather than an administrator. Almost every writer of a rule borrowed at least a little from some other writer of a rule—and yet the result is of an extreme variety if not a chaos.

During the ninth century Saint Benedict of Aniane catalogued the rules he could find. Among them he included "Extracts of a rule collected from all the Institutes of Cassian." This was known as "the Rule of Cassian." Yet the phrase has something in it foreign to Cassian's mentality. His aim was a body of moral and spiritual thought. Someone else must give that body of ideas a base in administration and canonical structure.

It was Cassian's fortune to be taken up by the greatest of the makers of rules; more than his fortune, because he deserved the fate. Saint Benedict drafted "a little rule for beginners." It made its way to dominate Europe. It was sensible, and easy or at least possible to keep. And it was taken up by the see of Rome, and in time became the specially Roman rule for monks, during centuries when the see of Rome extended its influence. Within his Rule Benedict included a recommendation that Cassian be read regularly. Therefore—not quickly but over five centuries—Cassian's ideas could hardly be escaped by the monks of the Western world. Though Cassian sat uneasily to a rule, he profited more than any other from someone else's rule. He became the guide of Western monasteries partly because his guidance was of a wisdom and stature that enabled him to sustain the role, and partly because through Saint Benedict he became one main part of the spiritual reading of monks. Naturally they interpreted him in the light of the practice and experience of their respective generations.

IV

A monastery does not always sit comfortably with a church. In the sixteenth century it came to a crunch, where half the Church made monks illegal.

Cassian did not wish monks to be an elite. Yet he showed in himself almost none of the popular superstitions that marked the ordinary congregations of his day. Whether he liked it or not, his monks and nuns were an elite. They grew out of the earlier groups, with specially pious practices, attached to ordinary congregations. Now they had moved away from the ordinary congregations, out into the desert or the woods. They were no longer attached to a congregation. They were their own congregation. They were no longer under the priest of a parish. They elected a priest of their own and sent him to the bishop to be ordained. Part of the reason for escaping the ordinary congregation was the flood of half-Christians who in that generation invaded the churches.

Does mysticism need a church? The individual experience of the divine is overwhelming. It passes beyond the memory of biblical texts and every other thought. Does it also pass beyond sacraments? Or sermons? If wordless apprehension is the highest, what need of congregations, where babies cry, and dogs bark, and young men ogle, and priests show off their voices, and old widows commit superstition? Might it be that holy anarchy is nearer to God than ordered ecclesiasticism? A monk is nothing but a simple Christian heart trying to find his Maker. Why does he need a church to intrude on his privacy, which is an experience of God unique to himself and incapable of being shared with another?

The point was important for Cassian. For the entire direction of his thought was toward the private, "mystical" experience of the divine.

In Cassian's monastic books, bishops are almost absent. Ordinations happen. But Cassian was not usually pleased with ordinations. To ordain a man may be to take him away from the life of the spirit and set him to serve tables, to be a treasurer for giving out alms, or for administering all the organizations of a congregation. He once apologized because he had not himself been able to avoid ordination (*Institutes* 11.18). He made this apology almost with a sense of shame. He met the Bishop of Panephysis in Egypt, by name Archebius. And Archebius had been "carried off" from his community of hermits to become a bishop and thought of his consecration as a sign of his moral failure in that he was found unworthy to go on in his hermitage (*Conferences* 11.2). And at times Cassian could be very rude about bishops. He had no feeling that to be a bishop protected a person from just criticism. He attacked a great Western bishop for profanity. He accused an eminent Eastern bishop of madness.

INTRODUCTION

Still in Cassian, to be a bishop is an honor. He protects the faith of the Church—usually. To be a priest in a monastery is an honor. Cassian, ashamed of his own ordination, looked back on the bishop who ordained him with a deep reverence and affection. Perhaps to be a priest is an honor that a monk should shrink from, but it is still an honor. Cassian met Daniel, who was an ordained priest, and admired him for not exercising his orders. This monastic ideal was not very ecclesiastical. The hierarchical structure of the Church meant little to its daily life. It had other things to think about.

Nevertheless, Cassian's monastery was part of the Catholic Church. The sacraments were part of the worshiping life. The great body of Christian doctrine was the structure of thought on which the monastic ideal rested. Cassian disapproved altogether of persons who avoided the sacrament. He wanted it weekly, even, for some, daily. To be a priest was perhaps a peril, because it was busy and because it was an honor, and might therefore lead, if one were not careful, to vanity or even pride; and because it took hours of time in visiting the sick or care for the sacraments and the children and the dying. Cassian preferred to avoid priesthood because it was an honor, not because it was not. To receive what the priest had to offer, that was a necessary part of the Christian life. He wholly disapproved of persons who avoided the sacrament because they thought themselves too sinful, or because they thought it to break into their solitude, or because they regarded it as not quite spiritual.

He did not settle the great problem—the link between the Church and the monasteries within the Church—which was to stay with the Church through all the centuries, never quite solved, until settled so fiercely by the Reformation in northern Europe and then by the Enlightenment in southern Europe.

V

During Cassian's life the barbarians broke the Rhine frontier. Less than half a century after his death the Roman Empire of the West came to an end. The falling world seemed to have fallen. The quest for the kingdom of God instead of the failed kingdom of men gained a new strength. The otherworldly streak was still stronger in the heirs of Cassian—the transitoriness of this society we are born into; the nearness of its end; the mothlike quality of human existence; the absence of any safety except in God; the imminence of the next world; man's longing for permanence; the need of stern acts of outward penitence to sustain

31

humankind in prayer and fasting and self-denial. And in this mood Cassian's moderate interpretation of Egypt was soon to be not the only interpretation known to Western monks. Other documents from the Egyptian desert were translated into Latin, and their anecdotes were more exciting to the reader. In that dangerous age readers admired the heroic asceticisms that Cassian preferred them not to admire to excess. A century after Cassian someone tried to imitate the stylites of the East by living on top of a pillar near Treves on the German border. "You are wrong," the bishops told him. "You fail to take account of the conditions of life in this country" (Gregory of Tours, *History of the Franks* 8.15).

This immoderate though temporary phase was most marked in the Celtic monks who came out of Ireland and traveled western Europe on "pilgrimage." Saint Columban traveled in France and Germany and Northern Italy during the sixth century and owed something to Cassian's writings. It was a fresh atmosphere out of a new background. But the way Columban proposed for his monks had little that was original, except in the changed atmosphere and the ferocity of the discipline to keep the monks in order, to sanctify them by the stick. The Irish memorized the Scripture with even more attention because they were simultaneously entering the general language of European culture. They experienced ecstasies in prayer and the visions of the night. Compared with the atmosphere in Cassian, the atmosphere in Columban is more remote. The man was a hero, and preached discretion in the way heroes preach discretion, and we wonder whether Cassian would have recognized him to share in the virtue of true discretion. Columban's influence rested not in his ideas but in the fervor of his piety. For a moment he led the monastic ideal of Europe. But not for long. Though he leaned in part on Cassian, he could not be compared with Cassian as a lasting influence on European thought. For moral ideas last when moral fervor is forgotten.

VI

One other of Cassian's successors, besides Saint Benedict and Saint Columban, must be mentioned when Cassian's place in Christian spirituality is considered: Saint Gregory the Great.

No doubt Cassian's moderation was derived from a wide range of human experience; in Romania perhaps, certainly in Bethlehem and in Egypt, then in the streets of great cities, Constantinople and Rome, and finally in Southern France. Gregory had as wide an experience. He was lay administrator, prefect of Rome, monk, ambassador in Constantinople, Pope—like Cassian he knew the world and the weakness of humanity, and the knowledge made him moderate. It also made him practical. And Gregory had behind him two authors of nearly two centuries before his time, Saint Augustine and Cassian. The literary texts prove the strong influence on him of both. Being a famous bishop, he was much more ecclesiastical than Cassian. But his career prevented him from being an "ecclesiastical" in the narrow sense of that term. And he shared this belief with Cassian, that he did not believe in prayer only for an elite. Anyone, in any profession or trade or vocation, may attain to the prayer of contemplation.

The light of God is a key idea; limitless light, unbounded light, an ocean of light. Prayer is full of light. To reach that light the soul must find total simplicity. But much more than Cassian, Gregory was willing to pile on descriptions; not very informative descriptions because negative—not to be seen, not bodily, not to be comprehended, not to be spoken of adequately, not to be bounded, not to be in time, not to suffer change, not to be able to suffer passion, not to be able to be corrupted. But the descriptions were not all negative—for He is all-wise, and all truth; like the sun, and like fire. He is in everything, and everything in Him. He is in everything and not enclosed in anything. As in Cassian, the moments of contemplation of God, or union with God, are in this life brief and not lasting; sudden shafts of light and not a steady illumination. As in Cassian there is the same vagueness, or rather restraint, of language. They both knew what they experienced. Neither thought it right or possible to try to describe that experience analytically. Gregory had a more articulate sense of the lasting quality of the direction of the mind toward God. The experience may be sudden and short. The attitude, within which the experiences sometimes come, can endure. Both Cassian and Gregory are very restrained in their descriptions of the sensations that accompany vision. Their differences are of emphasis; their kinship in the main ideas is marked. Together, they laid the foundations for the spirituality of the Western Middle Ages; Cassian the more monastic in atmosphere because he presupposed the enclosure in a community or a hermitage; Gregory moving out to the wider Church—monastic in essence, but unconfined by the walls of a cloister. He turned the spirituality of the desert, which retreated from the formal Church, into the spirituality of all the Church.

INTRODUCTION

VII

Already among the monasteries we find the normal provisions of daily worship being supplemented. Some monks who aspired were not content with the formal liturgy, nor even with the memorization of Scripture. They needed aids. These were little books, derived from the liturgy and Scripture, but framed as helps to guide the mind to prayer. The earliest examples were developed, probably out of Spanish patterns, in Ireland and England. We find the so-called Book of Cerne, now in the University Library at Cambridge, a manuscript written between 721 and 740 for Bishop Ethelwold of Lindisfarne. Shortly afterward we have a book of prayers handed down under the name of Alcuin, Charlemagne's advisor and educator.

As in Cassian the psalter remained dominant—and would always remain dominant. But its texts are woven with other words, litanies or hymns. The psalter began to be not only the public prayer book of the Church and the private prayer book of the monks, but the book of devotion for educated laity of the Church.

Some psalms were difficult to understand or translate. A few psalms were difficult to use as prayer. Therefore the Middle Ages made repeated efforts to make the psalms more easily available—by selection, or shortening, or brief explanation. The Benedictines did what they could. For the use of Carolingian kings they illuminated the psalms with lovely illustrations. For the people and for the monks, each psalm was given a heading or a little summary, with its Christian interpretation. These summaries became an important part of early medieval devotion.

This process of selection was the father of the numerous prayer books for private and devotional use. And these books made Cassian's ideals of private prayer easier for the less instructed to put into practice.

Whether Cassian would have approved a selection from the psalter instead of the whole psalter, which was the Word of God, is a question. But probably his conviction that ordinary men and women are called to the use of the psalter in private prayer would have triumphed over a hesitation based on dogma, and he would have been grateful for the work of his Benedictine heirs.

In that moment when other sources besides the psalms were allowed to come into the books of devotion, a chance of enrichment lay at hand. This made an opportunity never open to Cassian and never desired by Cassian.

INTRODUCTION

The Meditations and Prayers of Anselm, later to be Archbishop of Canterbury, were written or selected for his Benedictines at the abbey of Bec in Normandy. As a Benedictine, Anselm stood in the tradition of Cassian. His book has not only psalms. It has much devotion to the Blessed Virgin. It marks a stage in the development of the cult of Saint Mary during the Middle Ages. The division between the popular cult of the lay congregation and the pure prayer of the monastic community was bridged. Whether or not we think that bridge desirable, it was inevitable. Monks were not born out of nothing. They came from a people, accustomed to a people's devotion, and they still needed a people's devotion. In the high Middle Ages the devotion grew ever more Christ-centered in language, in minds like those of Saint Bernard of Clairvaux or Saint Bonaventura. Not that Cassian was not Christ-centered. On the contrary. But the *language* of Christ-centeredness, in its warmth and fullness as a Cistercian like Saint Bernard used it, could not be Cassian's because his central book of devotion was a hymnbook from a pre-Christian epoch and he did not think it right or possible to use nonbiblical language. Whether or not the particular enrichments that occurred were all good—and some were pious, some of doubtful taste, some touched with superstition—the history of monasticism proved that long hours of prayer needed much nourishment, at least for many souls. The multitude of later medieval books of devotion proves that Cassian was wrong in thinking his Bible a sufficient ground of religious meditation for the multitude, at least in the conditions of devotion and education that prevailed during the later Middle Ages. It must also be said that Cassian, though he may have guided nuns, wrote for an essentially male community. The spread of nunneries during the later Middle Ages meant that books of devotion needed to satisfy feminine psychology, which might not always be the same as masculine, and which at times tended to a warmth of affectionate expression that could hardly rest content with the austere prose of Cassian and his "pure prayer."

VIII

About 850, John the Scot, the Irishman known as Erigena, arrived at the court of France. He had a mystical spirit. And he knew Greek. He translated into Latin the works of the pseudo-Dionysius the Areopagite—ultra-Platonic mysticism from Constantinople. He was not at first influential. But so far as mystical experience went, or rather the language of analysis of mystical experience, the Western influence of

35

the Areopagite marked a new phase of spirituality. The restraint, the refusal to define or describe, found in Cassian or Gregory would give place to a loftier but more doubtful series of descriptions, at least among the minority who were drawn to the language of mysticism. Cassian was hardly a source for the language of later medieval mysticism. His language was too plain. For everyone believed the Areopagite to be the disciple and friend of Saint Paul the Apostle.

Most souls were not drawn to that more mystical language. Meditation on Scripture remained the normal instrument of devotional life. The influence of Cassian remained among the monks, and in several of their best theorists. Like the Rule of Saint Benedict, his work was a protection against excess, and a constant recall to that primitive simplicity where Eastern spirituality met Western.

Conference One

THE GOAL OR OBJECTIVE OF THE MONK

1

The most celebrated fathers of monasticism, the ultimate in excellence, were to be found in the desert of Scete. And among all these very beautiful flowers of holiness none was more outstanding than the abbot Moses, both for the fragrance of the virtue he practiced and for the preeminence of his contemplation.

I wanted to find some base that would be secured by his teaching. So too did the holy abbot Germanus. Both of us had been together since our days as recruits fighting the first of our battles of the spirit. We had been together in community life and in the desert and, to show our close friendship and our common purpose, each of us would say that we were one mind and one soul living in two bodies. Together now and with an outpouring of tears we begged of the abbot that he would talk to us in a constructive way. We had known very well that he had a very determined mind and that he would never throw open the gates of perfection except to those who longed for it in all faith and with saddened hearts, since here is certainly not something to be made known to the indifferent or to those with a lukewarm urge. The revelation can be made only to those longing for perfection, and by handing it over to the unworthy or to begrudgers he seemed to fear to do wrong or to run the risk of a betrayal.

But he was worn down at last by our entreaties. And this is how he began.

2

"Every art," he said, "and every discipline has a particular objective, that is to say, a target and an end peculiarly its own. Someone

37

keenly engaged in any one art calmly and freely endures every toil, danger, and loss. The farmer, for instance, does not shirk the burning rays of the sun or the frosts and the ice as he tirelessly cuts through the earth, as, over and over again, he ploughs the untamed sods of the field. All the time he pursues his objective, cleaning all brambles from the field, clearing away all grass, breaking up the earth until it is like fine sand. He is aware that there is no other way to achieve his aim, which is the prospect of an abundant harvest and a rich yield of crops so that he may live securely or add to his possessions. He draws the grain willingly from the fullness of his barns and, working intensively, he invests it in the loosened soil. He pays no attention to what he is losing now because he is thinking ahead to the coming harvests.

"Again, there are those who engage in commerce. They are not frightened by the hazards of the sea. No dangers terrify them. Borne up by their hope of profit they are carried toward their goal.

"It is the same with those inflamed by military ambitions. They look toward the goal of honors and power and as they do so they shrug off doom and danger while they venture afar. They are brought down neither by the sufferings of the moment nor by wars, so long as they keep before themselves the honored plan to which they aspire.

"So also with our profession. It too has its own objective and goal to which, not just tirelessly but with true joy, we devote all our labors. The hunger of fasts does not weary us. The tiredness from keeping vigil is a delight to us. The reading and the endless meditation on Scripture are never enough for us. The unfinished toil, the nakedness, the complete deprivation, the fear that goes with this enormous loneliness, do not frighten us off. And I have no doubt that it was for this goal that you gave up the love of your family, your native soil, the pleasures of the world, that you traveled through so many countries in search of men like us, ignorant backwoodsmen who live the rough life of this desert.

"So, tell me then what is the end and the objective which inspires you to endure all these trials so gladly."

3

Since he really wanted to know our answer to this question we replied that we had taken on all this for the sake of the kingdom of God.

4

"A good answer insofar as it concerns your goal," he said. "But now what should be our aim, what direction should we take which, if closely followed, will bring us to our objective? This, above all, is something of which you ought to be aware."

We admitted, in all honesty, that we did not know. "As I have remarked already, every art and discipline is preceded by some objective," he said. "The spirit points in a certain direction. There is an unwavering purpose in the mind. If this is not held on to with all eagerness and dedication there can be no coming to the longed-for fruits of the goal. The farmer, as I remarked, has the goal of living peacefully in sure abundance thanks to good rich harvests, and in order to reach that end he sets himself to clearing the brambles and the useless grasses from his land. He knows well that he will not enjoy that restful ease toward which he is striving unless somehow his work and his aspirations themselves become a sort of foretaste of what he hopes to actually enjoy one day.

"The merchant does not put aside his urge to amass goods, for it is through these that he can grow wealthy on the proceeds. It would be useless for him to have a wish for profit if he did not follow the road heading there.

"And there are those who have a wish for the honors of this world. They take on this job or follow that career, depending on the honor they want, and they do so in order to arrive at their wished-for plan by way of the right path along which hope leads them.

"In the same fashion the objective of our life is the kingdom of God, but we should carefully ask what we should aim for. If we do not look very carefully into this we will wear ourselves out in useless strivings. For those who travel without a marked road there is the toil of the journey—and no arrival at a destination."

Seeing our amazement at all this, the old man resumed: "As we have said, the aim of our profession is the kingdom of God or the kingdom of heaven. But our point of reference, our objective, is a clean heart, without which it is impossible for anyone to reach our target. If we keep to this point of reference we will proceed with all assurance, as though along a carefully drawn line. If our minds wander a little from this we can come back to it again and keep our eye on it, using it as a standard by which to give ourselves sure guidance. This standard will draw all our efforts toward the one point and will serve as a warning to us if our minds waver even a little from the proposed route.

5

"Take the example of those who are skilled in archery and who wish to demonstrate their prowess before some king of this world. They strive to hurl their darts or their arrows against tiny shields on which there are painted the rewards of achievement. They know well that they can attain the desired reward only if they come straight on target. It is there for them—if they can reach the set objective. Imagine, however, that the target was removed from their view and from the right line. They would fail to notice it was missing since they would lack a point of reference by which to demonstrate that their shot was accurate or poor. They would pour useless shots through the empty air and would have no idea of why they were going wrong and they would have no way of judging how far out of the way they were going nor could they therefore correct their own guideline nor summon it back.

"So too with our profession whose goal, as the apostle says, is eternal life. 'As a reward you have your sanctification and your goal is eternal life' (Rom 6:22). Our objective is purity of heart, which he so justly describes as sanctification, for without this the goal cannot be reached. In other words, it is as though he said that you have purity of heart for an objective and eternal life as the goal. And indeed, with regard to this sense of direction, the blessed apostle in the teaching he gives us actually makes significant use of the term 'objective.' 'I forget the past and push ahead to what is yet to come. I am rushing toward the objective, to the prize to which God calls me from on high' (Phil 3:13–14). The Greek has 'I am rushing toward the object,' that is, 'I am running with a finishing line in view.' It is as if the apostle said, 'Guided by this aim of forgetting my past, namely the sins of the earlier man, I am driving myself toward the goal of a heavenly reward.'

"Therefore, we must follow completely anything that can bring us to this objective, to this purity of heart, and anything which pulls us away from it must be avoided as being dangerous and damaging. After all, it is for the sake of this that we undertake all that we do and all that we endure. For its sake we hold family, country, honors, riches, the delight of this world and indeed all pleasure in low esteem, and we do so always so as to hold on to purity of heart. With this as our continuous aim, all our acts and thoughts are fully turned toward its achievement, and if it were not ever firmly before our eyes all our efforts would be empty, hesitant, futile, and wasted, and all the thoughts within us would be varied and at loggerheads with one another. For a mind which lacks an abiding sense of direction veers hither and yon by the hour, and by the minute is a prey to outside influences and is endlessly the prisoner of whatever strikes it first.

6

"This is why we see many who, having given up the greatest wealth not only in gold and silver but also in splendid estates, nevertheless become very upset over a knife, a scraper, a needle, or a pan. If they had looked unwaveringly to the purity of their hearts they would never have become involved with such trifles and they would have rejected these just as they did great and valuable possessions. There are some who guard a book so jealously that they can barely endure to have someone else read it or touch it. Such a situation, instead of gaining them the reward of gentleness and love, turns for them into occasions of impatience and even death. They have given away all their wealth out of love for Christ and yet they still hold on to their old heart-longings for things that do not matter, things for whose sake they grow angry. They are like those lacking the love of which the apostle spoke and in every way their lives turn fruitless and sterile. All this was foreseen in spirit by the blessed apostle. 'If I give all that I have to buy food for the poor,' he said, 'and if I hand over my body to be burnt, and yet have no love in me, then this is for nothing' (1 Cor 13:3). Perfection, then, is clearly not achieved simply by being naked, by the lack of wealth or by the rejection of honors, unless there is also that love whose ingredients the apostle described and which is to be found solely in purity of heart. Not to be jealous, not to be puffed up, not to act heedlessly, not to seek what does not belong to one, not to rejoice over some injustice, not to plan evil—what is this and its like if not the continuous offering to God of a heart that is perfect and truly pure, a heart kept free of all disturbance?

7

"Everything we do, our every objective, must be undertaken for the sake of this purity of heart. This is why we take on loneliness, fasting, vigils, work, nakedness. For this we must practice the reading of the Scripture, together with all the other virtuous activities, and we do so to trap and to hold our hearts free of the harm of every dangerous passion and in order to rise step by step to the high point of love.

"It may be that some good and necessary task prevents us from achieving fully all that we set out to do. Let us not on this account give way to sadness or anger or indignation, since it was precisely to repel these that we would have done what in fact we were compelled to omit. What we gain from fasting does not compensate for what we lose through anger. Our profit from scriptural reading in no way equals the damage we cause ourselves by showing contempt for a brother. We must practice fasting, vigils, withdrawal, and the meditation of Scripture as activities which are subordinate to our main objective, purity of heart, that is to say, love, and we must never disturb this principal virtue for the sake of those others. If this virtue remains whole and unharmed within us nothing can injure us, not even if we are forced to omit any of those other subordinate virtues. Nor will it be of any use to have practiced all these latter if there is missing in us that principal objective for the sake of which all else is undertaken.

"A worker takes the trouble to get hold of the instruments that he requires. He does so not simply to have them and not use them. Nor is there any profit for him in merely possessing the instruments. What he wants is, with their help, to produce the crafted objective for which these are the efficient means.

"In the same way, fasting, vigils, scriptural meditation, nakedness, and total deprivation do not constitute perfection but are the means to perfection. They are not themselves the end point of a discipline, but an end is attained through them. To practice them will therefore be useless if someone instead of regarding these as means to an end is satisfied to regard them as the highest good. One would possess the instruments of a profession without knowing the end where the hoped-for fruit is to be found.

"And so anything which can trouble the purity and the peace of our heart must be avoided as something very dangerous, regardless of how useful and necessary it might actually seem to be. With this for a rule we will be able to avoid the lack of concentration which comes as the mind follows highways and byways and we will be able to go with an assured sense of direction toward our longed-for goal.

8

"To cling always to God and to the things of God—this must be our major effort, this must be the road that the heart follows unswervingly. Any diversion, however impressive, must be regarded as secondary, low-grade, and certainly dangerous. Martha and Mary provide a most beautiful scriptural paradigm of this outlook and of this mode of activity. In looking after the Lord and His disciples Martha did a very holy service. Mary, however, was intent on the spiritual teaching of Jesus and she stayed by His feet, which she kissed and anointed with the oil of her good faith. And she got more credit from the Lord because she had chosen the better part, one which could not be taken away from her. For while Martha was working hard, responsibly and fully intent on her job, she realized that she could not do all the work herself and she demanded the help of her sister from the Lord. 'Does it not bother you that my sister leaves me to do the work alone?' she said. 'Tell her to come and help me' (Lk 10:40). Certainly she summons Mary to a task that is not inconsequential but is a praiseworthy service. Yet what does she hear from the Lord? 'Martha, Martha, you are full of worry and are upset over many things where actually it should be over a few or even one thing. Mary has chosen the good part and it will not be taken away from her' (Lk 10:41–42).

"You will note that the Lord establishes as the prime good contemplation, that is, the gaze turned in the direction of the things of God. Hence we say that the other virtues, however useful and good we may say they are, must nevertheless be put on a secondary level, since they are all practiced for the sake of this one. 'You are full of worry and are upset over many things when actually it should be over a few or even one.' In saying this the Lord locates the primary good not in activity, however praiseworthy, however abundantly fruitful, but in the truly simple and unified contemplation of Himself. He says that not much is needed for perfect blessedness. He means here that type of contemplation which is primarily concerned with the example of a few saints. Contemplating these, someone still on the upward road comes at last to that which is unique, namely the sight of God Himself, which comes with God's help. Having passed beyond the activities and the ministry of holy men he will live solely on the beauty and the knowledge of God. 'Mary therefore chose the good part and it will not be taken away from her.' But one must look carefully at this. In saying 'Mary chose the good part,' He was saying nothing about Martha and in no way was He giving the appearance of criticizing her. Still, by praising the one He was saying that the other was a step below her. Again, by saying 'it will not be taken away from her' He was showing that Martha's role could be taken away from her—since the service of the body can only last as long as the human being is there—whereas the zeal of Mary can never end."

9

We were deeply stirred by this. "So then" we said, "the toil of fasting, the constant scriptural reading, the works of mercy, justice, piety, and humanity will be taken away from us and will not remain as we remain? And this when the Lord Himself promised the reward of heaven to the people who do these things? 'Come you blessed of my Father,' He said. 'Take possession of the kingdom prepared for you from the beginning of the world. I was hungry and you gave me to eat. I was thirsty and you gave me to drink' (Mt 25:34–35). And all the rest. These things which bring the people who do them into the kingdom of heaven, how can they be taken away?"

10

Moses: "I did not say that the reward of a good deed must be taken away, for the same Lord said, 'Whoever will give even a glass of cold water to one of these little ones because he is one of my disciples, Amen I tell you, he will not lose his reward' (Mt 10:42). But what I do say is that an activity which takes place as a result of the needs of the body, the onslaught of the flesh, or the inequality of this world must come to an end. The dedication to scriptural reading or the infliction of fasts only serve the useful purpose of purifying the heart and punishing the flesh in this present life as long as it is the case that 'the flesh indulges itself against the spirit' (Gal 5:17). These activities are sometimes lifted from those who, wearied out by too much hard work, by sickness or by old age, are unable to practice them continuously. All the more reason, therefore, for these to cease in the next life when 'this corruption' will take on 'incorruptibility' (1 Cor 15:53), when this body which is now animal will rise as 'spirit' (1 Cor 15:44), when flesh will no longer indulge in conflict with the spirit. The blessed apostle spoke clearly about all this when he said that 'the exercising of the body has a limited value, whereas piety'—and no doubt he means love—'is useful for everything, holding as it does the promise of life both now and in the future' (1 Tm 4:8). What is said here about limited value is clearly right, since this is something which cannot be done for all time nor can it by itself bring us to the summit of perfection. The notion of limit can also indicate either the brevity of time, for bodily exercise is not something to last throughout the present and the future life, or else it refers to the minimal value of such exercise. The demands made on the body are actually only the beginning of the road to progress. They do not induce that perfect love which has within it the promise of life now and in the future. And so we consider the practice of such works to be necessary only because without them it is not possible to reach the high peaks of love.

"As for those works of piety and charity of which you speak, these are necessary in this present life for as long as inequality prevails. Their workings here would not be required were it not for the superabundant numbers of the poor, the needy, and the sick. These are there because of the iniquity of men who have held for their own private use what the common Creator has made available to all. As long as this inequity rages in the world, these good works will be necessary and valuable to anyone practicing them and they shall yield the reward of an everlasting inheritance to the man of good heart and concerned will.

"But all of this will cease in the time to come when equality shall reign, when there shall no longer be the injustice on account of which these good works must be undertaken, when from the multiplicity of what is done here and now everyone shall pass over to the love of God and to the contemplation of things divine. Men seized of the urge to have a knowledge of God and to be pure in mind devote all their gathered energies to this one task. While they still live in the corruption of the flesh they give themselves to that service in which they will persevere when that corruption has been laid aside. And already they come in sight of what the Lord and Savior held out when He said, 'Blessed are the clean of heart, for they will see God' (Mt 5:8).

11

"Why should you be surprised if these good works, referred to above, shall pass away? The blessed apostle described even the higher gifts of the Holy Spirit as things that would vanish. He points to love as alone without end. 'Prophecies will end, languages cease and knowledge will fail' (1 Cor 13:8). As for love, 'love will never cease.'

"Actually, all gifts have been given for reasons of temporal use and need and they will surely pass away at the end of the present dispensation. Love, however, will never be cut off. It works in us and for us, and not simply in this life. For when the burden of physical need has been laid aside in the time to come it will endure, more effectively, more excellently, forever unfailing, clinging to God with more fire and zeal through all the length of incorruption."

12

Germanus: "But, given the frailty of the flesh, who can ever be so intent on contemplation that his thoughts will never settle on the coming of a brother, the visit to a patient, the duties of hospitality which must be extended to travelers and to all passers-by? Who will not be turned aside by the requirements and need of his own body? What we really want to learn is the extent to which the spirit can actually be at one with the invisible, ungraspable God."

13

Moses: "As you say, a man surrounded by the frailty of the flesh cannot cling totally to God or be joined to Him in unbroken contemplation. Yet we certainly need to know the direction in which our mind must always go. We must be aware of the destination toward which we must always summon our spirit. And whenever the mind can succeed in this let it rejoice, and whenever it is distracted let it grieve and sigh, knowing that as often as it is turned aside from contemplation it has been cut off from the ultimate good, knowing that to veer for even a moment from beholding Christ is to be guilty of impurity. When our gaze has wandered even a little from Christ let us immediately turn the eyes of our heart back to Him and let our vision be directed to Him as though along the straightest line.

"For everything lies at the innermost recess of the soul. When the devil has been chased away from it and when sin is no longer in charge of it, then the kingdom of God is established there. This is what the evangelist conveys to us when he says, 'The kingdom of God will not come as something to be observed nor will people cry "Here it is! There it is!" Amen, I tell you the kingdom of God is within you' (Lk 17:20–21).

"Now there can be nothing else within us except the knowledge or unawareness of truth, the love of sin or of virtue, and with these we make a kingdom in the heart for the devil or for Christ. And what this kingdom is like is set out by the apostle when he says, 'The kingdom of God does not consist of eating and drinking, but in righteousness and peace and joy in the holy spirit' (Rom 14:17). If the kingdom of God is within us and that is a kingdom of justice, of peace, and of joy then whoever remains with these virtues is certainly in the kingdom of God. By contrast, all who deal in unrighteousness, in discord, and in death-bearing gloom have taken their stand in the kingdom of the devil, in hell and in lifelessness. It is by these tokens that the kingdom of God or of the devil is recognized.

"Actually, if we gaze upward in spirit to that condition enjoyed by the heavenly and celestial virtues who are truly in the kingdom of God, how else is this to be reckoned except as everlasting, continuous joy? What is more suitable and appropriate to true blessedness than an eternity of peace and joy?

"Do not imagine that what I am saying is simply my own point of view. Take it on the certain authority of the Lord Himself. Listen to Him as He gives a most luminous description of the character and condition of that world. 'Look, I am creating new heavens and a new earth. The past will not remain in the memory nor will it rise up over the heart. But you will delight and rejoice forever in these things which I bring forth' (Is 65:17–18). Or again, 'Joy and happiness will be found in this, a blessing and a voice of praise. And it will be so month after month, from sabbath to sabbath' (Is 51:3, 66:23). And again, 'They will have joy and gladness; pain and lamentation shall flee' (Is 35:10). If you want to have some clearer knowledge of that abode and realm of the saints, listen to the voice of the Lord speaking to the heavenly Jerusalem: 'I will give you peace for a visitor and will put justice as your judges. Iniquity shall no longer be heard of in your country nor ravage and ruin within your frontiers. Salvation will hold your walls and praise will be at your gates. No more will the sun light your day and the splendor of the moon will not shine upon you. You shall have the Lord for your everlasting light and your God for your glory. Your sun will set no more and your moon will not diminish. For you the Lord will be light eternal and the days of your mourning will be at an end' (Is 60:17–20).

"Accordingly, the blessed apostle does not describe joy in general or a particular joy as the kingdom of God but specifically and specially he points only to the joy in the Holy Spirit. He knows that there is another kind of joy, one which is blameworthy and of which it said 'this world shall rejoice' (Jn 16:20) and 'woe to you who laugh because you shall weep' (Lk 6:25).

"The kingdom of heaven can be understood in three ways. First, the heavens, that is to say, the saints shall rule over all the other men made subject to them, in accordance with the words 'You! Rule over five cities. And you! Rule over ten' (Lk 19:17, 19). And there is the statement to the apostles: 'You will sit on twelve thrones and you shall judge the twelve tribes of Israel' (Mt 19:28). Or, second, the skies themselves shall become the kingdom of Christ when all things have been put under His authority and when God shall be 'all in all' (1 Cor 15:28). Or, third, the blessed in heaven shall rule together with the Lord.

14

"Let everybody know this. He shall be assigned to the place and to the service to which he gave and devoted himself in this life and he can be sure that in eternity he will have as his lot the service and the companionship which he preferred in this life. This is what the Lord means when He says, 'If anyone is my servant let him follow me and where I am he will be there as my servant' (Jn 12:26).

"Just as the kingdom of the devil is raised up by the concourse of sin, the kingdom of God is possessed by way of the practice of virtue in purity of heart and in spiritual knowledge. Where the kingdom of God is, there certainly is eternal life, where the kingdom of the devil is, there surely is death and damnation, and there, in the words of the prophet, one cannot praise the Lord. 'The dead will not praise you, Lord, nor those who have gone down into hell'—sinners no doubt— 'but we who live'—not in sin, nor in the world, but in God—'we bless the Lord now and forever. No one who is dead remembers God, and in hell [i.e., sin] who shall utter his confession to the Lord?' (Ps 6:6). No one. Anyone who sins does not offer praise to the Lord, not even if he proclaims himself a thousand times to be a Christian and a monk. No one doing what the Lord abhors is mindful of God. Falsely he calls himself the servant of the One whose commands he rashly and contemptuously spurns. This is the kind of death of which the blessed apostle speaks when he refers to the widow who lives in luxury. 'The widow who lives for pleasure is in living death' (1 Tm 5:6).

"There are many indeed living in the body but actually dead. They lie in hell and cannot praise God.

"By contrast there are those who are dead to the body but who praise God in spirit and praise Him in accordance with the saying 'Spirits and souls of the just, give praise to the Lord' (Dn 3:86), and 'Let every spirit offer praise to the Lord' (Ps 150:6). In the Apocalypse the souls of those who have been killed are said not only to praise God but to cry out to Him. And in the gospel there is the clearer statement of the Lord when He says, 'Have you not read the utterance of God in the words "I am the God of Abraham and the God of Isaac and the God of Jacob." He is not the God of the dead but of the living' (Mt 22:31–32).

"Everyone therefore has life in him and regarding these the apostle says, 'That is why God was not ashamed to be called their God, since He has made ready a city for them' (Heb 11).

"The gospel parable of the poor man Lazarus and of the rich man clothed in purple shows us that souls separated from the body are neither inactive nor bereft of feeling. The one man wins as his blessed abode the peace that exists in the bosom of Abraham; the other is subjected to the unbearable scorchings of eternal fire. And if we wish to ponder what was said to the thief, namely, 'Today you shall be with me in paradise,' what other obvious meaning is there to this if not that souls continue to have their former sense of awareness and, further, that their lot is in keeping with their merits and with what they have done? The Lord would never have made this promise to the thief if He knew that the soul, once separated from the body, must lose all feeling and be turned into nothing. For it was the soul and not the body which would go with Christ to paradise.

"Now we must beware utterly of that most detestable distinction made by the heretics who do not wish to believe that Christ could not have been in heaven on the same day that He descended into hell. They break the sentence in two and have 'Amen, I say to you today' and then 'you shall be with me in paradise.' Hence the promise could not be considered to have been immediately fulfilled upon passing away from this life but rather after the resurrection. They do not understand what He said, quite some time before His resurrection, when speaking to the Jews who considered that He, like themselves, was locked into the limits and the fragility of human flesh: 'No one rises up to heaven except He who came down from heaven, the Son of man' (Jn 3:13).

"All of this clearly shows that not only are the souls of the dead not deprived of their intellectual faculties but that they also are not lacking in feelings such as hope and sadness, joy and fear. They already have a foretaste of what is in store for them after the general judgment. Nor does it happen, as some unbelievers would hold, that upon leaving this world they are turned to nothing. Actually they live more intensely and they concentrate more on the praises of God.

"If one might leave aside for a moment the evidence in Scripture and if I myself may be permitted to think a little about the nature of the soul, doing so to the extent possible to my poor intelligence, is it not the ultimate in stupidity, indeed of madness, to have a lightweight opinion of what is in fact the more valuable part of man? Here, as the blessed apostle says, is the image and likeness of God. Could this become devoid of awareness after having shed the corporeal burden by which it is held back in this life? All the power of reason lies here and gives consciousness to the dumb, unfeeling stuff of the flesh. It must surely follow, it must certainly happen that when the mind has shed the inhibiting grossness of the flesh it recovers in improved form its intellectual capacities, that it gathers, not loses, these in a purer and more penetrating condition.

"The blessed apostle is so convinced of what I am now saying that he goes so far as to long to depart from the flesh in order that by virtue of this separation he may be enabled to enter into the closest union with the Lord. 'I have a longing to be gone,' he says, 'and to be with Christ, which would be better' (Phil 1:23), 'because as long as we are in the body we are roaming from the Lord' (2 Cor 5:8–9). Thus, he is saying that the sojourn of spirit in this body is an exile from the Lord, an absence from Christ, and he believes totally that the separation and the departure from the body means a coming into the presence of Christ. And, more knowledgeably, the apostle has this to say about the most intense life of souls: 'But you have come to Mount Sion, to the city of the living God, to the heavenly Jerusalem, to the gathering of many millions of angels, to the church of the first-born who are enrolled as citizens of heaven, and to the spirits of the just who have been made perfect' (Heb 12:22–23). About these spirits he says elsewhere, 'Our fathers in the flesh have been our teachers and we have revered them. Should we not be all the more obedient to the father of the spirits and thereby have life?' (Heb 12:9).

15

"Contemplation of God can be understood in more than one fashion. For God is not solely known by way of that astonished gaze at His ungraspable nature, something hidden thus far in the hope that comes with what has been promised us. He can also be sensed in the magnificence of His creation, in the spectacle of His justice, and in the help He extends each day to the running of the world. He can be sensed too when with well-purified minds we consider what He has achieved in each generation by means of His saints. He can be sensed when we gaze with trembling hearts at that power of His which controls, guides, and rules everything, when we contemplate His immense knowledge and His knowing look which the secrets of the heart cannot evade. His presence is known when we meditate on the fact that the sands of the sea are numbered by Him, that He keeps a count of the waves. Astounded, we reflect that every drop of rain, every day and every hour of all the centuries, everything past and everything to come are all facts of which He is aware. Overwhelmed with wonder we think of that unspeakable mercy of His which allows Him to endure with unfailing patience the numberless crimes committed at every moment while He watches. We think of how in His pity for us He has called us to Him, though we had done nothing previously to deserve it. We think of all the times when He made it possible for us to be saved as His adopted sons. He ordained that our birth was to be such that His grace and the knowledge of His Law would be available to us from the cradle. And having overcome the adversary within us He offers us, in return merely for our goodwill, an eternity of happiness and of rewards. We think too of the incarnation, which He arranged for our salvation, and we think of how He spread to all people the wonder of His mysteries.

"There are innumerable other considerations of this kind. They surface within our sensibilities—depending on the quality of our living and purity of our hearts. By means of them God is seen and beheld in immaculate visions. And it is certain that none of them will be in the uninterrupted keeping of anyone who keeps alive in himself any of the desires of the flesh. 'You will not be able to look upon my face,' says the Lord, 'for a man will not look upon me and live' (Ex 33:20). Live, that is, in this world and amid earthly longings."

16

Germanus: "How is it then that despite ourselves, indeed without our even knowing it, useless thoughts slide into us, subtly and without our seeing them, so that it is no small thing not simply to drive them away but even to know and to grasp that they are there at all? Is it possible for the mind ever to be free of them, to remain unscathed by illusions of this sort?"

17

Moses: "It is impossible for the mind to remain undisturbed by thoughts, but anyone serious about the matter can certainly permit them entry or drive them away, and although their origin does not lie entirely under our control we can choose to approve of them and to adopt them.

"As I have said, it is not possible that the mind should be unapproached by thoughts. But these must not be attributed completely either to some incursion or those spirits which strive to slip them in among us. Otherwise man's free will would not remain nor would our task of self-discipline continue to be there. But I would say that to a great extent it is up to us to ensure the good character of our thoughts. It depends on us whether they turn holy and spiritual or else earthly and of the flesh. Now the regular reading and the continuous meditation on Scripture are undertaken so that a spiritual turn be given to our memory. The constant singing of the psalms is designed to produce a persistent compunction within us so that the mind, slimmed down, may not have a taste for the things of earth and will turn, instead, to behold the things of heaven. And if we carelessly neglect these, then of necessity the mind, filled with the squalor of sin, turns soon and comes rushing toward the domain of the flesh.

18

"This activity of the heart is compared, not inappropriately, to that of a mill which is activated by the circular motion of water. The mill cannot cease operations at all so long as it is driven round by the pressure of the water and it, then, becomes quite feasible for the person in charge to decide whether he prefers wheat or barley or darnel to be ground. And one thing is clear. Only that will be ground which is fed in by the one who is in charge.

"In a similar fashion, the mind is under pressure in this life. From all sides temptation comes in torrents to drive it along and in no way will it be free of turbulent thoughts. But the workings of zeal and diligence will decide which of those thoughts may be allowed in and cultivated. And, as I have said already, if we turn to the constant meditation on Scripture, if we lift up our memory to the things of the spirit, to the longing for perfection and to the hope of future blessedness, then the thoughts deriving from all this will of necessity be spiritual and they will hold the mind where the thoughts have been. However, if we are overcome by sloth or by carelessness, if we give ourselves over to dangerous and useless chattering, if we are caught up in worldly cares and in profitless worries, there will follow in effect from this a harvest of tares to serve as a ministry of death to our hearts. As the Lord our Savior proclaimed, where treasure lies for our works and for our hopes our hearts will of necessity abide there too.

19

"Above all we should realize that there are three sources for our thoughts—God, the devil, and ourselves.

52

"They come from God whenever He deigns to approach us through an illumination of the Holy Spirit, thereby lifting us up to a more sublime terrain. They come from Him whenever He brings a most saving compunction upon us amid the poverty of our efforts and the laziness of our activities. They come from Him whenever He opens up the mysteries of heaven to us, whenever He turns our thoughts to better deeds and to better resolutions.

"Consider King Asuerus, for example. Punished by the Lord, he was moved to search the records of his kingdom. These drew his attention to the good offices of Mardochaeus, for whom he proceeded to decree the highest honors, and forthwith he revoked the most cruel death sentence which he had passed on the Jewish people.

"Or again, there are the words of the prophet, 'I shall listen to what the Lord God has to say in me' (Ps 84:9). Also, 'The angel who was speaking within me had this to say' (Zec 1:14). Or again, when the Son promised that He would come with the Father to make a dwelling place in us, or when He said, 'It is not you who speak but it is the spirit of your Father who speaks in you' (Mt 10:20). And there are these words from Paul, the vessel of election, 'You are looking for a proof that it is Christ who is speaking in me' (2 Cor 13:3).

"A train of thoughts comes too into being from the devil when these undermine us with the attractiveness of sin and when the devil gets to us with his hidden snares, when with the subtlest of skills he deceitfully presents evil as good and on our behalf transforms himself into angel of light. Or, there is the story from the evangelist how 'during the supper the devil put it into the heart of Judas, son of Simon Iscariot, to betray the Lord' (Jn 13:2). And, again, 'After the morsel Satan entered into him' (Jn 13:27). Peter said to Ananias, 'Why has Satan tempted your heart, causing you to lie to the Holy Spirit?' (Acts 5:3). We read in the gospel what was said a long time before in Ecclesiastes: 'If the spirit of the one having power shall rise up against you, do not leave your place' (10:4). There is also what the unclean spirit said against Achab to God in book three of Kings: 'I shall go forth and I shall be a spirit of untruth in the mouths of all his prophets' (3 Kgs 22:12).

"Thoughts come from within ourselves when we think of what we do or have done or have heard. And this is natural. Regarding such matters, the blessed David said, 'I thought of the old days and in my mind I had the everlasting years; I gave myself to meditation and by night I was busy in my heart and I looked deeply into my own spirit' (Ps 76:6–7). Or again: 'The Lord knows the thoughts of men, for they are empty'

(Ps 93:11) and 'The thoughts of righteous men are thoughts of justice' (Prv 12:5). And in the gospel the Lord says to the Pharisees, 'Why do you think evil thoughts in your hearts?' (Mt 9:4).

20

"We must therefore keep a close eye on this threefold scheme of our thoughts and we must exercise a wise discretion concerning them as they surface in our hearts. Right from the beginning we will scrutinze their origins, their causes, their originators, deciding our necessary reaction to them in the light of who it is that suggests them. And we shall do this in order to become what the Lord described as skilled changers of currency whose greatest skill and knowledge consist in the fact that they can tell the difference between the purest gold and that which, having had the minimal testing in fire, is commonly described as *obryza* or standard gold. Or they can unfailingly observe when a cheap coin tries to look valuable, attempting with the gleaming color of gold to appear to be a precious item of money. It is not simply that they can tell which coins bear the heads of rulers but they can go farther and with their more informed skill they can spot the difference between fakes and those coins bearing a genuine likeness of the king. And they make careful use of the scales in case anything should be missing from the legal weight.

"We have the obligation to take the same precautions in all spiritual matters, as is clear from the use of the term *money-changers* in the gospel.

"So we must first scrutinize thoroughly anything appearing in our hearts or any saying suggested to us. Has it come purified from the divine and heavenly fire of the Holy Spirit? Or does it lean toward Jewish superstition? Is its surface piety something which has come down from bloated worldly philosophy? We must examine this most carefully, doing as the apostle bids us: 'Do not believe in every spirit, but make sure to find out if spirits are from God' (1 Jn 4:1).

"This is what has happened in the case of many who were actually fooled. Having solemnly undertaken monastic life, they were won over by the glitter of words or by the utterances of philosophers, all of which, as they heard them, seemed to be right and seemed to accord with religion, for they had the deceptive gleam of gold. And once they had enticed these men away it was as though they had deceived them with their spurious coinage and they thrust them down into unending nakedness and wretchedness. They dragged them back either into the tumult of the world or else into heretical error and swelling presumption.

"Such as the misfortune of Achor, of which we read in the book of Jesus, son of Nave. He turned a covetous eye on a golden ladle from the camp of the Philistines. He stole it, and for this he was condemned and earned an everlasting doom for himself.

"Secondly, it will be proper for us to watch very carefully in case a false interpretation, hammered out from the purest gold of Scripture, should deceive us with its merely metallic value. In this respect the devil, with his utmost skill, tried a deception on the Lord our Savior— as though he were dealing with a mere man. This is something which happens in the case of all the just. The devil changed scriptural sense by means of a maliciously intended interpretation and tried to make it fit particularly the very One who has no need at all of the guardianship of angels. 'He has given orders to his angels concerning you that they are to guard you in all your paths. And they will carry you in their hands lest you should happen to strike your foot against a stone' (Mt 4:6). By skilled abuse he disturbs the precious utterances of Scripture, twisting them to an opposite and dangerous sense in order that he might display the image of a tyrannous countenance in the deceptive guise of gold.

"He tries to fool us by means of counterfeit pieces. He urges us on to some task which has not the authentic stamp of the ancients and which, seemingly for the sake of virtue, leads us into sin. By means of excessive or inappropriate fasting, through unduly long vigils, through prayer out of turn or scriptural reading at the wrong time, he works deceit and leads on to a destructive end. He persuades us to undertake visitation for reasons of charity so as to drive us out of the spiritual enclosure of the monastery and from the quiet of friendly peace. He inspires us to show concern and care for women who are leading lives in religion and destitution, and all this so as to ensnare some monk beyond rescue in the coils of pernicious concerns. Or, again, he moves us to wish for clerical duties. The pretext is the edification of numerous souls or the desirability of spiritual gain. The purpose, however, is to draw us in this way from the lowliness and the austerity of our lives.

"All these activities run counter to what is safe for us and to our profession. However, since they are covered by the cloak of mercy and of religion they easily deceive the unskilled and the unwary. They put on the show of being the coinage of the true king, for they seem for the moment to abound in piety. But they do not come out of the lawful mint. That is, they are not given their shape by the authentic Catholic Fathers nor did they come forth from the official and public quarters of their learning. They are the furtive, fraudulent work of demons who hand them on to the unskilled and to the ignorant and do so to their detriment.

"However useful and necessary these may seem at the moment, if they afterward begin to be at variance with the stability of our profession and to bring great harm to our way of life, salvation requires that they be thrown away and cut off from us, for they are like some necessary but damaging limb, a right hand or a foot which has an essential function to perform. Better to be minus a limb—that is, to forgo the fulfillment and benefit of some precept—to remain healthy and vigorous, to enter with an infirmity into the kingdom of heaven, better this than to fall over some stumbling block while one is preoccupied with some valuable precept. A dangerous habit can draw us away from the penitential rule and from the discipline of our adopted way of life. It can plunge us into such disaster that, unable to make up for the losses to come, all our past merits and indeed the body of all our work are burned up in the fires of hell.

"The book of Proverbs spoke very aptly of such illusions: 'There are paths which seem right to a man, but their outcome is in the depths of hell' (Prv 16:25). Or again, 'The evil one does harm when he mingles with the just' (Prv 11:15). That is, the devil deceives whenever he is protected by the color of sanctity.

21

"Indeed, we know that the abbot John, who lives in Lyco, was recently deceived in this way. At a time when his body was worn and weakened he put off the taking of food by prolonging his fast for an extra two days. Then on the following day, while he was getting ready to eat, the devil came to him in the form of a ghastly Ethiopian and threw himself on his knees before him. 'Forgive me,' he said, 'It was I who imposed this toil on you.' This most excellent man, outstanding in his perspicacity, realized that in the very prolonged fast, undertaken in the guise of abstinence, he had been got at by the skill of the devil in order that he might impose on his weary body an unnecessary fatigue, one that would actually be harmful to his soul. He had been deceived by specious coinage. He had shown respect for the image there of the true king and had paid too little attention to its authenticity.

"Finally, there is the test to be applied to the money-changer, a test which, as I have already stated, has to do with checking the weight. This is how it is practiced. If our thoughts suggest something to us to be done we must handle it with the utmost scrupulosity. It must be placed on the scales of our heart and weighed with the most exacting care. Is it filled with what is good for all? Is it heavy with the fear of God? Is it genuine in the feelings which underlie it? Is it lightweight because of human show or because of some thrust toward novelty? Has the burden of vainglory lessened its merit or diminished its luster? This prompt testing will be done as something public. That is, it is measured against the acts and the witness of the apostles. If it looks to be whole, complete, and in conformity with these latter, then let us hold on to it. Or if it seems defective, dangerous, and not of equal weight with these, let us cautiously and carefully reject it.

22

"So, then, the four kinds of discernment to which I have been referring will be necessary to us. First, as to material, is it true gold or spurious? Second, we must reject as fake and counterfeit coinage those thoughts which have the deceptive appearance of piety. They bear a false and not the genuine image of the king. Then we must be able to detect and to abhor those which impose a viciously heretical stamp on the precious gold of Scripture. This is not the effigy of the true king but of a tyrant. Finally, we must drive away thoughts which are like underweight coins, dangerous and inadequate, thoughts which have lost weight and value because of the rust of vanity, thoughts which do not measure up to the standard of the ancients.

"In this way we shall avoid the misfortune against which the Lord warned us to be totally on our guard so as not to be cheated of the merit and the reward of our labors. 'Do not store up treasures for yourselves on earth where the moths and the worms destroy them and where thieves can break in and steal them' (Mt 6:19). Whatever we do for the sake of human glory this we know to be, as the Lord says, the treasure we gather on earth. Hence it is like something hidden in the ground and buried in the earth, and it is there to be filched by various demons, to be used up by the consuming rust of vainglory, or to be devoured by the worms of pride. And it will be of no use or profit to the one who concealed it.

"All the corners of our heart must therefore be examined thoroughly and the marks of all that rise up into them must be investigated with the utmost wisdom. And all this must be done in case some beast of the mind, some lion or serpent, has passed through and has left its dangerous hidden marks there, marks by which, as a result of the way we neglect our thoughts, a way into the sanctuary of our heart may be made available to others. Every hour and every moment working over the earth of our heart with the plough of Scripture, that is, with the memory of the Lord's cross, we shall manage to destroy the lairs of the wild beasts within us and the hiding places of the venomous serpents."

23

The old man looked at us and at how we were stirred by all this. He saw that we were inflamed by an unquenchable enthusiasm for what he had been saying. He even stopped talking for a moment because he was astonished by our eagerness. Then he added thus:

"My sons, it is your zeal which led me to speak for so long. Because of your eagerness, some kind of fire has given a more urgent sense to what I have been saying. But in order that I may observe more clearly your thirst for the doctrine of the life of perfection, I want to say a few things to you about the particular excellence and beauty of discernment. Among all the virtues it holds the scepter and the rule. I want to speak of its preeminence and its value, and I wish to do so not only by means of examples taken from every day but also by means of the old sayings and opinions of the fathers. For I am reminded of what happened to me many times. People came to me with groans and tears asking for a discourse of this kind, and I myself was eager to bestow some doctrine upon them. But I could not. Ideas failed me. Words too. I found myself having to send my visitors away without even a little consolation. By these signs it is easy to realize that the grace of the Lord inspires a speaker in direct proportion to the merit and the eagerness of those who are listening to him.

"Very little remains of the night and not enough for me to say what I have to say. Better then to give this time over to rest. The body will claim everything if denied the little to which it is entitled. So we will put off until tomorrow or the next night the discussion of this subject. It is only right that the masters of discernment should give evidence of the good workings of their minds! They should show themselves to possess the virtue which they teach so that while they talk of that virtue which is the mother of moderation they do not succumb to the very opposite vice. May the virtue of discernment, which I propose to investigate with the Lord's help, have this first advantage to confer on us, namely, that while I speak of its splendor and of that moderation in which its primary excellence is known to consist, it may not permit my words to drag far beyond the limits of time."

In this way the blessed Moses put an end to the discussion. We of course were eagerly hanging on to what he might say. But he urged us to enjoy a bit of sleep, suggesting to us that we might stretch out on the mats on which we had been sitting. Under our heads we put the coverlets he gave us. These are made out of the thicker papyruses which are drawn into big or small bundles tied together at every foot and a half. They are also the low seats used by the brethren when they meet together in assembly and they put them under their heads to sleep on. They are not too hard and they provide support which is easily shaped and manageable. They are most suitable for these various monastic uses and are convenient. They are yielding and they can be acquired for little work and expense, since the papyrus grows everywhere along the banks of the Nile. Being handled easily and also light they can be carried or moved as needed.

This is how, on the advice of the old man, we got ready to have a little sleep. But what a nuisance this sleep! And we hung between the pleasures of the discussion we had just heard and the expectation of that which had been promised us.

Conference Two

ON DISCERNMENT

1

We had a short morning sleep and then, joyously, we saw the coming of daylight. We began to beg for the talk which had been promised us, and so the blessed Moses began to speak.

"I see you are fired by a very great longing. That brief interval of rest which I set aside from our spiritual discussion for the sake of the flesh's repose can hardly have been of much benefit to the body. And as I now look upon your zeal I have a much greater worry. For the more insistent your demand, the greater the care I owe to your faith. As Scripture says: 'If you sit down to dine at the table of a great man, take careful note of what you are given and reach your hand out to it in the sure knowledge that you too must get the like ready' (Prv 23:1–2).

"We are going to talk about discernment, its goodness, its special excellence. We had reached it last night as the concluding point of our discussion, and I think I shall first establish its outstanding character by reference to the opinions of the fathers. When it is clear what our predecessors thought or said about it, I shall then cite the example of various people whose catastrophic downfall, in the past and in recent times, was due to the fact that they had paid it scant attention. Then, to the best of my ability, I shall deal with its use and benefit. Following on this, I shall study its goodness and value and we will consider how we may more effectively locate it and cultivate it.

"This is no minor virtue, nor one which can be seized anywhere merely by human effort. It is ours only as a gift from God and we read in the apostle that it is to be numbered among the most outstanding gifts of the Holy Spirit. 'To one the gift of preaching the word of wisdom is given by the spirit, to another is given a word of instruction by the same spirit, to another faith in the same spirit, to another the gift of healing through this one spirit' (1 Cor 12:8–9). Further on is 'to another is given the discernment of spirits' (ibid. 10). And following on the full list of the spiritual gifts he adds that 'it is the one and same spirit which works all of these, giving them out to each one as he chooses' (ibid. 11).

"So you see, then, that the gift of discernment is neither earthly nor of little account, but is, rather, a very great boon of divine grace. And if a monk does not do his utmost to acquire it and if he does not have a clear knowledge of the spirits rising up against him he will surely stray like someone in a dark night amid gruesome shadows and not only will he stumble into dangerous pits and down steep slopes but he will often fall even in the level, straightforward places.

2

"I remember the years when I was still a boy in that section of the Thebaid where the blessed Antony used to live. Some older men came to visit him and to talk to him about perfection. Their talk lasted from the evening hours until dawn and the problem we are now discussing took up the greatest part of the night.

"There was a most searching inquiry into which of the virtues and which observance could always preserve a monk from the snares and the deceptions of the devil and could lead him with firm tread on a sure path to the summit of perfection. Each one offered an opinion in accordance with the understanding he had of the matter. Some declared that by means of zealous fasting and the keeping of vigils the mind would be enlarged and would produce purity of heart and body so as to enable one to come all the more easily into union with God. Others posited detachment from everything in order that the mind, shorn of everything, freed from all the snares which were holding it back, would come more speedily to God. Others thought that what was necessary was to get completely away, to have the solitude and secrecy of the desert where a man, living there always, could converse more intimately with God and where union could be achieved more directly. Some opted for the practice of charity, that is to say, the works of hospitality, since it was to people of this kind that the Lord in the gospel promised especially that he would give the kingdom of heaven. 'Come, you blessed ones of my father, come and possess the kingdom which has been ready for you since the beginning of the world. I was hungry and you gave me food to eat. I was thirsty and you gave me a drink,' and so on (Mt 25:34–35).

61

"Thus it was that the different virtues were said to give a more certain access to God. And most of the night was spent in this inquiry.

"Finally, the blessed Antony spoke. 'All the things that you have spoken about are necessary and helpful to those thirsting for God and longing to reach him. But the countless disasters and experiences of many people do not permit that any one of these virtues should be said to be the prime influence for good. For very often we have seen people who have been most zealous in their fasts and vigils, who have lived wondrously solitary lives, who have endured such total privation of everything that they would not allow themselves to hold on to even a day's food or even a single coin of the lowest value, who have hastened to do all that is required in charity—and who have suddenly fallen prey to illusion with the result that not only could they not give a fitting end to the work they had undertaken but they brought to an abominable conclusion that high zeal of theirs and that praiseworthy mode of life. Hence if we probe the exact reason for their delusion and fall we will be able to recognize what it is that, above all else, leads us to God. The virtuous activities, of which you were talking, flourished among them. But the lack of discernment prevented them from reaching the end. No other cause can be found for their downfall. Lacking the training provided by older men they could in no way acquire this virtue of discernment which, avoiding extremes, teaches the monk to walk always on the royal road. It keeps him from veering to the right, that is, it keeps him from going with stupid presumption and excessive fervor beyond the boundary of reasonable restraint. It keeps him from going to the left to carelessness and sin, to sluggishness of spirit, and all this on the pretext of actually keeping the body under control.'

"It is discernment which in Scripture is described as the eye and the lamp of the body. This is what the Savior says, 'Your eye is the light of your body, and if your eye is sound then there is light in your whole body. But if your eye is diseased then your entire body will be in darkness' (Mt 6:22–23). This eye sees through all the thoughts and actions of a man, examining and illuminating everything which we must do. And if it is not sound in a man, that is, if it is not fortified by good judgment and by well-founded knowledge, if it is deluded by error and by presumption, this makes for darkness in our entire body. The clear thrust of the mind as well as everything we do will be shadowed and we shall be wrapped in the blindness of sin and the blackness of passion. 'If the light within you is darkness,' says the Savior, 'what a darkness that will be' (Mt 6:23). For let no one doubt that our thoughts and our works, which originate from the deliberative processes of discernment, will be caught up in the shadows of sin if ever the good judgment of our heart goes astray or is taken over by the night of ignorance.

3

"This is how it was with the one who, by a decision of God, was first to obtain the kingship of the people of Israel. He lacked this discerning eye and, as it were, he became darkened in his entire body. He was cast down from the throne. His was the glow of shadow and of error. He thought that his sacrifices would be more pleasing to God than any obedience to the commandment of Samuel. Hence his disgrace, even as he was hoping to make himself agreeable to God.

"And I say that this inability to discern was responsible for the fact that following the outstanding triumph accorded him by divine favor, King Achab of Israel was impelled to believe that his show of mercy was preferable to the very harsh execution of God's command, a command which seemed a cruel one to him. Thinking in this way he grew weaker. He preferred to temper a bloody victory with clemency and because of this unwise show of mercy he was, so to speak, reduced to darkness in his whole body and was condemned to a death from which there was no recall.

4

"Such, then, is discernment, and not only is it called the lamp of the body but is even described as 'the sun' by the apostle when he says 'may the sun not set upon your anger' (Eph 4:26).

"It is called the 'guide' of our life, in line with the words 'those without a guide will fall like the leaves' (Prv 11:14).

"Very rightly it is called 'good sense' and the full weight of Scripture forbids us to do anything without it, even to the extent that we are told not to drink the wine of the soul without being guided by it, that wine 'which gladdens the heart of a man' (Ps 103:15). These are the words: 'Do everything sensibly, drink wine sensibly' (Prv 31:3). Or again, 'Like a city with walls down and with no defense, such is the man who does anything without good sense' (Prv 25:28).

"How dangerous the lack of good sense can be to a monk is borne out by the witness and example of this last text, which compares him to a city which is ruined and without walls.

"Wisdom, intelligence, and sound judgment lie hereabout, and without these the house of our interior life cannot be built nor can the riches of the soul be amassed. This is what Scripture says: 'A house is built by wisdom and it rises strong and firm because of intelligence. And sound judgment fills up its cellars with every rich and good treasure' (Prov 24:3–4). This, I say, is the solid food which can be taken only by the mature and the strong. As Scripture says, 'Solid food is for mature men, for those trained by the habit of telling the difference between good and evil' (Heb 5:14). It is considered so helpful and necessary to us that it is linked to the Word of God and to His virtues. As Scripture says, 'The Word of God is living and active, more cutting than any two-edged sword, reaching through to mark off the soul from the spirit and the joints from the marrow, and discerning the thoughts and wishes of the heart' (Heb 4:12).

"Hence it is very clear that no virtue can come to full term or can endure without the grace of discernment. And thus it was the agreed opinion of the blessed Antony and of all those with him that it is discernment which with firm step leads the enduring monk to God and which holds utterly intact together all the virtues referred to above. With discernment it is possible to reach the utmost heights with the minimum of exhaustion. Without it there are many who despite the intensity of their struggle have been quite unable to arrive at the summit of perfection. For discernment is the mother, the guardian, and the guide of all the virtues.

5

"A recent example of the kind that I promised you will show the force of that description proclaimed of old by the blessed Antony and by the other fathers. Think of what you recently saw happening before your very eyes. Remember the old man Hero who was cast down from the heights to the lowest depths because of a diabolical illusion. I remember how he remained fifty years in this desert, keeping to the rigors of abstinence with a severity that was outstanding, loving the secrecy of the solitary life with a fervor marvelously greater than that of any one else dwelling here. After such toil how and why could he have been fooled by the deceiver? How could he have gone down into so great a ruin that all of us here in the desert were stricken with pain and grief? Surely the reason for it was that he had too little of the virtue of discernment and that he preferred to be guided by his own ideas rather than to bow to the advice and conferences of his brethren and to the rules laid down by our predecessors. He practiced fasting so rigorously and so relentlessly, he was so given to the loneliness and secrecy of his cell, that even the special respect due to the Easter day could not persuade him to join the brethren in their meal. He was the only one who could not come together with all his brethren assembled in church for the feast, and the reason for this was that by taking the tiniest share of the vegetables he might give the impression of having relaxed from what he had chosen to do.

"This presumptuousness led to his being fooled. He showed the utmost veneration for the angel of Satan, welcoming him as if he were actually an angel of light. Yielding totally to his bondage he threw himself headlong into a well, whose depths no eye could penetrate. He did so trusting completely in the assurance of the angel who had guaranteed that on account of the merit of his virtues and of his works he could never come to any harm. To experience his undoubted freedom from danger the deluded man threw himself in the darkness of night into this well. He would know at first hand the great merit of his own virtue when he emerged unscathed. He was pulled out half-dead by his brothers, who had to struggle very hard at it. He would die two days later. Worse, he was to cling firmly to his illusion, and the very experience of dying could not persuade him that he had been the sport of devilish skill. Those who pitied him his leaving had the greatest difficulty in obtaining the agreement of abbot Paphnutius that for the sake of the merit won by his very hard work and by the many years endured by him in the desert he should not be classed among the suicides and, hence, be deemed unworthy of the remembrance and prayers offered for the dead.

6

"And then there were the two brothers who lived on the far side of the desert at Thebais, where the blessed Antony had been. Traveling across the vast emptiness of that uninhabited region they were moved by a lapse of discernment to resolve that the only food they would take would be whatever the Lord Himself offered them. They were staggering through the desert, weak from hunger, when they were spotted from a distance by the Mazices. This is a people more savage and cruel than almost any other tribe. Some shed blood for the sake of loot but these are stirred by sheer ferocity. And yet in spite of their innate barbarism they rushed with bread to the two men.

"One of them, moved by discernment, accepted with joy and blessing the food offered him, as if it were the Lord Himself who was giving it. In his view the food had been made available by God Himself.

It had to be God's work that those who always rejoiced in the shedding of blood were now giving of what they had to weak and wasted men.

"The other man refused the food. It had been offered by man. And he died of hunger.

"Both had started out with a wrong decision. One, however, with the help of discernment changed his mind about something which he had rashly and imprudently decided. The other man stuck to his foolish presumptuousness. Knowing nothing about discernment he drew down upon himself the death which the Lord had wished to avert. He would not believe that at God's instigation wild barbarians had so forgotten their innate savagery as to come with bread instead of the sword.

7

"Then there is the man whose name I do not wish to mention since he is still alive. For a long while he saw the devil shining before him like an angel and he was so often granted innumerable revelations that he was fooled into believing him to be a messenger of justice. Besides, without the aid of any lamp the visitor illuminated his cell every night.

"Finally, he was commanded by the demon to offer up his own son, then living with him in the monastery, so that by this sacrifice he might equal the merit of Abraham the patriarch. He was so completely taken in that he would have done the deed of killing had it not been for the fact that his son, noticing that he was sharpening a knife in an unusual manner and that he was getting chains ready as a preliminary to sacrifice, guessed the crime to be committed and ran away in terror.

8

"It would take a long time to tell in detail how a monk from Mesopotamia was deceived. Very few in that province could imitate the abstemiousness which alone in his cell he had practiced in so singular a manner. And then after all those toils and virtues in which he surpassed every monk living there he was so deceived by devilish revelation and dreams that he lapsed wretchedly into Judaism and circumcision.

"At first the devil wanted him to get used to having visions so that he could be led on to a subsequent delusion. For a long time he told him things that were quite true, as though he himself were a messenger of truth. Finally he showed him the Christian people, together with the apostles and martyrs who are the founders of our religion and faith. There they were—in darkness and filth, lean, rotting, and misshapen.

By contrast, the Jewish people, together with Moses, the patriarchs, and the prophets, were dancing with the greatest joy and were sparkling with a most resplendent light. And the devil told him that if he wished to share in their merit and blessedness he should hurry to be circumcised.

"No one of these men would have been so sadly deluded if they had worked to acquire the guidance of discernment. The downfall and the experience of many give proof of how dangerous it is not to have this grace of discernment."

9

In reply, Germanus said this: "These recent examples and the authoritative statements of our predecessors show clearly the extent to which discernment is the source and root of all the virtues. What we want to know is how to acquire it. How can we recognize something to be true and from God or false and from the devil?

"Taking up that gospel story which you explained in the first conference—the one telling us to become genuine money-changers—when we see on a coin the image of the true king we ought to be able to know if it is spurious and, in the common usage referred to by you in yesterday's conference, we should be able to reject it as being counterfeit. You are men possessing this skill. You have followed it fully and completely. You have marked what it is that the money-changer has of the spiritual, of the gospel. What use is it to us to know the merit attached to the virtue and grace of discernment if we are unaware of how to find and to acquire it?"

10

Then Moses spoke. "True discernment is obtained only when one is really humble. The first evidence of this humility is when everything done or thought of is submitted to the scrutiny of our elders. This is to ensure that one trusts one's own judgment in nothing, that one yields to their authority in everything, that the norms for good and bad must be established in accordance with what they have handed down.

"Not only will this procedure teach the young monk to march directly along the true road of discernment but it will actually keep him safe from all the deceits and snares of the enemy. Someone who lives not by his own decisions but by the example of the ancients will never be deceived. The skill of the enemy will not be able to delude the ignorance of a man who does not, out of dangerous shame, conceal the thoughts arising in his heart and who rejects or accepts them following upon their quick examination by older men. An evil thought sheds its danger when it is brought out into the open, and even before the verdict of discernment is proferred the most foul serpent which, so to speak, has been dragged out of its dark subterranean lair into the light by the fact of open avowal retreats, disgraced and denounced. Its dangerous promptings hold sway in us as long as these are concealed in the heart.

"And in order that you may more readily understand the force of what I am saying, I will tell you something which happened to the Abbot Sarapion, something which he very often told his younger brethren for their own good.

11

"He said: 'When I was very young and living with the abbot Theo, a habit grew in me as a result of diabolical assault. After a meal shared by me with the old man at the ninth hour each day I would conceal on my person a bit of bread which I secretly devoured later, unknown to him. I continued to be guilty of this hidden act. My will cooperated and there was no restraint at all on my urges. However, when my greed was satisfied my cheating returned to me and I suffered guilty torment that was much worse than any gratification I had experienced while eating. It turned into a burden as painful to me as that endured of old under the overseers of Pharaoh. Each day my heart suffered the torment of this compulsion and yet I was unable to break free of this most cruel tyranny and I was too ashamed to reveal my thieving to the old man.

" 'But then as a result of God's wish to snatch me from my captivity some brethren came to the cell of the old man for the sake of edification. After a meal a spiritual discussion began and, in answer to questions put to him, the old man started to talk about the sin of greed and about the way secret thoughts take a grip on someone. He examined their nature and described the most appalling power they have when they are concealed.

" 'I was stung by the direct impact of this discussion and was deeply frightened by the awareness of my guilt. I began to believe that if these things were now being said the reason lay in the fact that the Lord had revealed the secrets of my heart to the old man. At first I was moved to a sadness hidden within myself. Then my heart grew ever more scalded until I broke openly into sobs and tears. I pulled out the piece of bread which in my sinful habit I had taken away to be eaten secretly. I pulled it out from my breast which had shared the knowledge of my furtiveness and which had gone along with it. I put it out in front of everyone and, prostrate on the ground, I begged for pardon and I confessed how each day I was eating secretly. I poured out a rich flood of tears and I implored them to ask of God that I be delivered from my captivity.'

"Then the old man said this to me: 'Take heart, my son. Without my saying anything, your confession has set you free from this captivity. Today you have won a victory over the adversary who had beaten you. Through your confession you have brought him down more completely than when you yourself were down as a result of that silence which he had prompted. No word uttered by you or by anyone else had stopped him, and until now you had given him the whip hand over you, just as Solomon said, "Because nothing is said against those doing wrong, the heart of the sons of man is so filled up that they do wrong" (Eccl 8:11). Now because of this open denunciation of him, that most evil spirit will not be able to trouble you, and this most loathsome serpent will not take up a hiding place within you, for he has been pulled out into the light from your shadowed heart by this saving confession of yours.'

"And the old man had scarcely finished these words when a lamp was lighted in my breast and it so filled the cell with its sulphurous smell that its fierce stink barely allowed us to remain.

"The old man continued: 'See! The Lord has given open proof to you of the truth of what I was saying. He wanted you to see the instigator of this passion expelled from your heart and before your very eyes as a result of this saving confession. He wanted you to realize that by this open expulsion no further place would lie open within you for the enemy.'

"It was just as the old man said. Through the power of this confession the grip of this diabolic tyranny was wiped out and forever laid to rest. The enemy never even bothered to revive in me the memory of this urge and after this I never again felt myself moved by the wish to engage in stealing of this kind. We read this notion expressed so very well in Ecclesiastes: 'If the serpent does not have a whistling bite there will be no abundance for the soothsayer' (Eccl 10:11). What he is noting there is the silent bite. That is to say, if one does not confess a diabolic idea or thought to some soothsayer, to some spiritual person well used to finding in the magic, all-powerful words of Scripture an immediate cure for these serpent bites and the means of driving the fatal poison from the heart, there can be no help for the one who is in danger and about to perish.

"We will most easily come to a precise knowledge of true discernment if we follow the paths of our elders, if we do nothing novel, and if we do not presume to decide anything on the basis of our own private judgment. Instead let us in all things travel the road laid down for us by the tradition of our elders and by the goodness of their lives. Strengthened by this routine a person will not only reach the summit of discernment but he will remain completely safe from all the snares of the enemy. For the devil drags a monk headlong to death by way of no other sin than that of submission to private judgment and the neglect of the advice of our elders.

"All the skills and disciplines devised by human talent for the benefit of this temporal life can be laid hold of, observed, and understood, but only with the necessary help of some instructor. Now the spiritual life is unseen and hidden, open to only the purest heart. Here the fact of going wrong brings harm that is not of this world and that cannot easily be rectified. Rather, it causes the loss of the soul and an everlasting death. So then how stupid it is to believe that only this way of life has no need of a teacher! Here the enemy to be encountered is not visible but is unseen and pitiless. Here the spiritual fight goes on day and night and is waged not against one or two but against countless hordes and is all the more dangerous for everyone because the enemy is more vicious and more secretive. And so the footsteps of our elders must always be followed with the utmost care and every thought in our hearts must be submitted to them, stripped of the cover of false modesty."

12

Germanus: "The main reason for this dangerous false modesty, leading to our urge to conceal bad thoughts, is something we have encountered. We knew someone in Syria who was deemed the most outstanding of the elders, but when a brother came to him to confess openly the thoughts which were troubling him he was moved to rage and he very sternly upbraided him. As a result, we bury our thoughts and we blush to tell our elders about them, so that we find ourselves unable to acquire the remedy for these problems."

13

Moses: "Just as all young people are not equally fervent nor equally trained in wisdom and virtue, so all elderly men are not found to be equally virtuous, equally of the most proven excellence. It is not white hair which constitutes the riches of old men but the zeal they showed in their youth and the toils which they undertook. 'How can you find in old age what you did not gather in your youth? Old age is honorable not because of length of days nor is it reckoned in the number of years. Understanding—that is whiteness of hair; an untarnished life—that is ripe old age' (Wis 4:8–9).

"Therefore we must not follow the tracks or the traditions or the advice of all old men of whom white hair and length of years are the sole recommendation. Rather, we must follow those who, we know, stamped their youth in a praiseworthy and admirable fashion and who were trained not by their own presumption but by the traditions of their elders. There are many—and, sad to say, they are the majority—who grow old in the lukewarm laziness which they adopted as youths and who look to be authoritative not because of mature character but because of the toll of their years. These are the ones so rightly criticized by the Lord in the words of the prophet: 'Foreigners eat his strength away and he knows nothing about it; grey hairs are scattered over him and he knows nothing of it' (Hos 7:9). These are the ones, I say, who are held up to the young not because of their life's probity nor because of any praiseworthy and admirable zeal but only because of the number of their years. That most skilled adversary makes use of their white hairs, presenting them as the foreordained signs of authority—and all this to deceive the young who could be led out on to the road of perfection by their own advice or the advice of others. The enemy hastens to undermine them, with cheating subtlety to deceive them through the example of these old men. He turns their teaching and their way of life into dangerous laziness or fatal hopelessness.

"I have an example of this for you. But I am omitting the name of the man responsible since, otherwise, I would be guilty of doing what he did, namely, telling the world of sins confided by a brother. I will simply confine myself to what happened so as to provide you with the guidance that you need.

"Someone, by no means the least dedicated among the young men, came to an old man whom I knew well. He came for help, and he explained that he was troubled by the urges of the flesh and by the spirit of fornication. He felt sure that the prayers of the old man would ease his troubles and cure his wounds.

"But the old man berated him in the bitterest terms, calling him an unworthy wretch, exclaiming that he had no right to bear the name of monk in view of the fact that he was stirred by this kind of sin and concupiscence. And he so hurt the other with his reproaches that, as a consequence, the young man left the cell in utter misery and deadly despair. Weighed down with sadness, thinking deeply not so much about the cure for his passionate longing as about the realization of his desire, he met Apollo, the holiest of all the old monks. Apollo could see how troubled he was and how fierce a battle he was silently waging in his heart. Observing the depressed look on his face he asked to know the reason for such distress. The other could muster no reply to the gentle persistence of the old man. More and more the old man felt that it was not for nothing that the reason for such wretchedness was being veiled in silence, and the other's expression could not hide what he really felt. So ever more insistently he began to demand to know the causes of such hidden grief. Cornered, the young man told his story and declared that since, according to the old man he had consulted, he was incapable of being a monk and since he could neither check the urges of the flesh nor get a cure for his temptation he was going to leave the monastery, get married, and return to the world.

"The old man soothed him with gentle consolation, claiming that he too was moved each day by the same urges and tossed by the same storms. He urged him not to fall headlong into despair and not to be astonished by the ferocity of temptation. This was something to be conquered, not so much by the thrust of one's own effort as by the mercy and grace of the Lord. He asked the young man to hold off for just this one day and he begged him to go back to his cell.

"He went as speedily as he could to the living quarters of the other old man and as he drew close to it he stretched out his hands and, weeping, he prayed. 'Lord,' he said, 'you alone are the blessed judge of our hidden strength and the secret healer of human weakness. Turn the temptation aside from the youngster and on to that old man. Do this so that in his old age he may learn to reach down in kindness to the weaknesses of those in toil and may sympathize with the frailty of the young.'

"Moaning, he finished this prayer, and just then caught sight of a loathsome Ethiopian standing by that man's cell and hurling fiery javelins at him. The old man was immediately wounded and he came out of the cell and he began to run here and there like somebody gone mad drunk. He went out and in but could not remain there and he began to rush off along the same road taken by the young man. It was, so far as the monk Abbas was concerned, as if he had been turned into a lunatic and as he watched him caught up in his ravings he understood that the devil's javelin, which he had seen, was now riveted in his heart and that it was producing in him a turmoil of the mind and an unbearably feverish upheaval of the senses. He drew near him. 'Where are you hurrying off to?' he said. 'What are the reasons which bring childish disturbance in you sufficient to make you forget the serious behavior of old age and make you gad about in all directions?'

"The old man, tormented in conscience and upset by his own disgraceful agitation, began to think that his heart's passion had been detected and that the deep secret of his soul had been uncovered by the other old man. He could venture no reply to the other's questioning. 'Go back to your cell,' the old man said, 'and understand that up to now the devil either did not know about you or else that he despised you. Certainly he did not include you among those against whose progress and zeal he is moved to wage a daily war and struggle. Here you are, for all these years a monk, and not only were you unable to ward off a mere one of his javelins but you could not even repel it for one day.

" 'The Lord has allowed you to be hurt so that in your old age you may learn to have sympathy for the weaknesses of others, so that you may learn, as a result of what has happened to yourself, to reach out to the frailty of the young. A young man came to you struggling with the torments of the devil, and not only did you offer him no consolation but you actually gave him over in his deadly despair to the hands of the enemy. It was your fault that he was to be lamentably devoured by the enemy. And there can be no doubt that the vehemence of the assault on him arose on account of the fact that the enemy, who had so far not bothered with you, was jealous of the young man's future progress. He rushed to get in ahead of him and to bring low with his fiery arrows the goodness which he saw in his spirit. I have no doubt at all that he realized that the young man is stronger than you are and so he thought it worth his while to attack him with such ferocity.

" 'From what has happened you had better learn to have a feeling for those who are at risk. Do not frighten off those who run the risk of damnable despair. Do not madden them with the harshest of words. Instead, bring them back by means of mild and gentle consolation. Follow the advice of Solomon that most wise man: "Rescue those who are being led away to death and do not be slow to hold back those who are to be killed" (Prv 24:11). And, like our Savior, do not break the crushed reed and do not extinguish the smouldering wick (Mt 12:20), and beg of the Lord the grace to sing confidently and well: "The Lord gave me a disciple's tongue so that I may know how to fortify the tired man with my word" (Is 50:4).

" 'And unless the grace of God comes to the help of our frailty, to protect and defend it, no man can withstand the isidious onslaughts of the enemy nor can he damp down or hold in check the fevers which burn in our flesh with nature's fire. So it comes about that the purpose of our Lord's saving activity has now been achieved. He has freed the young man from his dangerous fever and he has decided to teach you how vicious the attack can be and how necessary it is for us to be sympathetic. Let us therefore join together to beg the Lord to lift this affliction which he laid on you for your own good. "For it is He who makes the pain and again it is He who brings the healing; He strikes, and His hand has brought the cure" (Jb 5:18). "He lays low and lifts up high; he kills and grants life; he herds down to the kingdom of death and again is the leader out" (1 Kgs 2:6–7). May He spread the abundant dew of His spirit to extinguish the devil's fiery javelins which, at my behest, He permitted to strike you.'

"The old man's one prayer was enough. The Lord took away the temptation as speedily as he had inflicted it and that very obvious experience taught the lesson that not only must we not denounce the fault which someone has admitted but we must also avoid despising any pain, however slight.

"Furthermore, the lack of skill or the frivolity of one old man or indeed of a few must not turn you away from that road of salvation of which I have been speaking, nor cut you off from what our fathers have taught us. Our enemy, who is very cunning, uses the white hair of age to fool the young. Let there be no falsely modest veil. Everything must be told openly to our elders. From them must come the cure of injury and the example of life lived in all faith. There will be help and profit there for us, provided we do not undertake anything on our personal decision and initiative.

14

"Actually this is an idea so pleasing to God that we find the notion deliberately referred to in the holy Scriptures. He arranged that the boy Samuel should be chosen but instead of teaching him directly He had him turn once or twice to an old man. This youngster, to whom He had granted a direct encounter with Himself, had nevertheless to go for instruction to someone who had offended God, and all because that person was an old man. He decided that Samuel was most worthy of a high calling and yet He made him submit to the guidance of an old man so that once summoned to a divine ministry he might learn humility and might himself become for all the young a model of deference.

15

"Christ Himself summoned Paul and spoke to him. He could have straightaway disclosed the road to perfection. He chooses instead to send him to Ananias and tells him to discover the way of truth from him: 'Get up. Go into the city, and there you will be told what you must do' (Acts 9:6). He sends him to an old man, thinking it better that he should be taught by him. What would have been quite appropriate in the case of Paul might turn out to be a bad example of presumptuousness of those coming later and someone might become convinced that he should turn only to God for teaching and instruction rather than be educated by the teaching of older men. Indeed, not only in his letters but also in what he did and in the example he set the apostle himself shows that this presumptuousness is to be thoroughly abhorred. For this special reason he went up to Jerusalem, so that he might join his fellow apostles and predecessors in a private brotherly examination of that gospel which amid the accompanying grace of the Holy Spirit and amid powerful signs and wonders he was preaching to the gentiles. 'I laid before them the good news that I preach among the gentiles and I did so out of fear that the course I was adopting or had already adopted would not be allowed' (Gal 2:2).

"Who, then, could be so presumptuous, so blind, as to dare to rely upon his own judgment and his own power of discernment and to do this after the 'vessel of election' bears witness to the fact that he needed to confer with his fellow apostles? Hence it is clear that the road to perfection is revealed by the Lord to no man who is in a position to have teachers, who in fact has small regard for the ideas and the practices of older men and who makes light of that saying which he ought very properly to observe: 'Ask your father and He will teach you, ask your elders and they will tell you' (Dt 32:7).

16

"So, then, we must seek in all humility to acquire the grace of discernment which can keep us safe from the two kinds of excess. For there is an old saying: 'Excesses meet.' Too much fasting and too much eating come to the same end. Keeping too long a vigil brings the same disastrous cost as the sluggishness which plunges a monk into the longest sleep. Too much self-denial brings weakness and induces the same condition as carelessness. Often I have seen men who could not be snared by gluttony fall, nevertheless, through immoderate fasting and tumble in weakness into the very urge which they had overcome. Unmeasured vigils and foolish denial of rest overcame those whom sleep could not overcome. Therefore, 'fortified to right and to left in the armor of justice,' as the apostle says (2 Cor 6:7), life must be lived with due measure and, with discernment for a guide, the road must be traveled between the two kinds of excess so that in the end we may not allow ourselves to be diverted from the pathway of restraint which has been laid down for us nor fall through dangerous carelessness into the urgings of gluttony and self-indulgence.

17

"Now I remember so often resisting the appetite for food that, after two or three days of taking nothing, not even the reminder of eating would cross my mind. And the devil then worked it that the onset of sleep was so kept from my eyes that I spent many days and nights begging the Lord for a little rest. I came therefore to realize that this reluctance to eat and this lack of sleep put me in much greater danger than the promptings of laziness and gluttony.

"We must rapidly ensure that we do not slide into danger on account of the urge for bodily pleasure. We must not anticipate food before the time for it and we must not overdo it; on the other hand, when the due hour comes, we must have our food and our sleep, regardless of our reluctance. Each battle is raised by the devil. Yet too much restraint can be more harmful than a satisfied appetite. Where the latter is concerned, one may, as a result of saving compunction, move on to a measured austerity. But with the former this is impossible."

18

Germanus: "What, then, is the measure of self-restraint which is correct and by means of which we may pass unhurt between each kind of excess?"

19

Moses: "I know this was something often dealt with by our elders. They used to talk about the practices of self-restraint among many, those who lived solely on vegetables or herbs or fruit. They thought that what was better than this was the use of dry bread and they reckoned that the best measure was two small rolls, amounting in weight to barely one pound."

20

This was a measure which both of us gladly accepted and which, we said, we considered was what was at least the requirement for self-restraint. It was an amount which we ourselves could not fully manage.

21

Moses: "If you want to experience the effect of this regulated amount keep firmly to it. And on Sunday or Saturday or when a brother comes to visit you, do not take some cooked food as an addition, since even though extra food can be a help this relaxation makes it harder both to be satisfied the rest of the time and to fast completely without trouble. Someone sticking to this measure of food will not go on complete fasts nor postpone his food for a day. And I remember something that often happened among my elders. They would find this regime very difficult. They had to deal harshly with their appetites and they rose from table reluctantly, even with groans and sadness.

22

"The general rule to be followed in the case of abstinence is this. One should take cognizance of the state of one's strength and body and age and allow oneself as much food as will sustain the flesh but not satisfy its longings. There will be the greatest danger for anyone who either restrains his appetite by excessive fasting or who opens up his appetite by too much eating. The spirit, brought low by lack of food, loses the vigor of its prayerfulness. Too much weariness weighs it down into unlooked-for sleep. Or again, if it is caught in the grip of too much eating, it will not be able to utter pure and winged prayers to God. And the pure state of chastity will not be able to remain undisturbed either. For on those days when the flesh is under the whip of an extra rigorous abstinence, the very lack of food will stoke the fire of bodily longing.

23

"One has to do without that which abundance of eating has gathered together in the marrow; it must be driven out in accordance with the law of nature which ensures that any excess of an unnecessary moisture is a danger and must not be allowed to remain. In similar fashion, our body has to be checked by a restraint which is continuously reasonable and continuously observed in regular measure so that even though, while we remain in the flesh, we cannot escape completely from its necessary burden, still the course of a year will rarely—indeed, not more than three times—find us in the situation of being defiled by it. And this is something which should happen without any desire disturbing the calm of our sleep. Nor should any deceptive image, proof of hidden urges to pleasure, arise as a provocation.

"This was the thinking behind the just measures of restraint figured out, as I have said, by the fathers. Hence every day one should have dry bread, accompanied by hunger, and in this way soul and body will remain unchanged, neither brought low by too much fasting nor dragged down by having too much. Restraint of this sort is so marked that one neither has a feeling about nor a memory of having eaten.

24

"This of course is something which cannot be achieved without some trouble, and as a result those who know nothing of the perfection which is characteristic of discernment like to prolong their fast, to hold over their allowance of bread until the next day, and all this in order that at eating time they can really enjoy the anticipated satisfaction of their hunger. As you know, this was the persistent habit of Benjamin, your fellow countryman. He did not wish to be held to the penitential daily ration of two rolls. He preferred instead to fast for two days in a row and then, at eating time, to give way to his appetite by means of a double portion. Through the two days of fasting he was able to acquire his four rolls, thereby getting the chance both to satisfy his longings and to enjoy a full stomach. He obstinately chose his own decisions in preference to what had been handed down by the fathers, and I have no doubt that you remember the sort of end he came to. He left the

78

desert and slid back to the empty philosophy of this world and to the vanity of the day. His downfall is something which gives force to the rule handed on by the fathers, the teaching that whoever is guided solely by his own judgment and decision will never climb up to the summit of perfection and will not fail to be the victim of the devil's ruinous power to delude."

25

Germanus: "How can we hold unshakable to this guideline? The station fast is sometimes finished at the ninth hour. Brothers arrive and, in their honor, something has to be added to the regular measure or else we have to forgo that hospitality which we are commanded to display to everyone."

26

Moses: "Yes, we must observe each rule with the same attention. That is, we must on the one hand be very careful, for the sake of self-restraint and purity, to keep to the alloted measure of food. On the other hand, when our brothers arrive we must similarly fulfill the obligations of hospitality and fraternal concern, and all this for the sake of love. Indeed, it would be quite ridiculous to receive a brother at table— or, rather, Christ himself—and then to take nothing of the meal, to be there like a stranger.

"But we will be open to neither the one nor the other criticism if we observe the following plan. At the ninth hour let us eat only one of the two rolls allowed to us and let us put the other roll aside in anticipation of visitors. If someone of the brethren comes we can eat with him and have our roll and in this way we will not be adding to our usual measure. In this way the coming of a brother, which should afford us very much joy, will not turn into an occasion of distress. We will fulfill the requirement of hospitality without easing the rigor of our self-restraint. And if no one comes we can still freely eat the bread permitted us by rule. Since we will already have taken something at the ninth hour our stomach will not notice the extra little bite which our remaining roll provides. Furthermore, we will avoid the inconvenience normally experienced by those who put off their full meal until the ninth hour for the sake of a more rigorous fast. In fact, this food which they take prevents spiritual ease and freedom during the prayers in the evening and at night. There is a quite definite advantage in our freedom to eat at the ninth hour. The soul is free and ready for the vigils of the night and, with our food now digested, we are fully prepared for the solemnity of vespers."

Twice now the blessed Moses had nourished us with his teaching. With his learned words he had not only shown the grace and the power of discernment but had in his first talk revealed the character, the purpose, and the objective of the life of renunciation. What we had earlier followed with closed eyes, so to speak, with only the thrust of our spirit and our zeal for God, this now put to us in a light clearer than day. We had the feeling that until now we had wandered at random, far from a true sense of direction, far from purity of heart. All this became very obvious to us as we realized that even in the arts of the world, for all that we see of them, there has to be a precise objective. There is no arrival unless there is a definite plan to go.

Conference Three

THE THREE
RENUNCIATIONS

1

    In that troop of saints who shone like the purest stars in the night of this world there was Paphnutius, a holy man, and we saw his knowledge gleaming with the glow of a great fount of light. He was the priest for that group of ours which was in the desert at Scete. Even as a very old man he never moved from the cell occupied by him since the time when he was quite young and which was five miles from the church. He could have come closer, could have spared his old age the weariness of such a long journey every Saturday and Sunday. Nor would he return empty-handed. He would put on his shoulders and carry back to his cell the container for his week's drinking water. And when he was over ninety he still would permit none of his younger brethren to perform this task for him.

    From the days of his youth he was so committed to the cenobitic schools that after a short time among them he was enriched as much by his own spirit of submissiveness as by the knowledge he had acquired of all the virtues. Disciplined by humility and obedience, he kept a mortifying grip on the stirrings of his will and in this way every vice was extinguished and perfection was achieved in all those virtues which monastic practice and the most ancient teaching of the fathers had established.

    But he had a feverish urge to move ever higher and hurried forward to enter into the secrets of the desert. Living amid the throng of his brethren he thirsted to get away from the distraction of human company and to be totally at one with the Lord. And once again his immense zeal drove him to surpass the virtues of even the anchorites. Racked by his longing for unceasing contemplation of God, he kept away from the sight of all, pushed farther and farther into the remote and inaccessible regions of the desert and hid there for a long time. Indeed he was rarely—and only with difficulty—found by the anchorites themselves. There was a belief that he enjoyed each day the delight of meeting with the angels. And because of this longing of his to be away from everyone he was given the nickname Bubalis, the wild roamer.

2

We very much wished to get the benefit of his teaching and we were goaded on by our own thoughts. So one evening we arrived at his cell.

"After a little silence he began to speak about what we had set before us to do. We had left our home country and, out of love for God, we had traveled through so many provinces. We had striven to endure the poverty and the vastness of the desert. We had struggled to imitate the strictness of that monastic way which even those born and reared amid such need and want can scarcely endure.

Our answer to him was that we had come in search of his lore and of his teaching so that we could give ourselves up completely to the teachings of a man such as he and to the perfection which, for countless good reasons, we felt to be in him. Also, we did not wish to be burdened by praises of ourselves. His words must not move us to pride, especially when the devil himself was tempting us right in our very cells. So therefore what we were begging from him were words which would stir compunction and humility in us and not complacency or pride.

3

Then Paphnutius spoke: "There are three kinds of vocation and three kinds of renunciation, and all have a vital bearing for the monk, regardless of how he himself is called.

"First, the three kinds of vocation, and we must look very closely at them. If we accept that our call to the service of God has been by way of the most exalted of the vocations, we must make the living of our monastic life conform to the exalted status of that call. It will be profitless to have begun sublimely if we are not seen to end up in like fashion.

"But if we recognize that we were drawn from worldly preoccupation by the humblest of vocations, then however much we see the lowliness of our start in religious life we ought to ensure that our zeal will push us to reach an end better than our beginning.

4

"The distinction between the three types of vocation should be clarified. The first is from God, the second comes by way of man, and the third arises from necessity.

"The vocation from God comes whenever some inspiration is sent into our sleepy hearts, stirring us with a longing for eternal life and salvation, urging us to follow God and to cling with most saving compunction to His commands. And so we read in the holy Scriptures how God's voice called Abraham away from his native land, from the love of his family, and from the house of his father. The Lord said: 'Come away from your native land and your family and the house of your father' (Gn 12:1).

"I know that the blessed Antony was called in the same way. He realized that his summons to the monastic life came only from God. For he had gone into a church and there he heard the Lord saying in the Scriptures: 'He who does not hate his father and his mother, his children and his wife, his lands and even his own life, he cannot be my disciple' (Lk 14:26). And also this: 'If you want to be perfect, go and sell everything you have and give it to the poor and you will have treasure in heaven; then come and follow me' (Mt 19:21). It seemed to Antony that this advice was addressed directly to himself and, with utter compunction of heart, he accepted it and straightaway renouncing everything, he went and followed Christ. No human advice or teaching had called him.

"The second type of calling is, as I have said, that which comes through human agency when the example and the advice of holy people stirs us to long for salvation. By God's grace, this is how I was called. I was moved by the counsel and by the virtues of Antony and hence was seized by a zeal for this mode of life. In similar fashion, as we see in Scripture, the sons of Israel were freed from Egyptian slavery by Moses.

"The third kind of vocation is that which comes through necessity. Imprisoned by the riches and pleasures of this world, we are suddenly put to the test. The danger of death hangs over us. The loss or seizure of our property strikes us. The death of those we love reduces us to sadness. And we are moved to turn in haste to the God whom we had neglected in the good times.

"We find this kind of call, the call of compulsion, often referred to in Scripture. Delivered to their enemies as a punishment for their sins, the children of Israel were weighed down by a terrible and most cruel tyranny and they turned to God and cried out to him: 'And God sent them as a savior Aoth the son of Gera, the son of Gemini who used not just his right hand but both hands' (Jdt 3:15). And again: 'They cried out to the Lord who raised up a savior to free them, Othonihel the son of Cenez, the younger brother of Caleb' (Jdt 14:26). Likewise, there is this in the psalm: 'Whenever he killed them they then were seeking him, they came back to him and in the morning they came to God and they remembered that the God on high was their rescuer' (Ps 77:34–35). And again: 'And they cried out to the Lord in their distress and he freed them from their miseries' (Ps 106:109).

5

"Of these three types of call, the first two seem to have the better beginnings. Yet I have occasionally found that some who started from the third level, that which seems the lowliest and the least committed, have turned out to be perfect men, most fervent in spirit and very like those who, entering the Lord's service by way of the first and best of vocations, lived out the remainder of their lives with a praiseworthy zeal of soul. And, again, I have known many who began with this higher calling and who often grew lukewarm and fell down to a most lamentable end. It was as if for those of the third kind of vocation it did not matter that they had been converted not so much by their own decision as by the presence of necessity, for what the kindness of the Lord gave them was this chance to come to compunction. In the case of the others, the glorious beginnings of their entrance to the religious life profited them nothing since they did not strive to reach life's end with equal glory.

"Moses was a monk who lived in a part of this desert known as Calamus. He lacked nothing which would make a perfect saint of him. Yet he came to the monastery as a refugee because he was afraid that he would be put to death on a charge of murder. He seized upon the fact that he had to change his way of life. Stirred virtuously in his soul he willingly used his situation to reach the summit of perfection.

"By contrast there were many—and I must not recall them by name—for whom it was of no benefit to have gloriously begun their service of the Lord. They fell into the dangerous evil of being lukewarm and they tumbled into the deep pit of death because of their cowardly and hard hearts.

"We can clearly see the same thing in the calling of the apostles. What benefit was it to Judas to have taken up the most glorious rank of an apostle, that same to which Peter and the others were called? The beginnings of vocation were glorious, and yet because of his cupidity and his love of money he came to a most terrible end, a parricide of the utmost cruelty who betrayed his Lord.

"Again, there was Paul. Suddenly blinded, it was as if he had been dragged unwillingly along the route to salvation. Later he followed the Lord with utter zeal of spirit. After a forced beginning he gave himself freely and fully, and did he not crown a life, made glorious by so many great virtues, with an end that was incomparable?

"So it is the conclusion that counts. Someone committed by the beginnings of a glorious conversion can prove to be a lesser man because of carelessness, and someone constrained by some necessity to become a monk can, out of fear of God and out of diligence, reach up to perfection.

6

"Something must now be said about the renunciations. The tradition of the fathers and the authority of the Scriptures put them at three and it is right that we should strive with maximum zeal to achieve them.

"The first renunciation has to do with the body. We come to despise all the riches and all goods of the world. With the second renunciation we repel our past, our vices, the passions governing spirit and flesh. And in the third renunciation we draw our spirit away from the here and the visible and we do so in order solely to contemplate the things of the future. Our passion is for the unseen.

"We read that the Lord instructed Abraham to achieve all three together. He said to him: 'Come away from your native land and from your family and from the house of your father' (Gn 12:1). He said first 'from your native land,' that is, from the riches of this world and from the goods of the earth. Second, 'from your family,' that is, from one's past way of life, character, and faults, which cling to us from birth and are linked to us by a sort of close relationship and blood. He said, thirdly, 'from the house of your father,' that is, from all worldly memory arising before our eyes.

"God in the person of David sings of two fathers, the one to be left and the one to be sought: 'My daughter, hear and see and incline your ear. Forget your people and the house of your father' (Ps 44:11). Now whoever said 'My daughter' is certainly a father and, equally, a father is he who instructed his daughter to forget home and people.

"All this happens when, dead with Christ to all that is in this world, our gaze, as the apostle proclaims, is 'not upon those things which are seen but on the unseen; for the things which are seen belong to time and the things which are not seen are everlasting' (2 Cor 4:18). In our hearts we leave this time-ridden, visible house and we firmly turn our eyes and mind to where we will remain forever. And we will achieve this when, still in the flesh, we begin to soldier in the Lord, not as flesh would have it, but when our deeds and our virtues join the apostle in crying out, 'Our homeland is in heaven' (Phil 3:20).

"The three books of Solomon accord with these three renunciations. Corresponding to the first renunciation is Proverbs, in which the desire for the things of the flesh and for earthly sin are excoriated. Corresponding to the second renunciation is Ecclesiasticus, where the vanity of everything under the sun is proclaimed. And applicable to the third is the Song of Songs, in which the mind, rising beyond all things visible, contemplates all that is of heaven and is brought into union with the Word of God.

7

"Therefore it will not be of much benefit to us to undertake the first renunciation in all fidelity if we fail to take up the second with equal enthusiasm. And when we have achieved this we can arrive at the third. Away from the home of our first father, the old man of our birth, away from the time when by nature 'we were, like the others, the sons of anger' (Eph 2:3), we remember that we once had a father—and we turn the full gaze of our mind to the things of heaven. Something about this father is said to Jerusalem, which had despised God its true father: 'Your father was an Amorite and your mother a Hittite' (Ez 16:3). And in the gospel there is this: 'The devil is your father and you prefer to do what your father wishes' (Jn 8:44).

"So after we have left our father and have crossed over from the seen to the unseen we shall be able to say with the apostle: 'We know that when our dwelling place here on earth is pulled apart we have a house made ready for us by God, an eternal home in heaven and not made by human hands' (2 Cor 5:1). And we shall be able to say what I referred to a little while ago: 'Our homeland is in heaven and we expect our Savior the Lord Jesus to come from there and He will transform our lowly body into a copy of His glorious body' (Phil 3:20–21). We shall be able to utter the words of the blessed David: 'I live on earth, a stranger like all my fathers' (Ps 118:19, 38:13). We shall be like those of whom the Lord speaks in the gospel: 'They are not of this world, just as I am not of this world' (Jn 17:16). Or, as He said to the apostles, 'If you belonged to the world, then the world would love you as one of its own, but because you do not belong to this world, because I have chosen to take you away from this world, the world has a special hatred for you' (Jn 15:19).

"Now we shall be worthy of the true perfection of this third renunciation when the mind is no longer dulled by fleshly contagion, when every worldly wish and character has been expertly polished away, when unfaltering meditation on the things of God and the practice of contemplation has so passed over to the unseen that there the surrounding frailty and domain of the flesh are felt no longer and there is rapture amid the bodiless realms above. The mind is so caught up in this way that the hearing no longer takes in the voices of outside and images of the passers-by no longer come to sight and the eye no longer sees the mounds confronting it or the gigantic objects rising up against it.

"No one will possess the truth and the power of all this unless he has direct experience to teach him. The Lord will have turned the eyes of his heart away from everything of the here and now and he will think of these as not transitory so much as already gone, smoke scattered into nothing. He walks with God, like Enoch. He is gone from a human way of life, from human concerns. He is no longer to be found amid the vanity of this present world. The text of Genesis relates that this actually happened to Enoch in the body: 'Enoch walked with God and was not to be found because God had taken him away' (Gn 5:24). The apostle says: 'Because of his faith Enoch was taken up so that he did not have to encounter death' (Heb 11:5). And this is what the Lord has to say about death in the gospel: 'He who lives and believes in me shall never die' (Jn 11:26).

"If, therefore, we wish to arrive at true perfection, we must hurry to rise above parents, homeland, the riches and pleasures of the world. Our hearts must leave them all, and we must never turn back in longing for what we have left behind. We must not be like those who were led out by Moses, who could not go physically back to Egypt but are said to have returned there in their hearts. They abandoned the God who had brought them out amid such prodigious signs and they began to worship the Egyptian idols which they had once despised. This is what Scripture tells us: 'In their hearts they went back to Egypt and they said to Aaron, make gods for us who will walk ahead of us' (Acts 7:39–40). And the verdict against us will be the same as it was for them. They had eaten heavenly manna in the desert and yet they longed for the squalid food of sin and of worthlessness. It might seem that we too would join them in murmuring 'We were well off in Egypt, we used to sit before pots of meat and we ate onions and garlic, cucumbers and melons' (Nm 11:18; Ex 16:3; Nm 11:5).

"Figuratively, that is what happened to the Jewish people, but every day we see this happening within our own rank and profession. Everyone who, after his renunciation of this world, returns to his old wishes and longings cries out with the Jews in deed and thought, 'I was well off in Egypt.' And I have a fear that as many prevaricating monks can be found now as there were among the followers of Moses. Three thousand six hundred armed men are reckoned to have come out of Egypt and of these only two reached the promised land. That is why we must rush to find examples of virtue from the very few and the very rare, for, in line with the figure I quoted, it is said in Scripture that many are called and few are chosen.

"So, then, the appearance of renunciation will be useless for us. It will be merely the body coming out of Egypt. More exalted and more valuable will be the renunciation by the heart.

"The apostle had something to say about this appearance of renunciation: 'If I give all my goods to feed the poor and hand over my body to be burned and have no love, it is of no benefit to me' (1 Cor 13:3). The blessed apostle would never have said this if he had not foreseen in spirit what was to come, if he had not known that there would be some who would give all they possessed to feed the poor and would, nevertheless, fail to achieve gospel perfection and the high summit of love, and all because they continued to hold on to the sinful practices of their past, their unrestrained ways, with pride and impatience mastering their hearts, with no thought of how to cure them. And because of this they could never reach the unfailing love of God. Stumbling at the second renunciation they could hardly reach the third and higher one.

"But pay careful attention to the fact that the apostle did not merely say 'if I give all my goods.' It might seem that he was talking of the person who, ignoring the gospel command, kept something back for himself, as so many of the lukewarm manage to do. But what he actually said was 'if I give all my goods to feed the poor,' that is, 'if I make a total renunciation of the riches of the earth.' And to this renunciation he adds a greater: '. . . and hand over my body to be burned and have no love, I am nothing.'

"It is as if he had used other words to say this: If I give all my goods to feed the poor, doing so in accordance with that scriptural command in which is said, 'If you wish to be perfect, go and sell all you have and give it to the poor, and you will have treasure in heaven' (Mt 19:21); if I make this renunciation and hold back nothing for myself; if I add to this sacrifice the fiery martyrdom of my flesh; if I hand my body over for the sake of Christ; if, nevertheless, I am impatient, prone to anger, jealous, proud; if I become enraged when wrongs are done to me; if I am on the lookout for my own interest; if my thoughts are evil; if I do not patiently and gladly endure all that happens to me; then the renunciation and the martyrdom of the outer man will be of no benefit to me as long as the inner spirit wallows in its old and sinful ways. It will be of no value that when in the first zeal of conversion I despised the simple substance of the world, which is neither good nor bad but neutral, if I took no care to throw out at the same time the evil goods of a corrupt heart and made no effort to achieve a Godlike love, a love which is patient and kind, which is not jealous, not boastful, which does not show annoyance or is wrong-headed, which is not on the lookout for itself, which thinks no evil, which endures all and sustains all, and which, finally, never allows its faithful follower to slip into the snares of sin.

8

"We must hurry therefore to make a total effort to ensure that the inner man shall reject and scatter those sinful riches which he gathered during his earlier way of life. These riches belong to us and hold fast to us in body and soul and if we do not cut them out and throw them away while we are still alive they will continue to be our companions after death. Just as the virtues acquired in this life and the love which is their source clothe their possessor after death in shining beauty, so do sins cloak the soul and stain it with the foul colors which will cling to it. Beauty or ugliness of spirit come with the brand of virtue or of sin. Color comes upon the soul to make it shine and make it deserve to hear the prophetic words: 'The king will fall in love with your beauty' (Ps 44:11); or else there is the color that makes it dark, foul, and misshapen and it speaks out to admit the nastiness of its shame: 'My wounds stink and are festering, the result of my folly' (Ps 37:6) and the Lord Himself will ask, 'Why is there no cure for the wound of this daughter of my people?' (Jer 8:22).

"These, then, are the true riches for us. They cling firmly to the soul. No king can grant them and no enemy take them away. There they are, our very own riches which death itself cannot take away from our souls.

"With renunciation we can reach perfection. Bound to worldly riches we are visited with everlasting death.

9

"In Scripture riches are taken in three senses, good, evil, and neutral.

"Evil riches are those of which it is said: 'The rich have gone hungry and thirsty' (Ps 33:11). Again: 'Woe to you, the rich, because you have already received your consolation' (Lk 6:24).

"It is the height of perfection to have thrown away such riches. The signs are there. The truly poor are those praised in the gospel by the Lord: 'Blessed are the poor in spirit for theirs is the kingdom of heaven' (Mt 5:3). The psalm has this: 'The poor man cried out and the Lord heard him' (Ps 33:7). Or again: 'The poor and the indigent shall praise your name' (Ps 73:21).

"Then there are the good riches, and it is the mark of great virtue and merit to have acquired them. The just man who possesses them is praised in the words of David: 'The race of good men shall be blessed. Glory and riches are in his house and his justice remains forever' (Ps 111:2–3). Again: 'The riches of a man redeem his soul' (Prv 13:8). And in the Apocalypse the man who does not have such riches is denounced for being poor and naked: 'I will vomit you from out of my mouth. You say "I am rich and well-to-do and in need of nothing" and you have no idea that you are wretched and miserable, poor and blind and naked. My advice to you is to buy from me gold that has been tested in the fire so that you may become rich, to put on white clothing and to hide the confusion of your nakedness' (Apoc 3:16–18).

"Then there are the neutral riches, that is, those which can prove to be either good or bad. They lean to one or the other, depending on the will and character of those making use of them. The blessed apostle had this to say about them: 'Give a warning to those rich in this world's goods that they must not look down on other people. They must not

90

put their hope in the uncertainty of riches but, rather, on God who generously pours all we need out to us. Tell them to do good, to practice good works, to be generous, to store up for themselves in the future a solid treasure with which they may acquire a true life' (1 Tm 6:17–19).

"There are the riches which the wealthy man in the gospel hangs on to and therefore gives nothing by way of help to the needy. The poor man Lazarus lay in front of his gate hoping for a crumb. And the rich man was thrust into the unbearable fires and the everlasting heat of hell.

10

"Now when we abandon these visible riches of the world, it is strange goods and not our own that we are leaving. And this is so even if we boast that we acquired them through our own efforts or that they were passed on to us as an inheritance. I say nothing is ours except what is in our hearts, what belongs to our souls, what cannot be taken away by anyone.

"Christ speaks in criticism of those who cling to the visible riches of the world as though these were their own and who refuse to give a share to the needy: 'If you cannot be trusted with what is not yours, who will give you what is your very own?' (Lk 16:12). Clearly, then, it is not the experience of every day which proves these riches not to be yours but the opinion of the Lord proves it by these words of His.

"Peter, addressing the Lord, speaks of invisible and evil riches: 'We have left everything so as to follow you. What therefore will be in it for us?' (Mt 19:27). Actually, what they left was, clearly, nothing more than cheap and torn nets. If the 'everything' in this renunciation was not the great abundance of sin, then we will find that nothing very valuable was left behind by the apostles and that the Lord had no very compelling reason to bestow on them the glory of such blessedness that they could deserve to hear this from Him: 'At the time of regeneration, when the Son of Man sits on his throne of glory, you yourselves will sit on twelve thrones to judge the twelve tribes of Israel' (Mt 19:28).

"But should it happen that those who have completely abandoned the visible riches of the world are nevertheless, for some reasons, unable to attain that third more sublime step of renunciation, which is characteristic of only a few, what must they think of themselves? They falter in the full practice of the first renunciation, easy though that is, and holding on to the infidelity of their earlier days they cling to perishing riches, glory in being monks, and in fact are that only in name.

"So, then, the first renunciation is, as I have said, the giving up of goods which do not belong to us. Hence it is not enough in itself for the achievement of perfection. One must pass on to the second renunciation, by which we give up what really is ours.

"And having achieved this, having driven all sin out, we will climb up to the high point of the third by which we come to despise, in heart and mind, not only all that is done in this world or possessed individually by men but the very superabundance of all the elements which are deemed everywhere so magnificent. We pass beyond that superabundance which is the slave of vanity and soon to die, and, as the apostle says, 'we look not at the things which are seen but at the unseen, for the things which are seen belong to time and the things unseen are forever' (2 Cor 4:18). And we do this so that we may earn the right to hear what was said to Abraham: 'Come into the land which I shall show you' (Gn 12:1). And what this clearly means is that unless the three renunciations are achieved with all the fervor of the mind it will not be possible to reach this fourth, the return and reward for perfect renunciation, that is, to enter the promised land where the thorns and the spikes of sin do not grow, a land gained in this life when all passion is ousted and the heart is pure, a land which neither the virtue nor the effort of a toiling man will open up but which the Lord Himself promised to reveal. 'Come,' He said, 'into the land which I shall show you' (Gn 12:1).

"All this clearly demonstrates that the beginning of our salvation is the Lord's call to 'come out of your native land' and the end, the crowning perfection and purity, is when He says, 'Come into the land which I shall show you.' What He means is, 'You cannot come to know it by yourself nor find it by your own effort, and yet to you, ignorant and uninquiring as you are, I shall reveal it.' From all of which it is clear that, inspired by the Lord's call, we hasten on to the road of salvation and, with Him to guide and enlighten us, we are led along and come to the perfection of utter bliss."

11

Germanus: "What then constitutes the freedom of our will and what praise is due to our efforts if it is God who launches and who crowns everything that has to do with our perfection?"

12

Paphnutius: "You would be right to be upset over this if it were indeed the case that in every work and discipline there was only a beginning and an end—and no middle. Now we know that God arranges the opportunities for salvation in different ways. Our situation is that we respond eagerly or in a laggardly manner to these opportunities made available by God to us. God made the call 'come out of your homeland'; Abraham by coming out was exercising obedience. There was the instruction 'come into the land'; it was done, and that was the work of obedience. But the addition 'which I shall show you' has to do with the grace of God, who gave a command—and a promise.

"However, of this much we must be sure. Never by our sole diligence or zeal nor by our most tireless efforts can we reach perfection. Human zeal is not enough to win the sublime rewards of blessedness. The Lord must be there to help us and to guide our hearts toward what is good. Every moment we must join in the prayer of David: 'Direct my footsteps along your paths so that my feet do not move astray' (Ps 16:5) and 'He has settled my feet on a rock and guided my footsteps' (Ps 39:3)—all this so that the invisible guide of the human spirit may direct back toward love of virtue our free will, which in its ignorance of the good and its obsession with passion is carried headlong into sin.

"We read this clearly in the one verse of the prophet's song: 'I was pushed and whirled and about to fall' (Ps 117:13). There the weakness of the free will is manifested. 'And the Lord came to my rescue' (Ps 117:13). Thus, the Lord's help is always there. Lest our free will should bring us to utter ruin, He is there, a hand stretched out to rescue and strengthen us when He sees us stumbling.

"Again there is this: 'When I said I am slipping'—because of the vacillation of my free will—'your mercy, Lord, was there to help me' (Ps 93:18). Once again he links God's help to his own wavering, since if the footsteps of his faith do not go astray thus—as he admits—it is not as a result of his own efforts but because of the Lord's mercy.

"Again, 'In the middle of all my troubles,' which certainly arise out of the freedom of my will, 'your consolations reach my spirit and make me happy' (Ps 92:18). They come as a breath from you into my heart and restore the sight of the good things to come, the things which you have made ready for those toiling for the sake of your name, and not only have they taken all worry away from my heart but they have bestowed a supreme happiness.

" 'If the Lord had not helped me, my soul would soon have gone to live in hell' (Ps 93:17). He bears witness that because of the wickedness of his free will he would have dwelt in hell had he not been saved by the help and protection of the Lord. 'The footsteps of a man are guided by the Lord' (Ps 36:23) and not by the freedom of the will. 'When the just man stumbles' because of his free will, 'he shall not fall down' (Ps 36:24). Why? 'Because the Lord gives a hand to him in support' (Ps 36:24).

"The plain meaning of what is said here is this: No just man suffices unto himself for the winning of justification. The divine mercy must always hold out a hand to his footsteps as they falter and almost stumble, and this is so because the weakness of his free will may cause him to lose balance, and if he falls he may perish forever.

13

"Holy men have never claimed that their own efforts would have enabled them to find a sense of direction along the road they were traveling to perfect virtue. Rather, they sought it from the Lord, praying, 'Direct me in your truth' (Ps 24:5) and 'direct the road I take in your sight' (Ps 5:9). And someone else asserts that he grasped this not only through faith but in a direct experience of how things are: 'I learned, Lord, that a man is no master of the road he takes nor is it in man's power as he goes his way to control his steps' (Jer 10:23). The Lord Himself had this to say to Israel: 'I will lead him on, like a greening fir-tree, and the fruit you bear comes from me' (Hos 14:9).

14

"They long for a knowledge of the Law—not through the labor of their own reading but through the guidance and illumination of God. This is what they pray for each day. 'Lord, point out your ways to me; make your paths known to me' (Ps 24:4). 'Open my eyes and I will look upon the wonders of your Law' (Ps 118:18). 'Teach me to do what pleases you, because you are my God' (Ps 142:10), the God 'who teaches knowledge to men' (Ps 93:10).

15

"The blessed David asks the Lord for understanding with which to recognize those commands written, as he very well knew, in the book of the Law. 'I am your servant; give me understanding so that I may learn your decrees' (Ps 118:125). Now, understanding was something which nature had granted him, and as for a knowledge of God's commands, these were laid down in the readily available Law. Yet he prayed to the Lord for a better grasp of them, for he knew that natural endowment does not suffice unless God's light guides reason, enabling it to enter into the spirit of the Law and to see in a clearer light what it enjoins.

"What I am saying here is expressed very much more clearly by that 'vessel of election,' Saint Paul. 'It is God,' he says 'who, for His own kindly purpose, puts both the will and the action into you' (Phil 2:13). What could be plainer? He is saying that God is the author of our goodwill and of the completion of our task. 'You have been given the privilege not only of believing in Christ, but of suffering for him as well' (Phil 1:30). That is to say, the impetus to conversion, to faith, and to the endurance of suffering comes from the Lord. David recognized this and he too prayed for the mercy of the Lord: 'O God, make strong what you are hurting in us' (Ps 67:29). Here he is showing that the introduction to salvation, made available to us by God's gift and grace, is not itself sufficient. It has to be brought to perfection by God's mercy and His everyday assistance.

"It is not free will but 'it is the Lord who sets the captives free' (Ps 145:7). It is not our own virtue but 'it is the Lord who lifts up those who were laid low' (Ps 145:8). It is not application to reading but 'it is the Lord who brings light to the blind' (ibid.) (The Greek version is 'The Lord gives widsom to the blind.') It is not our cautiousness but 'it is the Lord who protects the stranger' (Ps 145:9). It is not our endurance but 'it is the Lord who raises or gives support to the fallen' (Ps 144:14).

"The teacher of the gentiles knew this too. He knew well that it was neither his efforts nor his merits which made him a suitable minister of the New Testament. 'We are not qualified to claim anything as our own work; our qualifications come from God' (2 Cor 3:5). And 'it is he who made us suitable ministers of the New Testament' (2 Cor 3:6).

16

"The apostles were very sure that everything of theirs which had to do with salvation was a gift to them from God. 'Increase our faith' (Lk 17:5). They did not presume that the fullness of faith would come to them merely because they freely opted for it. They believed, rather, that it was a gift of God which would have to be granted to them.

"Also, the Author of human salvation teaches us that our faith is wavering, weak, and unable to sustain itself unless the help of God comes to prop it up. This is what He said to Peter: 'Simon, Simon. You must know that Satan has got his wish to sift you all like wheat. But I have prayed to my father for you that your faith may not collapse' (Lk 22:31–32).

"And there was someone else who felt this happening within himself. He saw his faith carried, as it were, on a tide of unbelieving toward the rocks of dreadful shipwreck and he cried out to the Lord and asked Him to come to the aid of his faith. 'Lord, help my unbelief' (Mk 9:23).

"Yes, the evangelists and the apostles knew very well that every good is achieved through the help of the Lord, and such was the lack of confidence in their ability to hold on to their faith through their own efforts and through the workings of their own free will that they begged the Lord to help it along within them or even to make a gift of it to them. If the faith of Peter needed the help of God to keep from faltering, who will be so presumptuous and so blind as to think that he can preserve his own without daily help from the Lord? This is how it is, especially in view of what the Lord Himself says in the gospel: 'As a branch cannot bear fruit all by itself but must remain part of the vine, neither can you unless you remain in me' (Jn 15:4). 'You can do nothing without me' (Jn 15:5). Since He says this, since He asserts that nobody can show forth the fruits of the spirit unless he has been inspired by God and has worked with God, it would surely be foolish, indeed sacrilegious, to attribute any good actions of ours to our own effort rather than to the divine grace. 'Everything good and everything perfect comes from above from the father of light' (Jas 1:17). And Zechariah says: 'The good comes from Him and the best comes from Him' (Ze 9:17). The blessed apostle regularly says the same: 'What have you got that you did not receive? And if you received it why boast as though you had not received it?' (1 Cor 4:7).

17

"That supreme endurance by means of which we can withstand the onslaught of temptation comes not from our own virtue but from the mercy and the guidance of God. This is what the blessed apostle says: 'The trials that you have had to bear are what people have usually to suffer. But God is to be trusted. He will not allow you to be tempted beyond your strength. He will give you a way out of temptation so that you will be able to put up with it' (1 Cor 10:13).

"He also tells us that it is God who makes our souls ready and gives them help for every good work and that He works in us those things which please Him: 'The God of peace who brought Jesus Christ back from the dead to become the great shepherd of the sheep by the blood that sealed an eternal covenant, may He make you ready to do His will in any kind of good action and may He produce in you whatever is pleasing to him' (Heb 13:20–21). He prays that this might happen for the Thessalonians: 'May our Lord Jesus Christ and God our Father who has given us His love and, through His grace, such everlasting comfort and good hope, comfort your hearts and strengthen you in every work you do and in every good word you utter' (2 Thes 2:15–16).

18

"The prophet Jeremiah, speaking in the place of God, tells us that from above there comes the very fear of God by which we may cling to Him. 'I shall give them one heart and one way so that they may fear me during all their days, so that all will be well for them and for their sons after them. And I will make an everlasting covenant with them and I shall not cease to do good things for them and, as a gift, I shall put fear of me in their hearts so that they may never go away from me' (Jer 32:39–40). Ezechiel speaks in similar terms: 'And I shall give them a single heart and I will put a new spirit in them and I will remove the strong heart from their bodies and I will give them a heart of flesh instead. And I shall do this so that they may walk as I command and respect my decisions and carry them out. Then they shall be my people and I shall be their God' (Ez 11:19–20).

19

"Quite obviously all this teaches us that the first good stirring of the will in us comes under the Lord's inspiration. He brings us along the road to salvation either Himself or by way of the exhortation of some man or through necessity. And our virtues are perfected also as a gift from Him. Our task is, laxly or zealously, to play a role which corresponds to His grace and our reward or our punishment will depend on whether we strove or neglected to be at one, attentive and obedient, with the kindly dispensation of His providence toward us. This is something which is clearly and openly set out in Deuteronomy. 'When the Lord your God has led you into the land of which you are to take possession He will bring many peoples low before you, the Hittite and the Gergashite, the Amorite and the Canaanite, the Pherizite, the Hivite and the Jebusite, seven nations greater in number and stronger than yourselves, and He will hand them over to you and you will strike them until they are wiped out. You will make no covenant with them nor will you join them in marriage' (Dt 7:1–3). Scripture makes clear that it is a grace of God to be led to the promised land, to have peoples wiped out before one, to have the more populous and stronger nations delivered into one's hands.

"But Scripture makes clear that it is Israel itself which either lays them low in death or lets them live, which does or does not make a covenant, which does or does not make marriage alliances with them. So there is clearly expressed for us in this testimony what it is we must attribute either to free will or to the decision and daily assistance of the Lord. We are characterized by whether we respond zealously or lack-adaisically to the kindly dispensations of God.

"This perspective is plainly expressed in the healing of the two blind men. Jesus was passing by, a fact made possible by God's provident grace. And the achievement of their own faith and belief was to cry out 'Lord, son of David, have pity on us' (Mt 20:31). The restored sight of their eyes is the gift of divine mercy.

"That upon receiving a gift it is as much the working of reason and the free will as the grace of God which endure is manifested by the ten lepers who were cured at one and the same time. Only one of them freely chose to give thanks. The Lord praises him—and inquires about the nine others, thereby showing His unfailing concern even for those who are forgetful of the good He has done them. For this too is a gift of His coming—to receive and acknowledge the grateful one and to ask after the ingrates.

20

"It is right for us to believe, with unshaken faith, that nothing is done in this world without God. It must be admitted that everything happens either by His will or with His permission. The good is achieved with God's will and help; the opposite happens with His permission when as a punishment for our misdeeds and for the hardness of our hearts He abandons us to the devil's mastery or to the ignoble passions of our bodies. This is the very clear teaching of the apostle when he says: 'This is why God has handed them over to the ignoble passions' (Rom 1:26). 'Because they did not trouble to know God, God handed them over to reprobate sensuality so that they might do what was unfitting' (Rom 1:28). And the Lord Himself speaks through the prophet: 'My people did not listen to my voice and Israel has not obeyed me. That is why I have abandoned them to the contrivances of their own hearts and they shall walk in accordance with their own decisions' (Ps 80:12–13).

21

Germanus: "That indeed is a text which most openly shows the freedom of the will: 'If my people had only listened to me' (Ps 80:14) and 'my people did not listen to my voice' (Ps 80:12). The words 'if my people had listened' show that it was in the power of the people to say yes or no. But how is it that although God has given us the capacity to hear or to refuse to hear, yet salvation is not to be construed as depending on us?'

22

Paphnutius: "You have quite rightly judged 'if my people had listened.' But you have not given attention to who it is that addresses the one listening and the one refusing to listen. Nor have you paid attention to the rest of the text, which is: 'I would have surely laid low its enemies and I would have raised my hand against those who were disturbing it' (Ps 80:15). No one may twist the meaning of the texts I have cited through a faulty interpretation which, showing that nothing happens without God, tries then to assert the freedom of the will and tries to deny God's grace and daily assistance with the texts 'and my people did not listen to my voice,' 'if my people had listened to me, if Israel had walked in my ways,' and so forth. The fact is, if only one looks at it, that while the freedom of the will is demonstrated by the disobedience of the people, the daily providential help of God is shown by God as He cries out to His people and advises them. When He says, 'If my people had listened to me,' He shows that earlier He had actually spoken to them. And God does not speak solely by way of written law. But every day He is giving advice, as Isaiah proclaims: 'Every day I have stretched out my hands to my people, who do not believe in me and who speak out against me' (Is 65:2).

"In fact, free will and divine grace are shown by this text: 'If my people had listened to me, if Israel had walked in my ways, I would have surely laid low its enemies and I would have raised my hands against those who were disturbing it.' Free will is shown by the disobedience of the people. Providence and God's help appear at the beginning and the end of the passage where God reminds us that He had spoken earlier and that He would have laid low the enemies of Israel if only Israel had listened to Him.

"So in citing these texts I was not trying to undermine the freedom of the will. What I really wanted to show was that every day and every moment the help and grace of God are very necessary to the will."

The monk Paphnutius, having instructed us with these words, sent us away. It was just before midnight. We left his cell with more regret than joy. For what was the most obvious result of the talk he had given us? We had believed that in giving ourselves wholeheartedly to the first renunciation we had come within sight of the summit of perfection. And here we were now with the beginnings of an awareness that even in our dreams we had not glimpsed the heights of monastic life. In the cenobitic communities we had heard something about the second renunciation. But as for the third, in which all perfection is gathered and which surpasses the other two in every possible way, we knew that before now we had never heard tell of it.

Conference Nine

ON PRAYER

.·

1

. . . This is what the blessed Isaac said by way of a summing up.

2

"The whole purpose of the monk and indeed the perfection of his heart amount to this—total and uninterrupted dedication to prayer. He strives for unstirring calm of mind and for never-ending purity, and he does so to the extent that this is possible for human frailty. This is the reason for our tireless and unshaking practice of both physical work and contrition of heart. Indeed, there is a mutual and undivided link between these. For just as the edifice of all the virtues strives upward toward perfect prayer so will all these virtues be neither sturdy nor enduring unless they are drawn firmly together by the crown of prayer. This endless, unstirring calm of prayer that I have mentioned can neither be achieved nor consummated without these virtues. And likewise virtues are the prerequisite foundation of prayer and cannot be effected without it.

"So it is pointless for me simply to talk about prayer, simply to direct attention to its ultimate reality, with its presupposition of the practice of all the virtues. The first task is to look at the succession of obstacles to be overcome and then to examine the necessary preliminaries to success. With the gospel parable for a guide, one must carefully calculate and gather together everything required for the construction of this most sublime tower of the spirit. And preliminary work will be necessary if the assembled materials are to be of any use, for they will not be able to support the sublime reality of perfection unless we unload all our vices and rid our souls of the wreck and rubble of passion. Then simplicity and humility must be laid as sure foundations on, as they say, the living solid earth of our hearts, on that rock of which Scripture speaks. There the tower to be built with our virtues may rest unshakably and rise with utter assurance to the heights of the skies. That tower resting on such foundations will not crumble, will feel no shock even when the mighty torrents of passion come pouring against it, when the raging tides of persecution are like a battering ram against its walls, when the cruel hurricane of storming devils pounds and thunders against it.

3

Prayer, if it is to be fervent and pure, demands that the following be observed.

"First, there must be a complete removal of all concern for bodily things. Then not just the worry but even the memory of any business or worldly affair must be banished from within ourselves. Calumny, empty talk, nattering, low-grade clowning—suchlike must be cut out. Anger and the disturbance caused by gloominess are especially to be eradicated. The poisonous tinder of carnal desire and avarice must be pulled out by the roots.

"Having completely expelled and sliced away these and similar vices which are so manifest to the human eye, having, as I have said, undertaken this clearing away which results in purity and in the simplicity of innocence, we have then to lay the indestructible foundations of deep humility, foundations which can support that tower rising upward to the skies. Next comes the spiritual edifice of virtue. After that, the soul must be restrained from all meandering, from all slippery wanderings, so that it may rise bit by bit to the contemplation of God and to the gazing upon the realms of the spirit. Because of the workings of memory whatever has preoccupied our mind before the time for prayer must of necessity intrude on our actual prayers. Therefore in advance of prayer we must strive to dispose ourselves as we would wish to be during prayer. The praying spirit is shaped by its own earlier condition. As we prostrate ourselves for prayer our deeds, words, and fastings rise up in our imagination. They are as they were before our prayer, and they move us to anger or gloom. We turn back toward desire or worldly affairs. Stupidly—and I am ashamed to say it—we laugh as we recall some clownish word or act, and the mind flits back to the earlier concerns of our talk.

"So therefore before we pray we must hasten to drive from our heart's sanctuary anything we would not wish to intrude on our prayers, and all this so that we might do as the apostle bids us: 'Pray ceaselessly' (1 Thes 5:17). 'In every place lift up pure hands, with no anger and no rivalry' (1 Tm 2:8). But we will not be able to fulfill this injunction unless the mind within us is cleansed of the contagion of sin, is devoted to virtue as its natural good, and feeds continuously on the contemplation of the all-powerful God.

4

"The soul may quite sensibly be compared to the finest down and the lightest feather which, if spared the onset and penetration of dampness from without, have a nature so mobile that at the slightest breeze they rise up of themselves to the highest points of the sky. But if they are weighed down by any splash, any dampening of moisture, not only will there be no natural impulse to fly up into the air but the pressure of the absorbed liquid will drag them downward to earth.

"So too with our soul. If sin and worldly preoccupation have not weighed it down, if dangerous passion has not sullied it, then, lifted up by the natural goodness of its purity, it will rise to the heights on the lightest breath of meditation and, leaving the lowly things, the things of earth, it will travel upward to the heavenly and the invisible.

"And so we are quite rightly admonished by the Lord's command: 'See to it that your hearts are not weighed down in drunkenness and intoxication and in the concerns of every day' (Lk 21:34). Therefore if we wish our prayers to reach upward to the heavens and beyond we must ensure that our mind is cleared of every earthly defect and cleansed of all passion's grip and is so light of itself that its prayer, free of sin's weighty load, will rise upward to God.

5

"We should take care to observe the reasons mentioned by the Lord for the loading down of the mind. He was not talking of adultery, of fornication, of murder, of blasphemy, of robbery. These, as everyone knows, bring death and damnation. But what He mentioned were drunkenness, intoxication, and earthly worries and concerns. No man of the world thinks of such things as dangerous or judges them to be damnable. Indeed—and it shames me to say this—there are some bearing the title of monk who turn to such distractions as though they were innocent, even useful.

"These three vices literally weigh down the soul which indulges in them. They turn the soul away from God and drag it down to earth. Yet they can easily be shunned, especially by us who are so well removed from the world and from its way of life, and who have no reason at all to be caught up in such palpable concerns, in such intoxication and drunkenness.

"But there is another kind of drunkenness, one no less poisonous. There is an intoxication of the spirit which is harder to avoid. There is another type of worldly care and concern. And even after we have utterly renounced the good things that are ours, even as we completely renounce wine and good fare, even when we are totally alone, these things frequently ensnare us. 'Wake up,' says the prophet. 'You are drunk, but not on wine' (Jl 1:5). Another says: 'Be stupified and stunned, waver and change your minds. You are drunk, but not on wine. You stagger, but not from intoxication' (Is 29:9). The wine causing such intoxication must be what the prophet calls 'the rage of dragons' (Dt 32:33), and its source is, as he says 'the vine from the vineyard of Sodom, their branches from Gomorra' (Dt 32:32). And would you like to know more about the fruit of this vine and the product of this branch? 'Their grapes are poisonous grapes, their clusters are envenomed' (Dt 32:32).

"Therefore if we are not completely cleansed from all sin, if we are not free of the intoxication of all passion, our abandonment of too much wine and of well-laid meals will be useless, and our hearts will bear the weight of a much deadlier intoxication and drunkenness.

"It was laid down by the fathers that worldly cares may preoccupy us even though we are not at all involved in the doings of this world. The fathers affirmed that everything over and above the needs of daily life and the strict requirements of the body must be reckoned among the worries and concerns of the world, so that, for example, when a single coin would meet the necessities of our bodies we choose in our effort and in our work to earn two or even three. Similarly with a couple of tunics. It is sufficient to have one for the night and one for the day, but we try to have three or four. One or two cells would be enough to live in, but wishing as the world does for possessions, to have more and more, we build four or five cells and we aim to have them better furnished and more spacious than our needs require. In such things we display as much as we can of passion and covetousness.

6

"Experience shows us that all this is at the promptings of demons.

"One of the wisest of the fathers was passing by the cell of a brother who was afflicted by this spiritual sickness to which I have been referring. Every day this man toiled worriedly at useless additions and repairs, and from a distance the father saw him trying to break a hard rock with a heavy hammer. He saw too an Ethiopian standing beside him, lending a hand in striking the hammer blows and urging him on with blazing torches to continue his work. The father stood a long time, amazed at the impact of this most cruel demon and at the deceit worked by this immense illusion. When the exhausted brother wished to take a rest and to put an end to his work the spirit stirred and shook him up and he had to pick up the hammer and, with the same zeal, continue the work he had begun. Endlessly urged on he completely failed to understand the harm of such excessive labor.

"The old man was deeply moved by this diabolical trickery. He turned from the direction he had been taking and went to the cell of his brother. He greeted him.

'My brother,' he said, 'what is this work you are doing?'

'We are struggling with this extremely hard rock and we can barely manage to break it.'

'You are right to say "we" ' the old man remarked, 'for you have not been alone in tackling it. There was someone else with you, someone you did not see, someone who was not so much helping you as viciously driving you on.'

"It will not be sufficient proof of our souls' freedom from the disease of worldly ambition that we keep away from matters which are beyond our aspirations and with which we cannot deal, even if we wanted to. Nor will it be a proof if we show contempt for what is beyond our reach. What we have first to do is to show contempt for ourselves before spiritual men and before men of the world. And the proof in question will appear when we thrust aside that which lies within our control and which could be cloaked in seemingly good purposes. Such things must mean nothing to us. And yet we see men of our profession thoughtlessly preoccupied with them, and the reality is that such nothings weigh down our souls just as much as more substantial matters preoccupy men of the world. Such things ensure that the monk is loaded with the world's dross and unable to breathe freely before God, which, indeed, is what the monk should wish with all his heart to do. For him the least separation from the sovereign Good should appear to be a veritable death, the worst of all.

"When the soul is solidly rooted in this peacefulness, when it is freed of the bonds of every carnal urge, when the unshaking thrust of the heart is toward the one supreme Good, then the words of the apostle will be fulfilled. 'Pray without cease,' he said (1 Thes 5:17). 'In every place lift up pure hands, with no anger and no rivalry' (1 Tm 2:8). Sensibility is, so to speak, absorbed by this purity. It is reshaped in the likeness of the spiritual and the angelic so that all its dealings, all its activity will be prayer, utterly pure, utterly without tarnish."

7

Germanus: "If only we could continue to hold on to those seeds of spiritual thought in the same way and with the same ease as we originate them! They come alive in our hearts as we think back to Scripture, or at the reminder of some spiritual act or as we contemplate some heavenly mysteries, and then, without our knowing it, they very quickly fly away and vanish. No sooner does the mind discover some other opportunities for spiritual thoughts than something else breaks in and what was grasped now slips and glides off. The soul cannot hold still. It is unable to keep its grip on holy thoughts. Even when it seems to have caught on to them, it looks as if its possession of them is the result not of effort but of chance. Indeed, how can the fact that they rise up within us be ascribed to any choice of ours when we actually have no capacity to keep them there within us?

"But I would prefer not to allow the consideration of this matter to take us too far from our theme or to delay what you propose to explain regarding the nature of prayer. It can be looked at in due time. What we wish to ask you now is to tell us about the nature of prayer, and we do so particularly since the blessed apostle warns us never to cease from our prayer. 'Pray without cease' (1 Thes 5:17).

"First, then, we would like you to tell us about the nature of prayer, about the character it should always have. Then we would like you to tell us how to keep with it in all its forms, how to engage in it without interruption. It cannot be achieved by a poorly stirred heart. We know this from everyday experience and we know it too from those words of your holiness in which you defined the objective of the monk and the high-point of perfection as 'the consummation of prayer.' "

8

Isaac: "Apart from great purity of intent and of soul, as well as the illumination of the Holy Spirit, there is nothing, I believe, which can mark off all the forms of prayer from one another. The differences are as great and as numerous as can be encountered within a single soul or, rather, within all souls in all their various conditions and states. I recognize that my own insensitivity makes it impossible for me to perceive them all. Still, to the extent allowed by my own poor experience, I will try to describe them.

"Prayer changes at every moment in proportion to the degree of purity in the soul and in accordance with the extent to which the soul is moved either by outside influence or of itself. Certainly the same kind of prayers cannot be uttered continuously by any one person. A lively person prays one way. A person brought down by the weight of gloom or despair prays another. One prays another way when the life of the spirit is flourishing, and another way when pushed down by the mass of temptation. One prays differently, depending on whether one is seeking the gift of some grace or virtue or the removal of some sinful vice. The prayer is different once again when one is sorrowing at the thought of hell and the fear of future judgment, or when one is fired by hope and longing for future blessedness, when one is in need or peril, in peace or tranquility, when one is flooded with the light of heavenly mysteries or when one is hemmed in by aridity in virtue and staleness in one's thinking.

9

"So much for the differences within prayer, and they touch all too briefly on a theme of major substance. So much for them, however, since I have so little time in which to discuss them, and in any case the dimness of my own mind and the dullness of my own heart cannot fully take them in. But there is a more serious difficulty here, namely to describe the different types of prayers.

"The apostle notes four types. 'My advice is that first of all supplication should be offered up for everyone, prayers, pleas, and thanksgiving' (1 Tm 2:1). Now one may be sure that this division was not foolishly made by the apostle. So we must first inquire what is meant by prayer, by petitions, by intercessions, and by thanksgiving. Then we must discover whether all are linked together at the same time in the one supplication, or whether they must be utilized one by one and separately. Should one offer petitions now, prayers some other time, or should one person offer intercessions now, another prayers, another blessings to God—and all this in accordance with the measure of age in which each soul manifests the effort of its zeal.

10

"The first item to be discussed is the exact meaning of the terms. What is the difference between prayer, supplication, and plea? Then the question must be asked whether these must be utilized one by one or together. And thirdly there is the question of whether the order laid down by the authority of the apostle has something more by way of instruction for the listener. Can the distinction made by the apostle be taken simply as it stands? Did he make it without any further purpose in mind? Actually, this last would seem absurd to me. It is incredible that the Holy Spirit spoke through the apostle something that was transitory and purposeless. Therefore with the Lord's help we will consider these types one by one, in the sequence given above.

11

" 'My advice is that supplication should be offered up for everyone.' A supplication is a plea or petition made on account of present and past sin by someone who is moved by contrition to seek pardon.

12

"In prayers we offer or promise something to God. The Greek term means 'vow.' Greek has 'I shall offer my vows to the Lord' and in Latin it is 'I shall do what I have promised to the Lord' (Ps 117:14), which, according to the sense of the term, may be taken as 'I shall make my prayers to the Lord.' In Ecclesiastes we read: 'If you have made a promise to God do not delay in fulfilling it' (Eccl 5:3). The Greek has 'If you are to pray to the Lord, do not delay about it.'

"This is how each of us must do this. We pray when we renounce this world, when we undertake to die to all the world's deeds and mode of living and to serve the Lord with all our heart's zeal. We pray when we promise to despise worldly glory and earth's riches and to cling to the Lord with contrite hearts and poverty of spirit. We pray when we promise to put on the purest bodily chastity and unswerving patience or when we vow to drag completely from our hearts the root of anger and the gleam which is the harbinger of death. And if we are brought down by laziness, if we return to our old sinful ways because of not doing at all what we promised, we shall have to answer for our prayers and our commitments and it will be said of us, 'Better not to promise than to promise and not deliver.' As the Greek would have it, 'It is better that you do not pray than that, having prayed, you do not do as you had undertaken' (Eccl 5:4).

13

"Third come pleas. We usually make them for others when we ourselves are deeply moved in spirit. We offer them for those dear to us or when we beg for peace in the world or, to borrow the words of the apostle, when we are suppliants 'on behalf of all men, on behalf of rulers and on behalf of all those in high places' (1 Tm 2:1-2).

14

"Fourth are thanksgivings. Unspeakably moved by the memory of God's past kindnesses, by the vision of what he now grants or by all that He holds out as a future reward to those who love Him, the mind gives thanks. In this perspective richer prayers are often uttered. Looking with purest gaze at the rewards promised to the saints, our spirit is moved by measureless joy to pour out wordless thanksgiving to God.

15

"These, then, are the four rich sources of prayer. Out of contrition for sin is supplication born. Prayer comes of the fidelity to promises and the fulfillment of what we have undertaken for the sake of a pure conscience. Pleading comes forth from the warmth of our love. Thanksgiving is generated by the contemplation of God's goodness and greatness and faithfulness. And all this, as we know, often evokes the most fervent and fiery prayers.

"Hence all of these types of prayer of which I have been speaking are valuable for all men, and indeed quite necessary. And so one man will now offer supplication, prayer then, later the purest and most zealous pleas.

"Nevertheless, the first type seems especially appropriate for beginners, for they are still goaded by the stings and by the memory of past sin. The second type is appropriate for those who are making progress in the acquisition of virtue and in the exaltedness of their souls. The third is suitable for those who live as they have promised to do, who see the frailty of others and who speak out for them because of the charity that moves them. The fourth suits those who have pulled the painful thorn of penitence out of their hearts and who in the quiet of their purified spirit contemplate the kindness and mercy that the Lord has shown them in the past, that He gives them now and that He makes ready for them in the future. Aflame with all this their hearts are rapt in the burning prayer which human words can neither grasp nor utter. Sometimes the soul which has come to be rooted in this state of real purity takes on all the forms of prayer at the same time. It flies from one to the other, like an uncontrollable grasping fire. It becomes an outpouring of living pure prayer which the Holy Spirit, without our knowing it, lifts up to God in unspeakable groanings. It conceives so much within itself at that instant, unspeakably pours forth so much in supplication, that it could not tell you of it at another time nor even remember it all.

"It may also happen that one can pray intensely and purely even at the first and lowliest stage when the mind is on the judgment to come. The soul, trembling with fright and fear at the thought of the examination and judgment, is touched at that hour by contrition, and out from its supplication comes an abundance of spiritual fervor so that it is as possessed as that soul which in shining purity contemplates the goodness of God and dissolves in unspeakable joy and happiness. It is all the more loving, as the Lord said, because of all that extra forgiveness which it knows it has received.

16

"But with an ever more perfect life and by perfect virtue we especially must be carried along toward the types of prayer which are rooted in the contemplation of eternal goodness and in a fervor of love. If I may use humbler language and words more suited to the measure of beginners, we must be carried along toward the forms of prayer which arise out of the wish to acquire a virtue or the urge to kill off a vice. In no way can our spirit attain those more exalted modes of prayer of which I have been speaking except by the step-by-step journey upward through all those pleas we pour forth.

17

"The Lord Himself deigned to initiate those four types of prayer and He gave us examples of them, so that there was a fulfillment of those words said of Him: 'What Jesus began to do and to teach' (Acts 1:1).

"He offers a supplication when He says: 'Father, if possible, let this chalice pass from me' (Mt 26:39). And there are the words put in His mouth in the psalm 'My God, my God, look at me. Why have you abandoned me?' (Ps 21:2). And there are others like this.

"There is a prayer when He says: 'I have glorified you on earth and I have finished the work which you gave me to do' (Jn 17:4). And this: 'For their sake I consecrate myself so that they may be consecrated in the truth' (Jn 17:19).

"There is a plea when He says: 'Father, I wish those you have given me to be with me where I am so that they may see the glory which you have given me' (Jn 17:24). And He certainly makes a plea when He says: 'Father, forgive them for they do not know what they are doing' (Lk 23:24).

"There is blessing when He says: 'I confess to you, Father, Lord of heaven and of earth, for you have hidden these things from the wise and the prudent and have revealed them to the lowly. Yes indeed, Father, for this is what has pleased you' (Mt 11:25–26). A blessing there surely is when He says: 'Father, I thank you because you have listened to me. Indeed I knew that you always listened to me' (Jn 11:41–42).

"It is clear to us that these types of prayer can be distinguished and also used at different times. However, the Lord also showed by example that they can all be put together in one perfect prayer, as in that prayer which, as we read at the end of the gospel of John, He poured forth in such abundance. It would take too long to cite the whole text but a careful inquirer can discover for himself that matters are indeed as I have said.

"The apostle in his letter to the Philippians clearly expresses this same idea though he cites the four types of prayer in a somewhat different order. He shows that they must be offered up out of the one burning zeal. This is what he says: 'In your every prayer and supplication let your pleas be included in your blessings to God' (Phil 4:6). What he wanted in particular to teach us was that in our prayer and supplication blessings should be mingled with our pleas.

18

"A state of soul more exalted and more elevated will follow upon these types of prayer. It will be shaped by the contemplation of God alone and by the fire of love, and the mind, melted and cast down into this love, speaks freely and respectfully to God, as though to one's own father.

"We must be careful to aspire to this state of soul. This is what the beginning of the Lord's prayer tells us when it says 'Our Father' (Mt 6:9). With our own voice we proclaim that the God, the Lord of the universe, is our Father and we thereby assert that we have been called out of the state of servitude to adoption as sons.

"To this we add 'who are in heaven' and we do so to mark the fact that the delay we make during this life of ours on earth is a kind of exile keeping us very distant from our Father. In all terror let us hasten out of it and with all longing let us rush toward that domain which we proclaim to be the abode of our Father. May nothing we do make us unworthy of our profession and the dignity of so wonderful an adoption. May nothing deprive us, like degenerate sons, of the heritage of our Father. May nothing cause us to run into His justice and His anger.

"Drawn as we are to the rank and status of sons we will burn with that continuous respectfulness characteristic of good sons. We will think no more of our own advantage. Our zeal will be poured out, all of it, for the sake of our Father's glory. We will say 'hallowed be your name,' and we shall bear witness that our longing, our joy, is for the glory of our Father. We shall be imitators of the one who said thus: 'He who talks about himself is looking for his own glory. As for the one who seeks the glory of whoever sent him, he is telling the truth and there is no injustice in him' (Jn 7:18).

"Paul, the 'vessel of election,' was filled with such a sentiment. He is even prepared to be anathema to Christ so long as his household grows and so long as the salvation of the entire people of Israel adds to the glory of his Father. He is prepared to die for Christ because he knows that no one can die for the one who is Life itself. And, again, he says this: 'We are glad to be weak—provided you are strong' (2 Cor 13:9).

"There should be no amazement at the fact that Paul is ready to be anathema to Christ for the sake of the glory of Christ, the conversion of his brethren, and the privilege of his people. The prophet Micah was willing to be a liar and to be excluded from the inspiration of the Holy Spirit provided that the Jewish people could escape those sufferings and the disasters of exile foretold by his own prophecies. 'I would wish to be a man without the Spirit and would rather speak a lie' (Mi 2:11). And there is of course the love of the lawgiver himself who was not unwilling to die alongside his brothers: 'Lord, this people has committed a great sin. I beg you to pardon them their wrongdoing or else strike me out of the book which you have written' (Ex 32:31–32).

"The words 'hallowed be your name' could well be understood in the sense that God is hallowed by our perfection. In other words, when we say 'hallowed be your name' to Him what we are really saying is 'Father, make us such as to deserve knowledge and understanding of how holy you are, or at least let your holiness shine forth in the spiritual lives we lead.' And this surely happens as men 'see our good works and glorify our Father in heaven' (Mt 5:16).

19

"The second request of the very pure soul is to see the coming of the Father's kingdom.

"What this means first of all is that each day Christ should reign among holy men. And this happens when the devil's power has been driven out of our hearts through the expulsion of sinful foulness and when God has begun to reign within us amid the good odors of virtue. With fornication vanquished, chastity rules; with anger overcome, peace is king; with pride under foot, humility is sovereign.

"There is also the promise, definite in regard to its time of fulfillment, made to all the saints, to all the sons of God, the promise that Christ will say to them 'Come, you blessed ones of my Father, take possession of the kingdom prepared for you from the time of the world's creation' (Mt 25:34). Gazing eagerly toward that set time, the soul is filled with longing and expectation and it says to Him: 'May your kingdom come' (Mt 6:10). With its own conscience for a witness, the soul knows that it will enter as a partner at the time of the coming of the kingdom. No sinner will dare to say this or to hope for it, for he will have no wish to see the throne of judgment and he will be fully aware that there will be no palm, no reward for his merits, but rather that he will suffer punishment forthwith.

20

"The third petition of sons is this: 'May your will be done on earth as it is in heaven.' No greater prayer can be offered than that the things of earth should be put on a level with the things of heaven. 'May your will be done on earth as it is in heaven.' What else is this if not a declaration that men should be like angels, that just as the will of God is fulfilled by the angels in heaven so all men on earth should do, not their will, but His.

"The only man capable of offering up this prayer sincerely will be the one who believes that God arranges everything—the seemingly good and the seemingly bad—for our benefit, that the salvation and the well-being of His own people is more of a care and a concern to Him than to ourselves.

"This prayer can also be interpreted certainly in the following way. God wishes for the salvation of all. This is the opinion of the blessed Paul. 'He wishes all men to be saved and to come to the knowledge of the truth' (1 Tm 2:4). The prophet Isaiah, speaking as the voice of God the Father, says: 'My wish shall be entirely fulfilled' (Is 46:10).

"So then as we give voice to 'may your will be done on earth as it is in heaven' we are saying in other words that 'like those in heaven, Father, may those on earth be saved by the knowledge of your name.'

21

" 'Give us this day our supersubstantial bread' (Mt 6:11). Another evangelist uses the term 'daily' (Lk 11:3).

"The first expression indicates that this bread has a character that is noble and substantial by virtue of which its exalted splendor and holiness surpass all substances and all creatures.

"With 'daily' the evangelist shows that without this bread we cannot live a spiritual life for even a day. When he says 'this day' he shows that the bread must be eaten each day, that it will not be enough to have eaten yesterday unless we eat similarly today. May our daily poverty encourage us to pour forth this prayer at all times, for there is no day on which it is unnecessary for us to eat this bread so as to strengthen the heart of the person within us.

" 'Daily' can also be understood as referring to this present life of ours. That is, 'give us this bread while we linger in this present world. We know that in the time to come you will give it to whoever deserves it but we ask that you give it to us today, for he who has not received it in this life will not be able to partake of it in that next life.'

22

" 'And forgive us our debts as we forgive those in debt to us.' Oh, the unspeakable mercy of God! Not only has He handed to us a model of prayer, not only has He given us a discipline which will make us acceptable to Him, not only because of this necessary formula (by which He teaches us always to pray) has He pulled up the roots both of anger and of gloom, but He has also made a way and a route by which those praying to Him may call on Him to exercise a kindly and indulgent judgment over them. He bestows a means to soften the verdict on us. He gives us the means to urge Him to pardon us on account of the example of forgiveness we ourselves offer when we say 'forgive us as we ourselves have forgiven.' Someone, therefore, having forgiven his own debtors, not those of the Lord, will trust in this prayer and will ask pardon for the sins he has committed.

"But there is something which is not so good. Some of us show gentleness and indulgence to wrongs, no matter how great, which have been done to God. If, however, the wrongs no matter how small are done to us, we wreak punishment cruelly and inexorably. Hence anyone who has not forgiven from the bottom of his heart the wrong done by a brother will be condemned, not pardoned, as he says this prayer, since he will be asking for a more severe judgment. 'Forgive me as I have forgiven.' If he is dealt with as he requested, what is in store for him if not that God, following the example he set, is implacably angry and punishes him without mercy? If, then, we wish to be judged mercifully we must show ourselves to be merciful to those who have done us wrong. We shall be forgiven proportionately with the forgiveness we display to those who, whatever their malice, have injured us.

"Many grow fearful at this and when this prayer is uttered by all the people in church they silently skip this part in case it should seem that by their words they are condemning themselves instead of making excuses for themselves. They do not realize that it is with empty subtlety that they are striving, uselessly, to camouflage themselves before the great judge who had wished to give advance notice of how He would exercise judgment to those praying to Him. Precisely because He did not wish us to find Him cruel and inexorable, He made clear the yardstick by which he made judgment. That was that we would judge the brothers who wronged us as we would wish ourselves to be judged by Him, since 'a judgment without mercy awaits the man who has not shown mercy' (Jas 2:13).

23

"There follows 'lead us not into temptation,' out of which comes a problem that is not a minor one. If we pray that we be not permitted to be tempted, where will that constancy come from for which we are to be tested? There is the scriptural statement that every man who has not been tested has not been approved of. There is 'Blessed is the man who endures temptation' (Jas 1:12). So this cannot be the sense of 'lead us not into temptation.' It is not 'do not allow us ever to be tempted' but rather 'do not allow us to be overcome when we are tempted.'

"Job was tempted. But he was not actually led into temptation. He did not ascribe folly to God. He did not take the road of impiety or blasphemy along which the tempter wished to drag him.

"Abraham was tempted. Joseph was tempted. But neither was led into temptation, for neither of them yielded to the tempter.

"And then there follows 'but deliver us from evil,' that is, 'do not allow us to be tempted beyond endurance by the devil and ensure that "with every temptation there is a way out, so that we can put up with it" ' (1 Cor 10:13).

24

"You see then the brief mode and formula of prayer given us by the judge to whom our pleas must be offered. There is no request for riches, no reminder of honors, no plea for power or bravery, no reference to bodily well-being or to this present life. The Creator of eternity does not wish that something perishable, something cheap, something time-bound, is sought from Him. It would be a terrible wrong to His generosity and lavishness to ignore requests for what eternally endures in favor of petitions for what is transitory and perishable. This kind of spiritual poverty in our prayers would incur the wrath instead of the favor of our judge.

25

"It would seem, then, that this prayer, the Our Father, contains the fullness of perfection. It was the Lord Himself who gave it to us as both an example and a rule. It raises up those making use of it to that preeminent situation of which I spoke earlier. It lifts them up to that prayer of fire known to so few. It lifts them up, rather, to that ineffable prayer which rises above all human consciousness, with no voice sounding, no tongue moving, no words uttered. The soul lights up with heavenly illumination and no longer employs constricted, human speech. All sensibility is gathered together and, as though from some very abundant source, the soul breaks forth richly, bursts out unspeakably to God, and in the tiniest instant it pours out so much more than the soul can either describe or remember when it returns again to itself.

"Our Lord, with this formula of pleading, passed through this same condition or situation. He withdrew to the solitude of the mountain, and in the silent prayer of His agony He gave with His bloody sweat an inimitable example of ardor.

26

"Who could have the experience to describe the different varieties, the causes and the sources of the compunction by means of which the soul is inflamed and is lifted like a fire to the purest and the most fervent prayer? But by way of example and to the best of my ability I will say something about this and cast my mind back, with the Lord's help to guide me.

"Once while I was singing the psalms a verse of it put me in the way of the prayer of fire. Or sometimes the musical expression of a brother's voice has moved sluggish minds to the most intense prayer. I have known it to happen that the superiority and the seriousness of someone giving voice to the psalms has stirred a great onset of zeal in those who were merely bystanders. Sometimes the encouragement and the spiritual discourse of a perfect man have stirred to the richest prayers the sensibilities of those who were depressed. And I know that in my own case the death of a brother or of a friend has moved me to the fullest compunction. The memory too of my lack of warmth and of my carelessness has produced a saving ardor of soul within me.

"In this way, then, there are certainly countless opportunities when, with God's grace, the torpor and the sluggishness of our souls are shaken up.

27

"A no less difficult problem is that of trying to discover how and in what manner these movements of compunction are produced within the hidden recesses of the spirit. Often the fruit of saving compunction emerges as an unspeakable joy and a liveliness of soul. Joy in its immensity becomes unbearable and the soul bursts out in great cries, bringing to a neighboring cell the word of our heart's gladness and of the mightiness of our exultation.

"Sometimes the soul lies low, hidden in the depths of silence. The stunning onset of sudden light takes all sound of voice away. All its senses are withdrawn into its own depths or else are let go and with unspeakable groanings it pours out its longings to God.

"And sometimes it fills up with such sorrow and grief that it can only shake it off by melting into tears."

28

Germanus: "Lowly as I am, I have some experience of this sentiment of compunction. Often at the thought of my own sins my tears have flowed and at the coming of the Lord this unspeakable joy has, as you said, so revived me that its very immensity has made me not despair of gaining pardon.

"It seems to me that nothing would be more glorious than this condition, especially if it lay within our power to renew it. Sometimes it has happened to me that wishing once more for these tears of compunction to flow I have spent all my efforts on this. I recall to mind all my mistakes and all my sins, and still I cannot recover that rich abundance of tears. My eyes stay dry, like the hardest stone, and not even the tiniest drop is shed. And just as I rejoice in that outflowing of tears, so I grieve when I cannot recover it at will."

29

Isaac: "Not every outflowing of tears springs from the one feeling or the one virtue.

"It is one thing for the tears to run down when our heart, stirred by the thorn of our sins, overflows. About this it is said: 'I am worn out with my groans, each night I shall bathe my resting place with tears, I shall dampen my bed with my weeping' (Ps 6:7). Or again: 'Let your tears flow day and night like a stream. Give yourself no rest and let not your eye grow quiet' (Lam 2:18).

"It is another thing when the shedding of tears springs from the contemplation of the goods of eternity and from the longing for its coming glory. The tears flow more abundantly because our happiness is too great and our joy unlimited as our soul thirsts for the strong and the living God. 'When shall I go and appear before the face of my God? Day and night my tears were my sustenance' (Ps 41:3–4). Each day it howls its lament: 'Woe to me because my living here is too long' and 'my soul has lived on too much.'

"It is another thing when the tears flow not because conscience reproaches us for some deadly fault but because of our fear of hell and of its terrible judgment. The prophet, stricken with this fear, prays to God: 'Do not enter a judgment against your servant, for no living man will be found worthy before your face' (Ps 142:2).

"There is another kind of tears and this is stirred not by an awareness of one's own sins but by the hard-heartedness and the sins of oth-

118

ers. It was for this that Samuel wept over Saul, and in the gospel we see our Lord weeping for Jerusalem. Or in the past Jeremiah is said to have wept saying: 'Who will turn my head into a fountain and my eyes into a spring of tears? And I will weep day and night for the dead out of the daughter of my people' (Jer 9:1). These are the kind of tears about which he sings in the one hundred and first psalm: 'I ate ashes as though it were bread and I mixed my cup with my tears' (Ps 101:10). Quite certainly these tears do not come from the same emotion as that causing the penitent in the sixth psalm to weep. This latter emotion arises on account of the worries, the constraints, and the anxieties of life with which the just of this world are afflicted. This is shown clearly not only by the text of the psalm itself but also by the title, 'A prayer of a poor and worried man as he pours out his prayer before God.' The character presented is that of the poor man of the gospel about whom it is said: 'Blessed are the poor in spirit, for theirs is the kingdom of heaven' (Mt 5:3).

30

"Such weeping is far and away different from those tears squeezed out of dry eyes by a hardened heart, although we must not believe that such tears are fruitless. It is a good intention which seeks to shed them and is characteristic of those who have not yet acquired an assured knowledge of perfection and who have not been able to purify themselves completely of their past and present faults.

"But for those who have acquired a love of virtue this sort of torture is not needed. They should not set such a value on the tears of the man we see. And such squeezed-out tears can in no way match spontaneous outpourings. Indeed, the struggles for them will distract the soul from prayer and will lower it and plunge it into things human. They will pull it away from the sublime heights where it ought to be prayerfully anchored. They will compel it to relax the zeal of its prayer merely for the sake of wearing itself out on little, sterile, forced weepings.

31

"And in order that you may have an understanding of true prayer, I will give you not my own opinion but that of the blessed Antony.

"Sometimes I saw him so long at prayer and with a mind so ecstatic that the sunrise would catch up with him and I could hear him cry out from the ardor in the soul, 'Why, O sun, why are you getting in my

119

way? You are rising now to snatch me away from the brilliance of real light.'

"He too voiced this opinion—heavenly and more than human: 'Prayer is not perfect when the monk is conscious of himself and of the fact that he is actually praying.'

"Perhaps I, with my frailty, might dare to add something to this admirable opinion, and I would point out the signs which show, in my experience, that a prayer is listened to by the Lord.

32

"If, as we pray, no hesitation cuts across us and no uneasiness undermines our confidence in what we ask for, if we feel in the flush of prayer that we have been granted what we sought, then I have no doubt that our prayers have effectively reached through to God. Our conviction that God is looking at us and that He has the power to grant what we ask of Him earns us the right to be heard and to be given what we seek. For what the Lord Himself said to us cannot be withdrawn: 'Whatever you ask for in prayer, believe that you will receive it and it will come to you' (Mk 11:24)."

33

Germanus: "My belief is that this confidence of being heard comes from purity of conscience. But what about those of us whose hearts are sadly aware of the thorn of sin? How can we have this confidence? If we have no merits to give us assurance, how can we presume that our prayers have to be heard?"

34

Isaac: "The words of the gospels and of the prophets bear witness to the fact that the reasons for being heard are as different as souls and their dispositions.

"You have as the outcome of the harmony between two people what the Lord Himself laid down: 'If two of you on earth agree to ask anything it will be granted to you by my Father in heaven' (Mt 18:19).

"You have it in that fullness of faith which is compared to a mustard seed: 'If your faith were the size of a mustard seed you would say to this mountain move from here, and it will move and nothing will be impossible to you' (Mt 17:19).

"You have it in the persistence at prayer, that unwearying persistence which the Lord called importunity: 'Amen, I tell you, he will get up and give him what he wants if not for the sake of friendship then because of his importunity' (Lk 11:8).

"You have it in the good fruit of almsgiving: 'Give your alms into the heart of a poor man and your alms will pray for you on the day of tribulation.'

"You have it in a changed style of living and in the works of mercy: 'Break the chains of impiety, each the crushing loads' (Is 58:6). And the prophets add this after criticizing the sterility of a profitless fast: 'Then you will call out and the Lord will hear you; you will cry out and He will say here I am' (Is 58:9).

"Sometimes it is too great a burden of sorrows which causes us to be heard: 'I cried in distress to the Lord and he heard me' (Ps 119:1). 'Do not afflict the stranger because if he cries out to me I shall hear him, for I am merciful' (Ex 22:21, 27).

"So you see then the many ways in which the grace of being heard is won. No one, therefore, should allow the misery of his conscience to break him in discouragement when there is a question of salvation or of the things of heaven. I know well our wretchedness and I know we completely lack the virtues which I mentioned above. We lack that admirable harmony of two souls, the faith which has been compared to a mustard seed, and those deeds of piety described by the prophet. But can we not at least have that importunity which is available to anyone who wants it and by which the Lord has promised to give us what we ask?

"We must therefore not be hesitant and lacking in faith. We must persist in our prayers, and our persistence will quite certainly win us, as God has told us, everything we ask for. No doubt about this at all!

"The Lord, in His wish to grant the things that are everlasting and of heaven, urges us to coerce Him with our importunity. Not only does He not despise and reject the importunate, He calls them to Him and He praises them and with utter kindness He promises to grant them whatever they have consistently hoped for. He says: 'Ask and you shall receive, seek and you shall find, knock and it shall be opened to you. Everyone who asks receives, and the seeker finds and for the one who knocks there is opening' (Lk 11:9–10). Again this: 'Everything you believingly pray for you will receive and nothing will be impossible for you' (Mt 21:22, 17:19).

"So then if all the reasons I mentioned for us to be heard are completely lacking in us, at least let our insistent importunity animate us. This is something which is independent of all merit and hard work, and it can be grasped by anyone who wishes for it.

"But one thing is certain. Anyone who prays and who doubts that he will be heard will not be listened to at all.

"That unfaltering prayer must be offered up to the Lord is shown us by the example of the blessed David. He was heard on the very first day of his praying, but the outcome to his petition only came after twenty-one days. Hence we must never let up in the zeal of our prayers, even when the Lord seems to us to be slow to answer. It may well be that the Lord wishes this delay for our own good. It may be that the angel bringing our divine gift has indeed left the presence of God but has been delayed by the devil, and he will certainly not be able to hand over to us the favor we asked if he finds us to have cooled off in our praying. This is what would certainly have happened in the case of the prophet mentioned above had it not been for the fact that with incomparable virtue he hung on in his prayers until the twenty-first day. Therefore this full, confident belief within us must not be broken by any weakening of hope, especially when we feel that we have not yet received what we prayed for. And we should have no doubt of what the Lord promised us when He said: 'Everything you believingly pray for you will receive' (Mt 21:22). We should constantly meditate on the saying of the blessed evangelist John, that saying by which all doubt regarding this matter is dissolved, 'We have the assurance of being heard by God if we ask for something that accords with His will' (1 Jn 5:14). Note that John invites this full, assured confidence in respect of whatever accords with the will of God and not for whatever suits us or is a worldly satisfaction to us. This is what we are taught to say in the Lord's prayer with the words 'Thy will be done,' your will, not ours.

"We should remember too what the apostle said: 'We do know what we should pray for.' That is, we will understand that sometimes we ask for things which are contrary to our salvation and hence for the sake of what is better for us He who sees better and more clearly what we need refuses our requests. Certainly this was the case with the apostle of the gentiles. He begged that the devil's angel, which by God's will had been allowed near him to beat him, should be taken away. 'Three times I asked the Lord that he would go away from me. And he said to me: "My grace is enough for you. My power is at its best in weakness' " (2 Cor 12:8–9).

"This too was the idea exemplified by our Savior in His humanity so as to provide us here as with everything else a model to imitate. So this is how He prayed: 'Father, let this cup pass from me, if it is possible. Yet let it not be as I wish but as you wish' (Mt 26:39). And yet His will was certainly not different from that of His Father. 'For He had come to save what was lost and to give His life for the redemption of the multitude' (Mt 18:11, 20:28). About this He Himself said: 'No one takes my life from me, but I lay it down of my own accord. I have the power to lay it down and I have the power to take it up again' (Jn 10:18).

"Regarding the identity of will between the Father and Himself, the blessed David has him say in Psalm 39, 'I came to do your will, for this is what I wish, O my God' (Ps 39:9). True, we read the following about the Father: 'God so loved the world that He gave His only begotten son' (Jn 3:16). And we find regarding the Son that 'He gave Himself up for our sins' (Gal 1:4). About the Father it is said: 'He did not spare His own son but handed Him over for the sake of all of us' (Rom 8:32). Of the Son it is said: 'He gave Himself up because He wished it' (Is 53:7). This union of will between Father and Son is pointed to everywhere right up to the resurrection, where we see each of them acting in the one single event. The blessed apostle says that the resurrection of the body was the work of the Father 'God the Father who raised Him from the dead' (Gal 1:1). The Son proclaims that He will raise up the temple of His body: 'Destroy this temple and I will raise it up in three days' (Jn 2:19).

"Hence, following the example of the Lord, we should end all our prayers like His, adding to all our petitions the words 'However, not as I wish, but as you wish.' This is the meaning of the triple bow made at gatherings of the brethren when the rite has been completed. (Obviously, the one who is utterly absorbed in his prayer will not observe this.)

35

"We need to be especially careful to follow the gospel precept which instructs us to go into our room and to shut the door so that we may pray to our Father. And this is how we can do it.

"We pray in our room whenever we withdraw our hearts completely from the tumult and the noise of our thoughts and our worries and when secretly and intimately we offer our prayers to the Lord.

"We pray with the door shut when without opening our mouths and in perfect silence we offer our petitions to the One who pays no attention to words but who looks hard at our hearts.

"We pray in secret when in our hearts alone and in our recollected spirits we address God and reveal our wishes only to Him and in such a way that the hostile powers themselves have no inkling of their nature. Hence we must pray in utter silence, not simply in order that our whispers and our cries do not prove both a distraction to our brothers standing nearby and a nuisance to them when they themselves are praying but also so as to ensure that the thrust of our pleading be hidden from our enemies who are especially lying in wait to attack us during our prayers. In this way we shall fulfill the command 'Keep your mouth shut from the one who sleeps on your breast' (Mi 7:5).

36

"The reason why our prayers ought to be frequent and brief is in case the enemy, who is out to trap us, should slip a distraction to us if ever we are long-drawn-out. There lies true sacrifice. 'The sacrifice which God wants is a contrite heart' (Ps 50:19). This indeed is the saving oblation, the pure offering, the sacrifice of justification, the sacrifice of praise. These are the real and rich thank offerings, the fat holocausts offered up by contrite and humble hearts. If we offer them to God in the way and with zeal which I have mentioned we can be sure to be heard and we can sing: 'Let my prayer rise up like incense before your face and my hands like the evening offering' (Ps 140:2).

But time and the coming night suggest to us now that we fulfill this obligation. My talk has been a long one and relative to what I am it seems that I have said many things yet it is also very little, given so sublime and so difficult a theme."

We were amazed rather than filled to satisfaction by these words of the blessed Isaac. We held evening prayers and then we went off to rest. The first light of day was coming as we went to our cells.

Still, we were promised a second visit, with a more extensive discussion. The knowledge of what had been promised to us added to the joy we had already felt. What we had been shown was the excellence of prayer. But by what method and through what virtue prayer could remain always with us—that, we felt, was a secret which this first conference had not completely presented to us.

Conference Ten

ON PRAYER

1

But now amid these sublime teachings of the anchorites which, with God's help, I have set down in my own prosaic fashion, there is something demanded by the sequence of the narrative, something to be added and included, rather like a wart on a beautiful body. Still, those of simpler disposition will derive from this a valuable teaching concerning the image of the omnipotent God as described in Genesis. Indeed, the standing of this great teaching is being undermined, and to know nothing about it is surely a great blasphemy and a great danger to the Catholic faith.

2

In the Egyptian region there is an old custom that when Epiphany is over, that day which the priests of the area claim is the day of the Lord's baptism and of His birth (and this is why these two events are not, as in the West, celebrated on two solemn occasions but as one feast day), the bishop of Alexandria sends letters to all the churches of Egypt, to all the cities and the monasteries, in order to announce the date of the beginning of Lent and of Easter Sunday. Now only a few days after our first talk with the monk Isaac, there came, according to custom, the official letters of the bishop Theophilus. In these he made the announcement about Easter and he included a long discussion of the absurd heresy of the Anthropomorphites, a heresy which he leveled with great eloquence. This was received very bitterly by almost every sort of monk throughout all Egypt, monks who, in their simplicity, had been ensnared by the error. Indeed, the majority of the older men among the brethren asserted that in fact the bishop was to be condemned as someone corrupted by the most serious heresy, someone opposing the ideas of holy Scripture, someone who denied that almighty God was of human shape—and this despite the clear scriptural evidence that Adam was created in His image. Those living in the desert of Scete and who were far ahead of all the Egyptian monks in perfection and knowledge denounced the bishop's letter. Among all the priests only our own Paphnutius was an exception. Those in charge of the three other churches in the desert refused to allow the letter to be read or publicly presented at their assemblies.

3

Among the victims of this heresy there was a man named Sarapion. For a very long time he had lived a life of austerity and he had experience of every aspect of monastic discipline. Merit and age combined to bring him to the front ranks of the monks but his ignorance in this doctrinal matter made him all the more culpable in the eyes of those holding the true faith. Despite the many entreaties of the holy priest Paphnutius he could not be led back on to the path of the true faith. The concept seemed new-fangled to him. It was something unknown to his predecessors and not taught by them.

By chance a deacon named Photinus came along. He was a very well-versed man. He came from Cappadocia because he wished to visit the brethren living in the desert of Scete, and the blessed Paphnutius received him with great pleasure. In order to add strength to the doctrine contained in the bishop's letter he brought Photinus into a gathering of all the brethren. He asked him how the Catholic churches of the East interpreted the words in Genesis, "Let us make man in our own image and likeness" (Gn 1:26).

Photinus explained how all the leaders of the churches were unanimous in teaching that the image and likeness of God should be understood not in an earthly, literal sense but spiritually. He himself demonstrated the truth of this in a lengthy discourse and with abundant scriptural evidence. He showed that it was impossible for the boundless, incomprehensible, and invisible majesty to undergo anything typical of human experience and likeness, for here is something that is not corporeal or composite, something simple which can be observed neither by the eye nor by the mind.

At last the old man was moved by the many very powerful arguments of this extremely learned man and he was drawn back to the faith of the Catholic tradition. This agreement of his gave endless joy to the monk Paphnutius and to all of us, for clearly the Lord had not allowed an old man of great age and outstanding virtue, a man gone astray only because of ignorance and simplicity, to remain until the very end a stranger to the path of true faith. We stood up to bless the Lord and to pour out our prayers of thanks to Him. And then amid these prayers the old man became confused, for he sensed that the human image of God which he used to draw before him as he prayed was now gone from his heart. Suddenly he gave way to the bitterest, most abundant tears and sobs. He threw himself on the ground and with the mightiest howl he cried out: "Ah the misfortune! They've taken my God away from me. I have no one to hold on to, and I don't know whom to adore or to address."

We were deeply moved by this. And in our hearts was the memory of the earlier Conference. So we went back to the monk Isaac and when we saw him this is what we said to him:

4

"Even without these strange and recent events, our insistent memory of your Conference on prayer has persuaded us to abandon everything and to come back to Your Beatitude. Indeed, the serious error of the monk Sarapion has added something to this longing of ours. This error, it seems to us, comes as a result of the skill of most wicked demons. And we have fallen into no small discouragement as we think of his labor of the fifty wonderful years he has spent in this desert and of the fact that not only did he fall prey to this disastrous ignorance but even ran the risk of everlasting death.

"First, we want to know this. What is the source of so serious an error? Then we would like to learn how we achieve this level of prayer about which you spoke earlier with such abundant and magnificent eloquence. That wonderful conference of yours had such an effect on us that we fell into a stupor.

"How can we achieve this? How can we lay hold of it? This has not yet been revealed to us."

5

Isaac: "There is nothing surprising about the fact that a very simple man who never received instruction concerning the substance and the nature of the divinity could have remained until now a captive of ignorance and of long-standing error. Actually, he just remained stuck in old errors. It is not a question, as you think, of a recent diabolical trick, but rather of an old pagan misapprehension. Paganism gave human shape to the demons which it adored. And nowadays it is thought that the incomprehensible and unspeakable majesty of the true God can be adored amid the limitations of some image or other. People believe they are holding on to nothing at all if they do not have some image in front of them, an image to be prayed to, an image to be carried around in the mind, an image which is always there to be looked at. This is the error against which are directed the words: 'They have exchanged the glory of the incorruptible God for a likeness of corruptible man' (Rom 1:23). And Jeremiah says this: 'My people have exchanged their glory for an idol' (Jer 2:11).

"This error is ingrained in the minds of those I have mentioned. And among those untouched by pagan superstition the error arises under the influence of that declaration 'Let us make man in our own image and likeness' and it arises too out of ignorance and simplicity. It is from this abominable interpretation that there is really born that heresy of the Anthropomorphites, the heresy which obstinately and perversely claims that the infinite and simple divine substance is enclosed in what characterizes us and that it is of human shape.

"Anyone reared in Catholic teaching will reject this pagan blasphemy and will also achieve that purity in prayer of which I have been speaking. In its pleadings this prayer will not only reject all representation of the divine and all that is of human shape—an impossibly criminal utterance—but it will not give a place to even the memory of some statement of the appearance and shape of any act whatsoever.

6

"As I said in the first Conference, each soul in prayer is stirred and shaped in accordance with the measure of its purity. It loses sight of earthly and material things in proportion to the inspiration of its purity, so that it sees Jesus either in his lowly creaturehood or else, with the inner gaze of the soul, it sees the glorified Jesus coming in the splendor of His majesty. To look upon Jesus coming in the glory of His kingdom is not possible for those held back by that weakness, Jewish in character, which prevents them from saying with the apostle: 'Even if we did know Christ in the flesh, that is not how we know Him now' (2 Cor 5:16). Only those of purest eye can look upon His divinity, those who have risen up beyond lowly works and earthly thoughts and have gone off with Him to the high mountain of solitude. And that solitude is free from the entire swirl of worldly considerations, of worldly disturbances. It is safely removed from all the turbulence of sin. It is raised up high in the utter purity of faith and amid preeminent virtues. It makes known the glory of the face of Christ and reveals the image of His splendor to those worthy to look upon it with the clear gaze of the spirit.

"Jesus is seen by those who live in the cities and the towns and the villages of monastic life and work, but He is seen not with the clarity with which He has appeared to the Peter and the James and the John who can climb up with Him to that high mountain of virtue. In this kind of solitude He appeared to Moses and spoke to Elias.

"This was something which our Lord wished to lay down as something sure. He wished to leave us examples of perfect purity. Being Himself the inviolable source of holiness, He did not have to rely on withdrawal from the world in order to acquire it nor did He need the benefit of a solitary way of life. Being Himself the fullness of purity, He could not be touched by the stains of the mob nor, in consorting with men, would He be contaminated, He who purifies and sanctifies all that is polluted.

"Still, He withdrew to the mountain so as to pray there alone, and surely in this withdrawal He set us an example so that if we should have the wish to pray to God with a pure, clean heart, then we, likewise, must withdraw from all the worry and turbulence of the crowd. While we still hang around in this body we must reproduce some image of that blessedly eternal life promised for the future to the saints so that among us it may be a case of 'God—all in all' (1 Cor 15:28).

7

"Then there will be accomplished in us what our Savior prayed for when, speaking to His Father about His disciples, He said: 'So that the love you have for me may be in them, and they in us' (Jn 7:26). 'That they may all be one, as you, Father, are in me and I in you, and that they may be one in us' (Jn 17:21). The perfect love with which God 'first loved us' (1 Jn 4:10) will come into our hearts, for our faith tells us that this prayer of our Savior will not be in vain. And these will be the signs of God being all that we love and all that we want. He will be all that we are zealous for, all that we strive for. He will be all that we think about, all our living, all that we talk about, our very breath. And that union of Father and Son, of Son and Father, will fill our senses and our minds. As God loves us with a love that is true and pure, a love that never breaks, we too will be joined to Him in a never-ending unshakable love, and it will be such a union that our breathing and our thinking and our talking will be 'God.' And we will come at last to that objective which I have mentioned, the goal which the Lord prayed to be fulfilled in us: 'That they may all be one as we are one, as I am in them and you in me so that they are utterly one' (Jn 17:22–23). 'Father, I want those you have given me to be with me where I am' (Jn 17:24).

"This, then, is the goal of the monk. All his striving must be for this so that he may deserve to possess in this life an image of future happiness and may have the beginnings of a foretaste in this body of that life and glory of heaven. This, I say, is the objective of all perfection, to have the soul so removed from all dalliance with the body that it rises each day to the things of the spirit until all its living and all its wishing become one unending prayer."

8

Germanus: "We came here to you because of the astonishment we felt at that first Conference of yours. But an even greater amazement grows in us now. What you are teaching us is inflaming us with a desire for perfect blessedness. And yet we are very discouraged when we see how little we know of the route which would lead us to such sublimity.

"In our cells we have meditated for a long time and it may well be opportune to tell you the thoughts we have had. So please listen to us patiently. We know that Your Beatitude is not usually offended by the nonsense of the weak. And these things should be said openly so that anything foolish in them may be corrected.

"This is what we think. In any art or discipline, perfection can be reached only from beginnings which are necessarily very simple. One starts off from what is easier and gentler. The soul is nourished by the milk of reason, grows bit by bit, rises up gradually step by step from lowly things to the very highest. When one has taken hold of the simpler principles, when one has passed through the gates of one's profession, then as a consequence and without constraint one reaches the inner recesses, the high points of perfection. How can the child pronounce the simple gathering of syllables if he has not first learned to recognize the letters? How will skill in reading follow if one is unable to relate the brief and precise descriptions of words? How can someone ignorant of grammar achieve rhetorical eloquence or philosophic knowledge?

"The same goes for that most sublime discipline which teaches us to cling utterly to God. I am sure that it too possesses basic principles. After these have been very solidly established the high points can be grounded in them and raised up to the heights.

"The following, we humbly feel, would be the principles. First would be to know the method of finding and holding God in our thoughts. Second would be to hold unshakably to this method, whatever that may be, for in this perseverance, we feel, lies the ultimate perfection.

"Hence our anxiety to find a formula which will enable us to think of God and to hold incessantly to that thought so that, as we keep it in view, we may have something to return to immediately whenever we find that we have somehow slipped away from it. It will be there for us to take up once more without wasting time in searches or in painful detours.

"And here is what happens. When our thoughts slip away from spiritual contemplation and run here and there, we turn to ourselves as though coming from a sleep of forgetfulness. We wake up and look for the formula by which to revive our vanished spiritual thinking. The looking is a delay for us and before we have even found it we lapse a second time and before a contemplative gaze opens up and what our heart wishes for is vanished.

"The reason for this confusion is quite evident. It is that we had nothing settled, no special formula which we could hold constantly before our eyes, one to which the wandering mind could return after many wanderings and various travels, one that the mind could enter, as into a haven of peace after long shipwreck.

"So it happens that the mind, held back by ignorance of this and by this difficulty, is forever wandering and is tossed in all directions, like a drunk. If by chance—and not because of any effort of its own—it comes into direct encounter with something spiritual, it is powerless to hold on to it firmly and for a long time. One thought follows another, arriving, coming to being, ending and going away—all without the mind noticing."

9

Isaac: "Your query, in its precision and subtlety, shows how close to purity you are. Not everyone knows how to put questions about such things, let alone analyze and examine them, unless he has meditated carefully and deeply and is forever on the watch to scrutinize these issues in depth. His life has to be one of such constant mortification and effort that, so to speak, he can arrive at the threshold of purity and knock on its door.

"I am not suggesting that you are simply at the doorway of true prayer. Rather, your experience is such that you have touched upon the very central hidden mystery of prayer and have taken some hold of what it really is. And with the Lord as my guide it will not be too difficult for me to bring you in from the porch, where you walk uncertainly, and to lead you into the inner sanctum. Nor will you be prevented from understanding what I wish to show you. One is very close to knowledge when one clearly recognizes the questions to be asked. One is not far from true awareness when one begins to understand one's ignorance. And so I have no fear of being reproached for indiscretion or frivolity when I come to tell you what I left out of our earlier discussion of the perfection of prayer. In my view you have reached the point where even without any word from me the grace of God would have made such things known to you."

10

"You were quite right to make the comparison between training in continuous prayer and the teaching of children who at first do not know the alphabet, do not recognize letters, and are unable to write with a sure and firm hand. Models are put before them, carefully drawn in wax. By continually studying them, by practicing every day to reproduce them, they learn at last to write.

"The same happens with contemplation. You need a model and you keep it constantly before your eyes. You learn either to turn it in a salutary way over and over in your spirit or else, as you use it and meditate upon it, you lift yourself upward to the most sublime sights.

"And what follows now is the model to teach you, the prayer formula for which you are searching. Every monk who wants to think continuously about God should get accustomed to meditating endlessly on it and to banishing all other thoughts for its sake. But he will not hold on to it unless he breaks completely free from all bodily concerns and cares.

"This is something which has been handed on to us by some of the oldest of the Fathers and it is something which we hand on to only a very small number of the souls eager to know it:

"To keep the thought of God always in your mind you must cling totally to this formula for piety: 'Come to my help, O God; Lord, hurry to my rescue' (Ps 69:2).

"It is not without good reason that this verse has been chosen from the whole of Scripture as a device. It carries within it all the feelings of which human nature is capable. It can be adapted to every condition and can be usefully deployed against every temptation. It carries within it a cry of help to God in the face of every danger. It expresses the humility of a pious confession. It conveys the watchfulness born of unending worry and fear. It conveys a sense of our frailty, the assurance of being heard, the confidence in help that is always and everywhere present. Someone forever calling out to his protector is indeed very sure of having him close by. This is the voice filled with the ardor of love and of charity. This is the terrified cry of someone who sees the snares of the enemy, the cry of someone besieged day and night and exclaiming that he cannot escape unless his protector comes to the rescue.

"This short verse is an indomitable wall for all those struggling against the onslaught of demons. It is an impenetrable breastplate and the sturdiest of shields. Whatever the disgust, the anguish, or the gloom in our thoughts, this verse keeps us from despairing of our salvation since it reveals to us the One to whom we call, the One who sees our struggles and who is never far from those who pray to Him. If things go well for us in spirit, if there is joy in our hearts, this verse is a warning to us not to grow proud, not to get puffed up at being in a good condition which, as it demonstrates, cannot be retained without the protection of God for whose continuous and speedy help it prays. This little verse, I am saying, proves to be necessary and useful to each one of us and in all circumstances. For someone who needs help in all things is making clear that he requires the help of God not simply in hard and sad situations but equally amid fortunate and joyful conditions. He knows that God saves us from adversity and makes our joys linger and that in neither situation can human frailty survive without His help.

"I am assailed by a passion for good eating. I am on the watch for food of which the desert knows nothing. Into the drabness of my solitary life come the fragrances of royal dishes and I feel myself dragged unwillingly along by my longing for them. And so I must say 'Come to my help, O God; Lord, hurry to my rescue.'

"I am moved to think ahead to the time set aside for eating. With a great pain across the heart I struggle to hold on to my proper and accustomed measure of restraint. And so I must cry my groaning cry 'Come to my help, O God; Lord, hurry to my rescue.'

"The flesh attacks me, and I should fast more strictly. But weariness, or my parched, closed-in appetite keep me back. And if my hopes

are to be fulfilled, if the fevered stirrings of fleshly desire are to be quietened down, then I must pray 'Come to my help, O God; Lord, hurry
to my rescue.'

"The due hour has come to bid me eat, but the bread disgusts me
and I am held back from necessary food. And so I must howl 'Come to
my help, O God; Lord, hurry to my rescue.'

"I want to read, so as to keep my thoughts in order. A headache
keeps me from it. Or, at the third hour, sleepiness inclines my face onto
the sacred page and I have an urge either to skip the appointed time for
rest or to anticipate it. During assembly sleep weighs so much on me
that I am forced to interrupt the canonical recitation of the psalms. And
so too I must cry 'Come to my help, O God; Lord, hurry to my rescue.'

"Sleep has left my eyes. I see myself worn down by sleeplessness
over many nights and shut away from all the refreshment of my night's
rest. And so I must sigh and pray 'Come to my help, O God; Lord,
hurry to my rescue.'

"Here I am, still fighting against my sins. The temptation of the
flesh suddenly stirs me and with its smooth delight it tries as I sleep to
drag me into giving my consent. And so if an alien raging fire is not to
burn the sweetly fragrant flowers of chastity I must cry 'Come to my
help, O God; Lord, hurry to my rescue.'

"I feel the goad of desire gone dead, the fever in my loins gone cold.
And if this acquired virtue is to stay, if the grace of God is to remain
longer or indeed forever, I must be sure to say 'Come to my help, O
God; Lord, hurry to my rescue.'

"I am troubled by the pangs of rage, of greed, of gloom. I am
drawn to scatter that gentleness which I had embraced as my own. And
so if I am not to be carried off by turbulent rage into bitterness I must
groan mightily and call out 'Come to my help, O God; Lord, hurry to
my rescue.'

"I am tempted by boredom, by vainglory, by the surge of pride.
My mind takes subtle pleasure in the negligence or the easy-going attitude of others. And so if this devilish prompting of the enemy is not
to overcome me I must pray in all contrition of heart 'Come to my help,
O God; Lord, hurry to my rescue.'

"I have won the grace of humility and simplicity. With contrite
spirit I have laid off the yoke of pride. But I am afraid that 'the arrogant
fast may come against me, that the hand of the sinner may drive me
out' (Ps 35:12). And so if I am not to suffer a more grievous wound as

a consequence of the joy of my victory I must use all my strength to say aloud 'Come to my help, O God; Lord hurry to my rescue.'

"In my soul are countless and varied distractions. I am in a fever as my heart moves this way and that. I have no strength to hold in check the scatterings of my thoughts. I cannot utter my prayer without interruption, without being visited by empty images and by the memory of words and doings. I feel myself bound in by such sterility that I cannot bring to birth any spiritual feelings within me. And so if I am to deserve liberation from this bleakness of spirit from which my groans and sighs have been unable to save me I shall be obliged to cry out 'Come to my help, O God; Lord, hurry to my rescue.'

"I feel that my spirit has once more found a sense of direction, that my thinking has grown purposeful, that because of a visit of the Holy Spirit my heart is unspeakably glad and my mind ecstatic. Here is a great overflow of spiritual thoughts, thanks to a sudden illumination and to the coming of the Savior. The holiest ideas, hitherto concealed from me, have been revealed to me. And so if I am to deserve to remain thus for much longer, I must anxiously and regularly cry 'Come to my help, O God; Lord, hurry to my rescue.'

"At night the devils surround me with their horrors. I am bothered by the images of unclean spirits. My quivering terror drags away my very hope of salvation and of life. And so I shall fly to the saving port of this little verse and with all my strength I will exclaim 'Come to my help, O God; Lord, hurry to my rescue.'

"Again, when I have been made whole by the consolation of the Lord, when I have been encouraged by His coming, when I feel myself guarded by countless thousands of angels, when I have the daring to seek out and call to battle those whom I once feared more than death, those whose mere touch or presence filled me, mind and body, with terror, then indeed if I am to hold on to this strength of purpose I must, with all my strength, cry 'Come to my help, O God; Lord, hurry to my rescue.'

"Our prayer for rescue in bad times and for protection against pride in good times should be founded on this verse. The thought of this verse should be turning unceasingly in your heart. Never cease to recite it in whatever task or service or journey you find yourself. Think upon it as you sleep, as you eat, as you submit to the most basic demands of nature. This heartfelt thought will prove to be a formula of salvation for you. Not only will it protect you against all devilish attack,

JOHN CASSIAN

but it will purify you from the stain of all earthly sin and will lead you on to the contemplation of the unseen and the heavenly and to that fiery urgency of prayer which is indescribable and which is experienced by very few. Sleep should come upon you as you meditate on this verse until as a result of your habit of resorting to its words you get in the habit of repeating them even in your slumbers.

"This verse should be the first thing to occur to you when you wake up. It should precede all your thoughts as you keep vigil. It should take you over as you rise from your bed and go to kneel. After this it should accompany you in all your works and deeds. It should be at your side at all times. Following the precept of Moses, you will think upon it 'as you sit at home or walk along your way' (Dt 6:7), as you sleep or when you get up. You will write it upon the threshold and gateway of your mouth, you will place it on the walls of your house and in the inner sanctum of your heart. It will be a continuous prayer, an endless refrain when you bow down in prostration and when you rise up to do all the necessary things of life.

11

"The soul must grab fiercely onto this formula so that after saying it over and over again, after meditating upon it without pause, it has the strength to reject and to refuse all the abundant riches of thought. Grasping the poverty of this little verse it will come all the more easily to that first of all the gospel beatitudes, 'Blessed are the poor in spirit for theirs is the kingdom of heaven' (Mt 5:3). The one who is outstanding because of this kind of poverty will fulfill the word of the prophet, 'The poor man and the indigent man will praise the name of the Lord' (Ps 73:21).

"Indeed, what poverty can be greater and more holy than that of the man who recognizing that he has no defense and no strength begs each day for the largess of another and who understands that his life and being are at every moment sustained by divine help? He will rightly be called the Lord's mendicant as he cries out to Him in daily supplication, 'I am a mendicant and a poor man, but God helps me' (Ps 39:18). God Himself will give him light to rise up to the many-shaped knowledge of His being. He will enable him to feast on the sight of the most sublime and hidden mysteries.

"The prophet puts the matter thus: 'The mountain-tops are for the deer and the rocks for the hedgehogs' (Ps 103:18). And this fits in very well with the point I have been making. Someone who perseveres in

136

simplicity and innocence is a danger and a menace to no one. He is satisfied with his simplicity. All he wants is to be protected from being a
prey to his enemies. He is a sort of hedgehog of the spirit hidden under
that protective rock of which Scripture speaks. That is to say, he is protected by the memory of the Lord's passion and by his unceasing meditation upon the little verse of which I have been speaking, and so he is
protected against the ambushes of the circling enemy. Concerning these
hedgehogs of the spirit the following is said in Proverbs: 'The hedgehogs, a weak race, make their homes among the rocks' (Prv 30:26).

"To tell the truth, what is weaker than a Christian? What is more
drained than a monk who lacks not only the means to avenge the wrongs
done to him but who cannot even allow the lightest and the most silent
emotion to stir within him?

"Someone like this, someone who has not only reached the state
of having the simplicity of the innocent but who is fortified by the virtue of discernment, becomes the exterminator of the most vicious serpents and he keeps Satan under foot. The zeal of his soul makes him
like a spiritual deer who feeds on the high mountains of the prophets
and the apostles, that is, on their most high and most exalted teachings.
Nourished by this food, which he continually eats, he penetrates so
deeply into the thinking of the psalms that he sings them not as though
they had been composed by the prophet but as if he himself had written
them, as if this were his own private prayer uttered amid the deepest
compunction of heart. Certainly he thinks of them as having been specially composed for him and he recognizes that what they express was
made real not simply once upon a time in the person of the prophet but
that now, every day, they are being fulfilled in himself.

"Then indeed the Scriptures lie ever more clearly open to us. They
are revealed, heart and sinew. Our experience not only brings us to
know them but actually anticipates what they convey. The meaning of
the words comes through to us not just by way of commentaries but by
what we ourselves have gone through. Seized of the identical feelings
in which the psalm was composed or sung we become, as it were, its
author. We anticipate its idea instead of following it. We have a sense
of it even before we make out the meaning of the words. The sacred
words stir memories within us, memories of the daily attacks which we
have endured and are enduring, the cost of our negligence or the profits
of our zeal, the good things of providence and the deceits of the enemy,
the slippery subtle tricks of memory, the blemishes of human frailty,
the improvidence of ignorance. As we sing we are reminded of all this.

We find all these sentiments expressed in the psalms. We see very clearly, as in a mirror, what is being said to us and we have a deeper understanding of it. Instructed by our own experiences we are not really learning through hearsay but have a feeling for these sentiments as things that we have already seen. They are not like things confided to our capacity for remembrance but, rather, we bring them to birth in the depths of our hearts as if they were feelings naturally there and part of our being. We enter into their meaning not because of what we read but because of what we have experienced earlier.

"And so our soul will arrive at that purity of prayer reached, to the extent that the Lord permitted it, by the sequence of discussion in my earlier Conference.

"This prayer centers on no contemplation of some image or other. It is masked by no attendant sounds or words. It is a fiery outbreak, an indescribable exaltation, an insatiable thrust of the soul. Free of what is sensed and seen, ineffable in its groans and sighs, the soul pours itself out to God."

12

Germanus: "We have asked you for what was handed on as a tradition of spirituality. But you have given us more, for we think that it is perfection itself which you have described in an open and clear way. What could be more perfect and more sublime than to be able to latch onto God in a brief meditation, to leave all the boundaries of the visible world by means of reflection upon one little verse, and to pull together in a few words the sentiments engendered by all the forms of prayer?

"But we must ask you to explain our last point. How can we firmly hold on to this verse which you have given us as a formula? How can we keep it in such a way that, by God's grace, we are freed from the follies of earthly thoughts and are enabled to keep spiritual ideas unshakably within us?

13

"Our minds think of some passage of a psalm. But it is taken away from us without our noticing it, and, stupidly, unknowingly, the spirit slips on to some other text of Scripture. It begins to think about it, but before it gets to fully grasp it another text slides into the memory and drives out the earlier one. Meanwhile another one arrives and there is a further turnabout. The spirit rolls along from psalm to psalm, leaps from the gospel to Saint Paul, from Paul to the prophets, from there to incidents of spirituality. Ever on the move, forever wandering, it is tossed along through all the body of Scripture, unable to settle on anything, unable to reject anything or to hold on to anything, powerless to arrive at any full and judicious study, a dilettante and speedy taster of spiritual ideas rather than their creator and possessor. And so the mind is always on the move, and at the time of assembly it is pulled, like a drunk, in every direction and it performs no task competently. When it is speaking aloud in prayer, it thinks of a psalm or something else. When it is singing it is preoccupied with something other than the text of the psalm. When it is engaged in reading aloud it remembers something it wishes to do or to have done. In this way it neither turns to nor leaves any theme in a disciplined or opportune manner. It seems to be a victim of chance. It has not the power either to hold on to or to linger over what pleases it.

"Therefore it is essential for us to know above all else how we can properly perform these spiritual duties. And certainly we ought to know how we are to keep a firm hold of that little verse which you have given us as a formula so that all our ideas should cease to appear and disappear in their own inconstant way but should remain under our control."

14

Isaac: "I think I have already answered your question in what I had to say earlier about the condition of prayer. Nevertheless, since you have asked me to repeat it, I will briefly explain the method of keeping our hearts still.

"Three things keep a wandering mind in place—vigils, meditation, and prayer. Constant attention to them and a firm concentration upon them will give stability to the soul. But such stability cannot be obtained except by a continuous effort made not for the sake of ambitiousness but because of the requirements of the present way of life. This is the way to break out of the worries and the cares of the present life and to make possible for us the realization of the apostolic injunction 'Pray without cease' (1 Thes 5:17).

"The one accustomed to prayer only when he bends the knee prays very little. The one who on bended knee gives himself over to distraction is not praying at all. Before the time of prayer we must put ourselves in the state of mind we would wish to have in us when we actually pray. It is an inexorable fact that the condition of the soul at the time of prayer depends upon what shaped it beforehand. The soul will rise to the heights of heaven or plunge into the things of earth, depending upon where it lingered before the time of prayer."

Thus, then, was the second Conference of the monk Isaac on the nature of prayer. We listened to it with deep amazement. We were full of astonishment at what he taught concerning the meditation upon this verse which was under discussion and which he urged upon beginners as a way of formation. We very much wanted to put it into practice. We thought we had here a short and easy method. But in fact we found that it proved less easy than our regular habit of looking here and there in the body of Scripture for meditation themes without being bound by any one of them.

"But at least this much is clear. No one is shut off from perfection because of illiteracy. Lack of culture is no bar to that purity of heart and soul which lies quite close by to everyone. Constant meditation upon this verse will keep the mind wholly and entirely upon God."

Conference Eleven

ON PERFECTION

1

Living in a Syrian monastery we had learned the elements of the faith and had made some progress in it. But we began to wish for the grace of increased perfection. We quickly decided to go to Egypt and to visit the greatest possible number of holy men in the remotest areas of the desert of Thebais. Their renown had spread throughout the world and our urge was not so much to rival them as to get to know them. And so we sailed to an Egyptian city named Thennesus, which is washed on all sides either by the sea or by salt lakes. The people living there devote themselves entirely to business, since there is no land, and they earn their money and their living entirely by naval commerce. Indeed the earth which they need for the construction of their buildings has to be brought in from afar by sea.

2

The God who supports us in our longings arranged that our arrival should coincide with that of bishop Archebius, a most blessed and outstanding man. He had been hijacked from a group of anchorites to be made bishop of the town of Panephysis. Throughout his life he lived with the same austerity which he had set himself as a solitary. He relaxed none of his earlier humility and was in no way beguiled by the honor thrust upon him. He claimed that he was in no way suited to this job. Indeed he lamented that he had been expelled from the anchoritic life because he was unworthy of it and that in the thirty-seven years during which he was himself an anchorite he had never been able to achieve the purity required by so exalted a vocation.

This man had come to Thennesus for the election of a bishop there and he received us in a very holy and humane fashion. When he learned that we wished to visit the holy fathers in the remotest parts of Egypt, he said to us: "Before you go, come and see the old men who live not far from our monastery. Their old age is clear in their bent bodies and their saintliness shines in their faces. To those looking at them the very sight of them can bestow knowledge. Not from their words but from the example of their holy way of living you may learn that which I grieve to have lost and which, because it is lost, I cannot hand on to you. Still, I think that what I lack may somehow be eased by my concern for you and by ensuring that you can more easily acquire that gospel pearl for which you are seeking and which I do not possess."

3

He took the stick and the wallet which are customary for all monks traveling there and he himself was our guide on the journey to his town, Panephysis. The land here, together with most of the neighboring territory, was once so fertile that, according to reports, it was able to supply the table of the king. But it was overrun by the sea, which had broken its limits after a sudden earthquake. It destroyed nearly all the villages and it covered the once rich land with salt marshes. One could take as a literal prophecy for this region what was sung in a spiritual sense: "He turned rivers into desert and springs of water into thirsty ground and a fertile country into salt flats because of the wickedness of the people living there" (Ps 106:33).

Similarly, there were many towns in these areas built on higher ground. The flood drove out the inhabitants and made the towns look like islands, which now give holy men in search of retreat the solitude they long for.

Three very old anchorites were living there, namely, Chaeremon, Nesteros, and Joseph.

4

The blessed Archebius decided to bring us first to Chaeremon, since he was nearer the monastery and because he was older than the other two. He was over a hundred years old and only the spirit remained energetic within him. Old age and zeal for prayer had so bent his back that he was like someone in his first childhood, for he moved around with hands reaching to the ground. And so we gazed at a wonderful face and at this way of moving about. His limbs were dried up and dead, and still he had not lost the rigor of his earliest austerity.

Very humbly we asked him to speak to us and to teach us. We urgently maintained that the reason for our coming was a longing for the Rules of the spiritual life.

He sighed deeply.

"What teaching could I give you? The frailty of age has compelled me to relax my former austerity and has taken away any confidence in what I might have to say. How could I presume to teach what I myself do not practice? How could I instruct someone else in what, as I know, I do very little or lukewarmly? That is why I have allowed none of my juniors to live with me when I am this age. My example might weaken the austerity of someone else. The authority of a teacher will never be effective unless the fruit of deeds is impressed upon the heart of whoever is listening to him."

5

These words caused us no slight embarrassment, and, stirred by compunction, we gave him this answer: "A quite adequate lesson to us would be the very hardship of this place and that solitary life which even sturdy youth can scarcely enjoy. Even with you silent these things have abundant instruction to offer and they move us very deeply. But still we ask you to break your silence in some small way and to please tell us how it might be possible for us not so much to imitate as to contemplate that excellence which we so clearly see in you. It may be that our tepid enthusiasm has been made known to you so that we do not deserve to obtain what we seek. But this lack of warmth should be ascribed to the weariness of a very long journey which has brought us from the rudimentary training of the monastery at Bethlehem to here, where we wished so much to listen to your teaching and because we wanted so much to make progress."

6

Then Chaeremon said thus: "Three things keep men from giving themselves over to sin. There is the fear either of hell or of earthly laws. There is the hope and the desire for the kingdom of heaven. Or there is the attraction of good itself and the love of virtue.

"There is the text concerning how fear drives out the contagion of evil. 'The fear of the Lord hates evil' (Prv 8:13).

"Hope too shuts out the onset of all sins. 'Those who hope in Him do not commit sin' (Ps 33:23).

"Love is not nervous of the ruin of sin because 'love never falls' and 'love covers a multitude of sins' (1 Cor 13:8; 1 Pt 4:8).

"Further, the blessed apostle offers as a summary of salvation the perfection of these three virtues. 'Now,' he says, 'these three things remain—faith, hope, love' (1 Cor 13:13). For it is faith—with its fear of the judgment and punishment to come—which brings about the decline of sin's contagion. It is hope which draws our mind from the things of the present and which in its anticipation of heavenly rewards spurns all the pleasures of the body. And it is love which fires us to long for Christ, to be zealous for the fruit of the spiritual virtues and to detest utterly whatever is contrary to these virtues.

"All three seem to tend toward the one end. They summon us to abstain from everything unlawful. But they differ from one another in their degree of excellence. The first two are appropriate to men who seek perfection but who are not yet moved by zeal for the virtues. The third is particularly characteristic of God and of those who have really taken the image and likeness of God unto themselves. For only God does good, not out of fear nor in hopes of a reward but simply out of a love of goodness. 'The Lord has worked everything on His own account' (Prv 16:4). This is what Solomon declares. From the workings of His own goodness He lavishes all good things on the worthy and the unworthy and He can be wearied by no wrongs. Nor can He be provoked to painful emotion by human wickedness. But always and forever He remains what He is, perfect goodness and an unchanging nature.

7

"If anyone has a wish for perfection he will start off from that first step of fear which we describe as appropriate to a servant and of which it is said: 'When you have done everything say "we are useless servants" ' (Lk 17:10). He will rise up progressively to the higher path of hope which is made ready not for the servant but for the hired hand since such a one expects to be rewarded. Hope is sure of pardon and is without fear of being punished. Hope knows of the good works done. Hope is able to be on the lookout for the promised reward.

"But it has not yet reached the feeling of being a son who trusts in the abundant generosity of his father and who has no doubt that everything belonging to the father is also his. This was something which the prodigal son did not aspire to after he had lost both the name of son and the wealth of his father. 'I do not now deserve to be called your son'

(Lk 15:9). He turned back to become himself again after even the husks of pigs, that is, the squalid food of sin, had denied him satisfaction. He was moved by a saving fear. He began now to have a horror of the filth of pigs. He grew fearful of the torments of dreadful hunger. He turned, as it were, into something servile. Then he began to think of the reward attached to the condition of being a hired hand. He thinks he would like to be one and says: 'How many of my father's hired hands have more food than they want and here am I dying of hunger. I will go back to my father and I will say to him "Father, I have sinned against heaven and against you. I no longer deserve to be called your son. Treat me as one of your hired hands" ' (Lk 15:17–19).

"But the father rushed forward to meet him and received him with a fondness of feeling that was greater than those humble words expressing regret. And the father was not satisfied to give him the less valuable things. He moved him beyond the two lower grades and restored him to his former rank as son.

"So we too must hurry, and beg the grace of indissoluble love. We must climb to the third rank of sons who deem everything of the father to be their own. Let us earn the right to receive the image and likeness of the Father within us so that like that true Son we can cry out, 'Everything belonging to the Father is mine' (Jn 16:15). This too is what the blessed apostle says for us: 'All belongs to you, whether it be Paul, Apollo, Cephas, the world, life, death, the present or the future—all belong to you' (1 Cor 3:22). And this likeness to the Father is something to which we are called by the precepts of the Savior when He says: 'Be perfect as your heavenly Father is perfect' (Mt 5:48).

"Among those of lower standing the love of goodness is normally interrupted whenever lack of warmth, contentment, or pleasure unwind the vigor of the soul and cause a temporary withdrawal of the fear of hell or of the longing for the future. Still, these are stages on a way of progress causing us at the beginning to avoid sin, out of our fear of punishment or out of a hope for reward. Then we can move on to the stage of love for 'there is no fearfulness in love. Indeed perfect love expels fear, because to fear is to expect punishment and anyone who is afraid is still not perfect in love. So we are to love because God first loved us' (1 Jn 4:18–19).

"Therefore in no other way can we rise up to true perfection. God loved us first and this was for no other reason than that we should be saved and so we ought to love Him solely for His love of us. For this reason we should strive to rise from fear to hope and from hope to love

145

of God and of virtue. We should pass over to love of goodness itself, and so far as is possible for human nature, we should cling immovably to it.

8

"There is a great difference between the one who extinguishes the fires of sin out of fear of hell or hope of future reward and the one who, moved by love of God, turns in horror from evil and uncleanliness. He holds purity as a good because he loves and longs for chastity. He does not look to the reward promised for the future. Rather, he has the pleasurable sense of a present good and all his activities spring not from a consideration of punishment but out of his delight in virtue. For someone in this situation the removal of all human witnesses will lead to no abuse nor will he be able to pollute by the hidden delights of his thoughts. He holds the love of virtue deep in the marrow of his bones and with regard to anything opposed to this not only does he not allow it in his heart but he looks upon it with the utmost horror.

"To hate the contagion of sin and of the flesh while one is drawn to an existing good—this is one thing. And something else is the reining in of unlawful urges out of regard for the reward to come. It is one thing to be frightened of a present danger and another to be afraid of a future punishment. Finally, however, it is much better that for the sake of goodness itself one never wishes to desert the good rather than that one does not yield to evil out of fear of evil. In the one case the good is deliberately chosen, in the other, it is, as it were, forced, violently dragged out of someone unwilling, and this because of fear of punishment or thirst for reward.

"Furthermore, someone who keeps away from the blandishments of sin because he is afraid will return to the object of his choice as soon as the obstacle of fear is removed. Hence he will not acquire any firm stand in what is good. He will have no rest from temptation since he will not be possessed by the sturdy and continuous peace of chastity. Where the tension of war is to be found the danger of getting hurt cannot be escaped. Someone found in a place of struggle, however good a fighter he may be and however bravely and often he inflicts deadly wounds on the enemy, still he will often be set upon by the sword of the foe.

"But if someone has really conquered the onslaught of sin, he enjoys a secure peace and passes over to the love of virtue itself and he will have an unshaken place by that good of which he is utterly seized, for in his eyes there is nothing more deadly than some wreckage in the heart of his own chaste disposition. To him nothing is dearer, nothing more precious, than the purity which he now possesses. For him some deadly transgression against virtue or the poisonous contagion of sin itself is a grievous punishment. The deference shown him by men or total solitude will neither add to nor take from his own goodness. Everywhere and always he will strive to ensure that the supreme arbiter not only of his acts but of his thoughts will be his own conscience which, as he knows well, he cannot circumvent, deceive, or avoid.

9

"If with God's help and without a presumptuous reliance on his own efforts someone comes to win this condition, he will pass over to the status of an adopted son. He will leave behind servility with its fear. He will leave aside the mercenary hope of reward, a hope which seeks a reward and not the goodness of the giver. There will be no more fear, no more desiring. Instead, there will be forever the love which never fails.

"The Lord has critical words for some concerning this fear and this love and He indicates the kind of person to whom they apply. 'The son honors his father and the slave fears his master. If I am indeed father, where is my honor? And if I am master, where is the fear of me?' (Mal 1:6). The slave has to fear him because 'if knowing the wishes of his master he does things worthy of blows, he will be well flogged' (Lk 12:47).

"But anyone whose charity makes him to be an image and likeness of God, such a one will delight in the good because of the pleasure he takes in what is good, and with equal love he will embrace patience and gentleness. The failures of sinners will no longer enrage him. Rather, he will beg pardon for their weaknesses and out of sympathy he will plead for them. He remembers how long he too was besieged by the promptings of similar passions until the day when he was saved by the Lord's pity. It was not by his own efforts but rather by God's protectiveness that he was saved from the temptation of the flesh, and so he understands that it is mercy, not anger, which must be shown to those gone astray. And in all peace of heart he sings to the Lord the little verse 'You have broken my chains and I will offer you a sacrifice of praise' (Ps 115:16–17). 'Had it not been for the Lord's help my soul would soon have been dwelling in hell' (Ps 93:17).

Persisting in this lowliness of mind he will then be able to fulfill that gospel command of perfection, 'Love your enemies, do good to those who hate you, pray for those who persecute you and utter calumnies against you' (Mt 5:44). In this way we will earn the right to reach the reward mentioned a bit later, namely, that not only will we bear before us the image and likeness of God but we will even be truly called sons of God, 'that you may be described as sons of your Father in heaven who makes His sun shine on good and bad and who makes the rain fall on the just and the unjust' (Mt 5:45).

"The blessed John, knowing he had arrived at this feeling, says 'that we may be trustful on the day of judgment because in this world we have become as He is' (1 Jn 4:17). How could the nature of a human being—so frail, so fragile—hope to be like the Lord if it were not for the fact that to good and bad, just and unjust, he gives his heart's peaceful love—as God does—and does good because of his love of good? And so he comes to true adoption as son of God, regarding which the same blessed apostle says, 'Everyone born of God does not sin because the seed of God is within him, so he cannot sin because of his birth from God' (1 Jn 3:9). 'We know that everyone born of God does not sin. The birth which he has had of God protects him and the evil one does not touch him' (1 Jn 5:18). This, of course, is not to be understood of every kind of sin but rather of the sins that carry death. And if there is someone who does not wish to drag himself from this latter sort of sin, the above-mentioned apostle says, in another place, that one should not even pray for him. 'If anyone knows that his brother is committing a sin that is not mortal, he has only to pray and God will give him life, though not to those committing deadly sin. For there is a sin that brings death, and I do not say that you must pray about that' (1 Jn 5:16).

"Regarding those not engaged in sins that are not mortal, sins from which even the faithful servants of Christ are not exempt, despite all their vigilant effort to be careful, this is what is said: 'If we say we have no sin in us, we are fooling ourselves and the truth is not within us' (1 Jn 1:8). 'If we say we have not sinned we make a liar of God and His word is not within us' (1 Jn 1:10). Among any holy men it is impossible not to fall into those small lapses which occur because of something said, some thought, some unawareness, some forgetfulness, some urge, some wish, some surreptitious act. They are quite different from that sin which is declared to be mortal, but they cannot be innocent of blame or reproach.

10

"When someone has attained this love of the good and this imitation of God, about which I have been speaking, then he will put on the Lord's long-suffering patience and like Him he will pray for those who persecute him. He will say, 'Father, forgive them for they do not know what they are doing' (Lk 23:34).

"A very clear proof of the fact that a soul has not yet cut loose from the corruption of sin is when it feels no sympathizing pity for the wrongdoing of others but holds instead to the strict censoriousness of a judge. For how can someone attain perfection of heart if he does not possess what the apostle described as the Law's consummation when he said, 'Carry one another's burdens and in this way you will fulfill the law of Christ' (Gal 6:2)? How can he do so if he does not possess that virtue of charity 'which is not annoyed, is not boastful, which does not think evil, which endures everything and is a support for everything' (1 Cor 13:4–7). For 'the just man has compassion for the lives of his beasts, but there is no pity in the hearts of the unjust' (Prv 12:10). And therefore it is most certain that he yields to the very sins which he condemns in someone else with unmerciful and inhuman severity. 'The stern king will tumble into evil' (Prv 13:17). 'He who shuts his ears to the cry of the poor will himself call out, and there will be none to listen to him' (Prv 21:13)."

11

Germanus: "You have spoken powerfully and splendidly about the perfect love of God. But, to be honest, there is something which troubles us. Despite all your praise, you have said that fear and the hope of reward are imperfect. Now the prophet seems to have thought quite differently. 'Fear the Lord,' he says, 'all of you who are His holy ones. For nothing is lacking to those who fear Him' (Ps 33:10). Again, he admits that he is preoccupied with observing the commandments of God for the sake of reward. 'I have inclined my heart to obey your commands for the sake of an everlasting reward' (Ps 118:112). The apostle said thus: 'It was by faith that when he reached manhood Moses denied that he was a son of the daughter of Pharaoh. He preferred to be afflicted along with the people of God than to have the passing joy of sin. He considered that the insult offered to the anointed one was a greater treasure than the riches of Egypt, for he had his eyes fixed on the reward' (Heb 11:24–26).

"How, then, can these things be considered imperfect when the blessed David boasts that he followed the divine commandments for the sake of reward and when the lawgiver, as we are told, despised the adoption which would have given him royal status, preferred the most cruel suffering to the treasures of Egypt, and all this because he was looking to a future reward?"

12

Chaeremon: "Scripture summons our free will to different degrees of perfection, and this in proportion to the condition and the measure of the individual soul. It was not at all possible to propose to all together the same crown of perfection, since everyone does not have the same virtue, the same disposition of will, or the same zeal. Hence the Word of God lays down the different degrees and the different measures of perfection.

"A clear proof of all this is to be seen in the varied gospel beatitudes. Happy are those, it is said, to whom the kingdom of heaven belongs, happy those who will possess the earth, happy those who will be consoled, happy those who shall have their fill. And yet we believe there is quite a difference between living in heaven and possessing the earth such as it is; that there is quite a difference between an awareness of consolation and the plenitude, the satiety, of justice; that there is a great distance between those who will obtain mercy and those who will deserve to enjoy the most glorious vision of God. 'The brightness of the sun is one thing and the brightness of the moon another and something else again is the brightness of the stars. Star differs from star in brightness. And so it is with the resurrection of the dead' (1 Cor 15:41–42).

"Now Scripture praises those who fear God. 'Blessed are all those who fear the Lord' (Ps 127:1). It promises them blessedness for this. Again, it says, 'There is no fear in love. Rather, perfect love casts out fear, for it is fear which has an expectation of punishment. Anyone who is fearful is not yet perfect in love' (1 Jn 4:18).

"Again, since it is a glorious thing to serve God, it is said, 'Serve the Lord in fear' (Ps 2:11). 'It is a great thing for you to be called my servant' (Is 49:6). 'Blessed is the servant whom the master, upon his return, will find acting in this way' (Mt 24:26). And yet the following is said to the apostle, 'I do not call you servants any more, for the servant does not know what his master is doing. But I have called you friends because I have let you know all that I heard from my Father'

(Jn 15:14–15). And again, 'You are friends of mine if you do what I command you' (Jn 15:13).

"So you see, then, that there are different grades of perfection and that from some high points the Lord summons us to go higher. Someone blessed and perfect in the fear of God will walk, as is written, 'from virtue to virtue' (Ps 83:8), from perfection to some other perfection. That is, with eager spirit he will rise up from fear to hope and then he will be invited to a holier state, that of love. He who was 'the faithful and prudent servant' (Mt 24:25) will pass to the relationship of a friend and the adopted condition of sons.

"This, then, is how my words are to be interpreted. I do not wish to be understood as saying that the thought of everlasting punishment or of a most blessed reward has no value. They are indeed valuable because those given over to them are introduced to the first stages of blessedness. In love, however, there is a greater faith, and the joy of it is forever. Taking hold of them it will lead them from servile fear and from the hope of reward to the love of God and to being adopted as sons. It will, so to speak, make of the perfect those who are still more perfect. 'There are many mansions in my Father's house,' says the Lord (Jn 14:2). All the stars can be seen in the sky, and still there is a great difference between the brilliance of the sun, of the moon, of Venus, and of the other stars.

"And so it is that the blessed apostle makes out that love is not only higher than fear and hope, but higher than all the charisms, however great and however marvelous these may be in human reckoning. Having gone through the entire list of the spiritual charisms he decides to speak of the various facets of love and this is what he says: 'Furthermore, I will show you a way more excellent than the others. If I speak the language of men and angels, if I have the gift of prophecy, know all the mysteries and all that there is to know, if I have all faith so as to move mountains, if I give all my wealth to feed the poor and deliver my body to be burned—it will be of no use to me if I have not love' (1 Cor 12:31, 13:1–3).

"You see, then, that there is nothing more precious, nothing more perfect, nothing more sublime, and, as it were, nothing more enduring than love. 'Prophesying will go empty, languages will fail, knowledge will be undermined, but love will never die' (1 Cor 13:8). Without love not only are all these outstanding kinds of charisms but even the very glory of the martyr brought to nothing.

13

"It must follow that anyone solidly established in the perfection of this love will rise to that more excellent and more sublime stage which is the fear of love. This is not a terror in the face of punishment nor a desire for reward. Rather it is something which comes from the very greatness of love. It is the mixture of respect and affection which a son has for a very indulgent father, a brother for a brother, a friend for a friend, a wife for a husband. This is the fear whose splendor has been elegantly described by one of the prophets. 'Wisdom and knowledge are the riches of salvation, but its treasure is the fear of the Lord' (Is 33:6). He could not have more clearly described the dignity and the merit of this fear when he said that the riches of our salvation, namely true wisdom and the knowledge of God, cannot be preserved except by the fear of the Lord. This is the fear to which saints, and not sinners, are invited by the prophetic oracles. The psalmist says: 'Fear the Lord, all you who are His holy ones, because nothing is lacking to those who fear Him' (Ps 33:10). Someone holding to this fear of the Lord is certain to lack no perfection.

"As for the fear of punishment, it was of this that the apostle John spoke when he said, 'He who is fearful is not perfected in love, because fear anticipates punishment' (1 Jn 4:18). Hence there is a considerable distance between that fear which lacks nothing, which is the treasure of wisdom and of knowledge, and that fear which is imperfect. This latter is only 'the beginning of wisdom' (Ps 110:10) and because it implies punishment it is manifestly banished from the hearts of the perfect when love is at its most superabundant, 'Love has no fear and perfect love drives out fear' (1 Jn 4:18). Actually, if the beginning of wisdom lies in fear, what will be its perfection if not in that love of Christ which comprises the fear of perfect love and which therefore deserves to be called not a beginning but, rather, the treasure of wisdom and of knowledge?

"Hence there are two degrees of fear. The first characterizes beginners, namely, those who are servants, yoked and fearful. Of such a one it is said, 'And the servant will be frightened of his lord' (Mal 1:6). And in the gospel this is what is said: 'I do not call you servants because the servant does not know what his master is doing' (Jn 15:14). Hence too: 'The servant does not always remain in the house, but the son always remains there' (Jn 8:35). It is borne in upon us that we should pass from fear of punishment to the full freedom of love and to that trust which characterizes the friends and sons of God.

"Then there is the blessed apostle who by virtue of his love of God had once risen beyond the stage of servile fear. Looking down to the lowlier gifts, he asserts that the Lord enriched him with much more splendid gifts. 'God did not give me a spirit of fear, but rather of virtue, of love, and of moderation' (2 Tm 1:7). And this is what he has to say as an encouragement to those who were burning with perfect love of the heavenly Father and whom adoption out of the rank of servants had turned into sons: 'The spirit you received is not the spirit of slaves bringing fear once more into your lives, but you have received the spirit of adoption, which makes us cry out Abba, Father' (Rom 8:15).

"The prophet too is speaking of love's fear when he describes that septi-form spirit which undoubtedly came down upon the Lord-man, in accordance with the economy of the incarnation. 'The spirit of the Lord will come to rest upon him, the spirit of wisdom and of insight, the spirit of counsel and of strength, the spirit of knowledge and of piety' (Is 11:2). Then, finally, as a kind of crown to all this he says: 'And the spirit of fear of the Lord shall fill him' (Is 11:2). And what must be noted most carefully is the fact that he does not say 'The spirit of the fear of the Lord will come to rest upon him,' as he had earlier said, but, rather, 'the spirit of fear of the Lord shall fill him.' Such indeed is the splendor of the spirit's richness that when it takes possession of a soul, it does so not in part but entirely. Nor is this without good reason. Seizing upon that love which will never pass away, not only does he fill but he possesses inseparably and forever the one of whom he has laid hold, and he is never diminished by any worldly joys or pleasures, a thing which happens from time to time to that fear which drives out love.

"This then is the fear of perfection with which the Lord-man Himself was said to have been filled. He came not only to redeem us but also to give us in Himself a model of perfection and an example of virtue. As for the servile fear of punishment, this was something out of His reach, for He was the true Son of God 'who committed no sin and in whose mouth no guile was to be found' (1 Pt 2:22)."

14

Germanus: "Now that you have spoken to us about perfect love we would like to put some questions to you about the objective of chastity. For we have no doubt that those sublime reaches of love by which, as you have shown, one rises up to the image and likeness of love can hardly exist without the perfection of chastity. We would like to know if that virtue can be so steadfast that our purified hearts need never suffer the blandishments of concupiscence. Living in the flesh can we remain so free from the body's passions that we will never feel their goading fires?"

15

Chaeremon: "Truly it would be a sign of the utmost blessedness and of outstanding merit to take a stand unceasingly in that feeling, learned or taught, which makes us cling to the Lord. As the psalmist says, all our days and nights would pass by in the contemplation of it. Our souls, devoured by a hunger and by an insatiable thirst for justice, would ceaselessly feed upon this heavenly food.

"But we have to take thought for this animal body of ours and we must do so in accordance with the most kindly providence of our Savior. 'For the spirit is willing but the flesh is weak' (Mt 26:41).

"So we must make sure to give it a little food. When the body is refreshed, the spirit will be readier for that problem which you wish to investigate more thoroughly."

Conference Fourteen

ON SPIRITUAL
KNOWLEDGE

1

The sequence ordained by what I have undertaken to do, and also by my travels, demands that the teachings of abba Nesteros should come up now. He was a man outstanding in every way and possessed of the deepest knowledge.

We had memorized certain passages of the holy Scripture and he knew that we very much wished to know their meaning and so he began to speak to us as follows:

"There are many kinds of knowledge in this world. Indeed they are as varied as the arts and the professions. But though all of them are either of no practical value or else merely of benefit to the present world, still no one of them lacks its own appropriate sequence of knowledge, its own logical order, which is then open to those seeking to acquire it.

"Now if knowledge of these arts is to be gathered within fixed and appropriate limits, how much more is it the case that the professed discipline of our religious belief exists with its own definite sequence and rationale, for the discipline reaches out to contemplate the hidden depths of unseen mysteries and it seeks not today's advantage but the payment of everlasting reward. And the knowledge of it has a twofold aspect. There is first the practical side which is achieved through the correction of one's moral acts and through the purging of sin. Second, there is theory, that is, the contemplation of things divine and the awareness of very sacred meanings.

2

"Anyone wishing to master contemplation must, with all zeal and energy, acquire first the practical side. This practical mode can be reached independently of contemplation. But in no way can contemplation be arrived at without the practical. There are two arranged and separate stages by which human lowliness can reach up to the sublime. With these in the order which I have indicated, the human can attain the heights. But take away the first stage and there is no flying across it. Therefore the one who does not avoid the stains of sin strives vainly for a sight of God: 'For the spirit of God hates pretense and it does not make its abode in a body subdued by sin.' (Wis 1:4, 5)

3

"The active stage of perfection has a two-fold schema. First is to know the nature of one's sins and the means of curing them. Second is to discern the order of the virtues and to have our spirit shaped by their perfection, so that the soul is not, as it were, in thrall to them and violently subjected to their rule but, rather, is filled with a natural pleasure at their goodness, feeding upon them, delightedly climbing that high and narrow road. When someone is unable to understand the nature of his sins and makes no effort to root them out, how will he be able to arrive at that sense of the virtues which is the second stage in the practical discipline, or how will he come to the mysteries of things spiritual and heavenly? It will have to be said that progress toward the higher things is not possible for someone who has not coped with what is lower down, and still less will he lay hold of what is outside him if he has no understanding of what is within himself.

"But we should be clear about the fact that we must work twice as hard to drive out sin as to acquire virtue. In this I am not simply taking up my own opinion. Rather, we are instructed by the opinion of the One who alone knows the strength and the rational working of His own creation. 'Look, today I am setting you over nations and over kingdoms to tear up and destroy, to scatter and overthrow, to build and to plant' (Jer 1:10).

"He notes that four things are necessary for the driving out of destructive things, to tear up, to destroy, to scatter, to overthrow. For the achievement of virtue and for the acquisition of all having to do with justice what is necessary is to build and to plant. Clearly, then, it is harder to snatch away and to uproot the inveterate passions of the body and of the spirit than to build and to plant the virtues of the spirit.

4

"This practical mode has a twofold aspect, as I have said. But it is subdivided into many professions and many goals.

"Some direct all their efforts toward the secrets of the desert and purity of heart. In the past there were Elias and Elisaeus. In our own day there are the blessed Antony and those others who follow the same purpose, and we know that in the quiet of their solitude they enjoy the closest union with God.

"Some have given all their concern and zeal to the teaching of their brothers and to the care of cenobitic houses. This was so in the recent case of abba John who had charge of the great monastery in the neighborhood of the city named Thmuis. It was true also of some other monks of like merit and outstanding, as we remember, for the apostolic signs worked by them.

"Others like to engage in the holy work of welcoming strangers at hostels. In past times this was the work with which the patriarch Abraham and Lot pleased the Lord. In more recent days this was so in the case of the blessed Macarius, a man of outstanding gentleness and patience who ran the hostel in Alexandria and who did so in such a way that no one could think of him as being in any way inferior to any of the lovers of solitude.

"Some chose to take care of the sick. Others worked for the wretched and the oppressed. Others took up teaching. Others brought help to the poor, and in their love and their piety they flourished in the company of the great and of the holy.

5

"Hence it is valuable and proper that each one should strive with zeal and diligence to achieve perfection in whatever work he has undertaken, whether this be something he has chosen to do or something he has been given the grace to do. He can praise and admire the virtues of others, but he ought never to depart from the profession which he himself has picked. For, as the apostle says, he knows that the body of the church is one but its members numerous, that 'our gifts differ in accordance with the grace given to us. If one's gift is administration then let it be used for administration, if teaching then let it be used for teaching, if exhortation then let it be used in exhortation. Let the one who distributes do so in all simplicity. Let the one who is in charge be so solicitously and let the one doing the works of mercy be cheerful' (Rom 12:6–8). One member cannot undertake the work of others. The eyes do not perform the task of the hands nor does the nose do the work of the ears. Not everyone can be apostle, prophet, or doctor. Not everyone has the grace of healing. Not everyone speaks in tongues. Not everyone is an interpreter.

6

"What usually happens to those not yet established in their chosen profession is this. They hear people talked about because of zeal or virtues which are different from their own. Straight away they want to take up a discipline like theirs, and because of human frailty their efforts are necessarily in vain. For it is quite impossible for one and the same man to shine outstandingly with all the virtues mentioned above. And if one tries to pursue them all together what happens of necessity is that in chasing them all one does not really catch any of them, and out of this changing about and this variety one draws loss rather than gain.

"The journey to God follows many routes. So let each person take to the end and with no turning back the way he first chose so that he may be perfect, no matter what his profession may be.

7

"We have already spoken of the harm done to the monk who, out of spiritual turmoil, wishes to take up pursuits different from his own. Actually he runs a deadly danger here because it sometimes happens that what some do quite rightly others mistakenly imitate. What has turned out well for some has been observed to be dangerous for others. If we might give an example, it is as if one wished to imitate the virtue of that man whom abba John used to refer to, not as a model to be followed but in order to cause some wonder.

"Someone came to this old man, and he was dressed in civilian clothes and he brought to him some of his first fruits. The old man found that the other was in the grip of a most ferocious demon. Abba John gave him orders and commands, but he treated them with contempt and he proclaimed that he would never quit the body of which he had taken possession. But he grew frightened at the approach of the old man and having spoken his name with the utmost respect the spirit departed.

"The old man was amazed that such a grace had been revealed and his wonder grew when he observed that his new visitor was dressed in civilian clothes. So he began most diligently to ask him about his life and his profession.

"The other man said he was a civilian and that he was bound by the ties of marriage. The blessed John, thinking of the excellence of this man's virtue and of the grace that he had been given, began more eagerly to enquire about his way of life.

"The man said he was of rural background and that he sought his living with the daily work of his hands. He claimed that he did not think of himself as being any way good, merely that each morning before going to work and again in the evening when going home he was in the habit of going into the church to thank God for the gift of his daily bread. He never took anything of what he had grown until he had given a tithe of his first fruits to God. He never drove his cattle through another's meadows without first binding their mouths lest his neighbors should suffer some damage because of his negligence.

"In all of this, abba John saw nothing to match the outstanding grace which had drawn him to pick out this village. So he continued to ask questions. He tried to figure out the hidden virtue which could be on a level with so precious a grace.

"The other man was drawn by the deference shown in such persistent questioning. He admitted he had wished to be a monk but that twelve years earlier the compulsion and the authority of his parents had driven to him to take a wife. But without anyone knowing about it he had kept her a virgin, like a sister.

"Hearing this the old man in his amazement said openly that it was no wonder that the demon had despised him and had not been able to endure his presence. And as for himself he would not dare to risk his chastity in the imitation of such virtue, and this would be true not only of the feverish days of his youth but even now.

"Despite his admiration for such a deed abba John nevertheless advised strongly that no monk should try it. He understood that many things which are rightly done by some can bring great danger to those others who imitate them and that not everyone can hope for those special favors which the Lord has granted as a privilege to some few.

8

"But let us return to the discussion of that knowledge which was the original theme of this talk.

"As I said earlier, the practical side of knowledge is hived off among many professions and disciplines. The contemplative side is divided into two parts, namely, historical interpretation and spiritual insight. Hence, Solomon, having listed the multiform grace present in the Church, goes on to say, 'All those of her household are clothed twice over' (Prv 31:21).

"Now there are three kinds of spiritual lore, namely, tropology, allegory, and anagoge. This is what Proverbs has to say about them: 'Write these three times over the spread of your heart' (Prv 22:20).

"History embraces the knowledge of things which are past and which are perceptible. The apostle gives an example: 'It is written that Abraham had two sons, one by a servant and one by a free woman. The offspring of the slave was born in accordance with the flesh; the child of the free woman was born as a result of a promise' (Gal 4:22–23).

"What follows is allegorical, because the things which actually happened are said to have prefigured another mystery. 'These two women stand for the two covenants. The first, who comes from Mount Sinai and whose children are born to slavery, is Hagar. For Sinai is a mountain in Arabia, and she corresponds to the present-day Jerusalem and is a slave along with her children' (Gal 4:24–25).

"Anagoge climbs up from spiritual mysteries to the higher and more august secrets of heaven, such as what the apostle adds: 'The Jerusalem above is free and is our mother. For it is written, "Shout for joy you barren women who have borne no children, break forth and shout because you never knew the pain of childbirth. For there are more sons of the forsaken one than sons of the wedded wife" ' (Gal 4:26–27).

"Tropology is moral teaching designed for the amendment of life and for instruction in asceticism. It is as if by these two covenants we were to mean the practical discipline and the contemplative, or else we could take Jerusalem or Sion to be the human soul, as the following words express it: 'Praise Jerusalem the Lord, praise Sion your God' (Ps 147:12).

"And if we wish it, these four modes of representation flow into a unity so that the one Jerusalem can be understood in four different ways, in the historical sense as the city of the Jews, in allegory as the church of Christ, in anagoge as the heavenly city of God 'which is mother to us all' (Gal 4:26), in the tropological sense as the human soul which, under this name, is frequently criticized or blamed by the Lord.

"The blessed apostle spoke as follows about these four modes of explanation: 'Now, brothers, if I were to come to you with the gift of tongues, of what use will I be to you if my talking to you reveals nothing, tells you nothing, is no inspiration to you and does not instruct you?' (1 Cor 14:6).

"Revelation is linked to allegory insofar as it explains in a spiritual sense the truths hidden under the historical account. For example, suppose we wished to discover how 'our fathers were all beneath the cloud and all were baptized in Moses in the cloud and in the sea and [how] all ate the same spiritual food and drank the same spiritual drink from the rock and that rock was Christ' (1 Cor 10:1–4). This way of stating the matter prefigures allegorically the body and blood of Christ which we receive every day.

"The telling of things similarly referred to by the apostle is tropology. With this we prudently discern the value and the worth of everything in the domain of practical judgment. An example of this is when we are instructed to consider whether 'it is fitting that a woman should pray to God with an uncovered head' (1 Cor 11–13). As has been said, this way of thinking has a moral content.

"Then there is prophecy, which the apostle puts in third place. He means anagoge, by means of which words are moved to the plane of the invisible and the future: 'Brothers, we do not wish you to be in ignorance with regard to the dead, so that you will not grieve like those others who have no hope. If we believe that Christ died and rose again then we must believe that God will raise up along with Jesus those who are asleep in Him. We tell you this from the Lord's own teaching that any of us left alive until the Lord's coming will not have any advantage over those who are asleep in Christ. For the Lord Himself will come down from heaven at a sign given by the voice of an angel and the sound of a trumpet and those who are dead in Christ will be the first to rise' (1 Thes 4:12–15). Here in this type of exhortation the mode of anagoge is used.

"Doctrine makes plain the straightforward sequence of historical explanation. In it there is no more hidden meaning than what is in the words themselves, for example, the following: 'In the first place I handed on to you what I had been taught myself, namely, that Christ died for our sins in accordance with the Scriptures, that He was buried and that He rose on the third day and that He was seen by Cephas' (1 Cor 15:3–5); 'God sent His Son who was born of a woman, born under the Law, so that He might redeem those under the Law' (Gal 4:4–5); 'Listen, Israel, the Lord your God is a unique God' (Dt 6:4).

161

9

"So if your concern is to reach the light of spiritual knowledge and to do so not through the sin of empty boastfulness but rather by a purifying grace, then be enflamed first of all by the longing for this blessedness, concerning which is said, 'Happy are the clean of heart for they shall see God' (Mt 5:8). Do this in order that you may achieve what the angel spoke of to Daniel: 'The learned will shine like the splendor of the skies and those who have taught virtue to many will be like the stars for all eternity' (Dn 12:3). There is this about it in another prophet: 'While there is time light up within you the lamp of knowledge' (Hos 10:12).

"Preserve that eagnerness for reading which I believe is in you and hasten in all eagerness to acquire practical, that is, moral, knowledge. Without it, this contemplative purity, of which I spoke, cannot be acquired. This purity comes to those who are made perfect not by the words of those who teach them but rather through the virtuousness of their own acts. It comes as a kind of reward after so much work and labor. They will acquire knowledge not from meditation upon the Law but as the fruit of their work. They sing along with the psalmist: 'Knowledge has come to me from your commands' (Ps 118:104) and after they have driven out all passion they assert confidently, 'I will sing psalms and I will have knowledge on the road of innocence' (Ps 100:1–2). For the man singing the psalms understands what is sung, the man traveling the road of innocence with a pure heart.

"If, then, you wish to build in your heart the sacred tabernacle of spiritual knowledge, clear all the stain of sin away from you and wipe out all the concerns of this present world. For it is impossible that a soul which is in the slightest way taken up with worldly cares should win the gift of knowledge or should bear the fruit of spiritual awareness or should concentrate on spiritual readings.

"So be careful—you especially, John, whose youthfulness must especially heed what I say—be careful to completely hold your tongue unless you want your zeal for reading and your eager effort be raised up uselessly. For this is the first step in practical knowledge, namely, to receive the instructions and the opinions of all the older men with an attentive heart and a silent mouth, to place them carefully in your heart, and to hasten to put them in practice rather than to lecture about them. For on the one side is the flourishing harvest of spiritual knowledge.

CONFERENCE FOURTEEN

"During discussions with older men do not dare to speak up unless it be either to ask for something which it would be harmful for you not to know or else to seek what you ought to know. There are some people who are so puffed up by a love of vainglory that for the sake of showing off they go through the public motions of asking questions about doctrinal matters which they very well know. It is therefore quite impossible that someone who devotes himself to scriptural reading merely for the sake of winning human praise should indeed earn the gift of spiritual knowledge. For if he is bound by this passion he will necessarily be chained by other vices, especially that of pride. And in any case by being brought low in moral and ethical practice then the contemplative lore which follows from this will in fact scarcely arise.

"Therefore in all things be 'quick to listen and slow to speak' (Jas 1:19) lest the remark of Solomon be fulfilled in you: 'If you see a man too ready of speech know that a fool has more hope than he' (Prv 29:20). And never dare to teach someone what you have not practiced yourself.

"Our Lord taught by His example that this was the procedure which we should follow. This is what is stated: 'Jesus began to do and to teach these things' (Acts 1:1). So have a care that you do not rush to teach something you have not done yourself. Otherwise, you will be counted among those in regard to whom Jesus had the following to say to His disciples: 'Do what they tell you and listen to what they say, but do not act as they do. They talk and do not act. They tie up heavy burdens and lay them on men's shoulders but they will not lift a finger to move them' (Mt 23:3–4). Therefore 'he who breaks the least of the commandments and teaches men to do so shall be called least in the kingdom of heaven' (Mt 5:19). But as for the man who dares to teach the many greater commands and also neglects them himself, not only will he not be least in the kingdom but he shall be foremost for punishment in hell. So be careful not to be caught doing as some others do. They give lessons. They manage to be articulate in discussion. And because they know how to talk elegantly and abundantly they seem to have spiritual knowledge, or so it appears to those who have not learned to recognize its true character. For it is one thing to be a skilled talker and a shining speaker. It is something else to enter into the very heart and core of heavenly utterances, to contemplate with heart's purest gaze the deep and hidden mysteries. This is not something to be possessed by humanistic lore and worldly erudition. It will be gained only by purity of heart and through the illumination of the Holy Spirit.

10

"If you wish to achieve true knowledge of Scripture you must hurry to achieve unshakable humility of heart. This is what will lead you not to the knowledge which puffs a man up but to the lore which illuminates through the achievement of love. It is impossible for the unclean of heart to acquire the gift of spiritual knowledge. Therefore be very careful that your zeal for scriptural reading does not, because of empty pretentiousness, prove to be a cause of perdition, instead of being for you the source of knowledgeable light and of the endless glory promised to the man enlightened by knowledge.

"Then, having banished all worldly concerns and thoughts, strive in every way to devote yourself constantly to the sacred reading so that continuous meditation will seep into your soul and, as it were, will shape it to its image. Somehow it will form that 'ark' of the Scriptures (cf. Heb 9:4–5) and will contain the two stone tablets, that is, the perpetual strength of the two testaments. There will be the golden urn which is a pure and unstained memory and which will preserve firmly within itself the everlasting manna, that is, the eternal, heavenly sweetness of spiritual meanings and of that bread which belongs to the angels. The branch of Aaron is the saving standard of our exalted and true high priest Jesus Christ. It leafs out forever in the greenness of undying memory. This is the branch which was cut from the root of Jesse and which after death comes more truly alive.

"Now all of these things are covered over by the two cherubim, that is, by the plenitude of historical and spiritual lore. *Cherubim* means knowledge in abundance. They provide an everlasting protection for that which appeases God, namely, the calm of your heart, and they will cast a shadow of protection against all the attacks of malign spirits.

"And thus your soul will not only become the ark of God's testament but it will be carried forward into a priestly realm and, by its unfailing love of purity, its concentration upon the disciplines of the spirit, it will implement the priestly command imposed by the Lawgiver: 'He will not emerge from the holy place, lest he profane the sanctuary of God' (Lv 21:12). That is, he will not depart from his own heart where the Lord promised to live continuously when He said, 'I will live and walk among them' (2 Cor 6:16).

"Therefore the sequences of holy Scripture must be committed to memory and they must be pondered ceaselessly. Such meditation will profit us in two ways. First, when the thrust of the mind is occupied by the study and perusal of the readings it will, of necessity, avoid being taken over by the snares of dangerous thoughts. Second, as we strive with constant repetition to commit these readings to memory, we have not the time to understand them because our minds have been occupied. But later when we are free from the attractions of all that we do and see and, especially, when we are quietly meditating during the hours of darkness, we think them over and we understand them more closely. And so it happens that when we are at ease and when, as it were, we are plunged into the dullness of sleep, the hidden meanings, of which we were utterly unaware during our waking hours, and the sense of them are bared to our minds.

11

"As our mind is increasingly renewed by this study, Scripture begins to take on a new face. A mysteriously deeper sense of it comes to us and somehow the beauty of it stands out more and more as we get farther into it. Scripture shapes itself to human capacity. It will be earthly for the men of the flesh, divine for those of the spirit, so that those who once thought of it as somehow wrapped up in thick clouds find themselves unable either to grasp its subtlety or to endure its brilliance.

"The truth of what I am trying to say will become clearer from an example. It will be enough to cite one testimony of the Law and in this way I can show that all the commands of heaven apply to the whole human race in proportion to our capacity. Now this is what is written in the Law: 'You will not fornicate' (Ex 20:14). This is observed—and rightly—in a literal sense by the man who is tied down by the obscene passions of the flesh.

"But the man who has got away from the morass of such carry-on and from this impure outlook observes it in a spiritual sense. Therefore he stays away not only from idolatrous ceremonies but from all pagan superstition, from augury, from all the study of signs and days and times. Certainly he will not be tied up in the speculations which corrupt the purity of our faith and which have to do with words and names. This is the fornication by which Jerusalem is said to have been corrupted, the fornication 'on every high hill and beneath every leafing tree' (Jer 3:6). It was for this that the Lord criticized her through the words of the prophet: 'Let them stand and save you, these augurs of the heavens who studied the stars and reckoned the months so as to tell from these what was coming to you' (Is 47:13). This is the fornication of which the Lord accuses them elsewhere: 'A spirit of fornication has misled them and they have fornicated themselves away from their God' (Hos 4:12).

"Anyone free of this double fornication will have a third one to avoid, namely, that which is found in the superstitions of the Law and of Judaism. This is what the apostle said: 'You make observations of the months and of the times and of the years' (Gal 4:10). Or again: 'Do not touch, do not taste, do not pick up' (Col 2:21). And there is no doubt that this is said about the superstitions of the Law. To plunge into them is to be an adulterer from Christ and one no longer earns the right to hear the following from the apostle: 'I arranged for you to marry Christ so that I might give you away as a chaste virgin to this one husband' (2 Cor 11:2). But the voice of the same apostle has this to add: 'I fear that just as the serpent in its cleverness seduced Eve, so your thoughts will be corrupted away from the simplicity which is in Christ Jesus' (2 Cor 11:3).

"And if one has avoided the uncleanness of this fornication he will have a fourth to escape, the adultery wrought by heretical doctrine. The same blessed apostle has this to say: 'I know that after my departure fierce wolves will come in among you. They will not spare the flock. And even among yourselves men will rise up to say perverse things so as to lead disciples away after them' (Acts 20:29–30).

"If someone has been able to avoid this, let him be careful not to slip into the sin of a subtler kind of fornication which consists of the straying of thoughts. For every thought which is not simply disgraceful but valueless or which shifts in the slightest way from God will be deemed a most unclean fornication by the perfect man."

12

Upon hearing all this, I was first moved by a secret sorrow. And then I groaned heavily.

"All of what you have discussed so very fully has caused me more discouragement than I have ever felt before. Leaving aside those things in general which imprison the soul, leaving aside the distractions which come battering from without against souls that are weak, I feel that a particular obstacle to my salvation is the very slight knowledge I seem to have of literature. The insistence of my teacher and my own urge for continuous reading have so softened me that at this point my mind is, as it were, infected by those poetic works, worthless stories, tales of war in which I was steeped from the beginning of my basic studies when I was very young. I think of them even when I am praying. When I am singing the psalms or else begging pardon for my sins the shameful memory of poems slips in or the image of warring heroes turns before my eyes. And the conjuring up of such fantasies makes such a sport of me that my mind is unable to aspire to the contemplation of heavenly things, and my daily tears are unable to drive them out."

13

Nesteros: "This very thing from which comes your desperate urge to be cleansed can actually give rise to a speedy and effective cure. All you need is to transfer to the reading and meditation of the spiritual Scriptures the same care and the same zeal which, you said, you had for worldly studies.

"Of necessity, your mind will be taken up by those poems for as long as it fails to show equal application and zeal in dealing with those other matters which occupy it and for as long as it fails to give birth to things spiritual and divine instead of profitless and earthly thoughts. If it manages to enter deeply into these new ideas, if it feeds upon them, these previous topics of thought can be driven out one by one or expelled entirely. The human mind is unable to be empty of all thought. If it is not taken up with spiritual concerns it will necessarily be wrapped up in what it previously learned. As long as it has nowhere to go at every moment while engaging in its tireless activity then it has to slide toward those things which preoccupied it from the days of infancy. Always it thinks over and over about what concerned it during long practice and study.

"Spiritual knowledge must have a solid lasting strength in you. It is not something to be enjoyed occasionally, as happens with those who do not work for it, who only know of it from what others tell them or whose acquaintance with it is, so to speak, like that of some fragrance in the air. It is something to be hidden, perceived, and felt in one's innards. But for this to happen there is something you must note. It can happen that you know already something you hear at a discussion. Do not listen to this in a contemptuous or disdainful way. Rather, take it to heart with the same eagerness which we should always display when either hearing desirable, saving words or when speaking them ourselves. No matter how often there is talk that has to do with holy subjects, a soul thirsting for true knowledge will never have too much of it or never grow tired of it. Such matters will be received every day as something new, something longed for. The more frequently the soul hears it, the more eagerly it will listen to it or speak of it. Repetition will confirm what the soul knows, and the soul will not grow bored with continuous discussion. A sure sign of a lukewarm and proud soul is to listen carelessly and negligently to the saving medicine of words which are too zealously and too constantly uttered to it. 'The overfed soul mocks the honey, but to the hungry soul everything bitter is sweet' (Prv 27:7).

"If, then, such matters are carefully received, if they are hidden and consigned within the quiet places of the mind, if they are marked in silence, they will later be like a wine of sweet aroma bringing gladness to the heart of a man. Matured by long reflection and by patience, they will be poured out as a great fragrance from the vessel of your heart. Like some everlasting spring they will flow out from the channels of experience and from the flowing waters of virtue. They will come bounding forth, running, unceasing, from, as it were, the abyss of your heart. There will happen to you what is said in Proverbs to the man for whom all such things have become utterly real: 'Drink the waters from your own wells, fresh water from your own source. May the waters of your own spring pour out for you and may your waters pass over all your ways' (Prv 5:15–16). And, as the prophet Isaiah declares, 'You will be like a well-watered garden, like a flowing spring whose waters will never fail. And places emptied for ages will be built up in you. You will lift up the foundations laid by generation after generation. You will be called the builder of fences, the one who turns the pathways toward peace' (Is 58:11–12). That blessing promised by the prophet will come to you: 'And the Lord will not cause your teacher to fly far away from you and your eyes will look upon your guide. And your ears shall hear the word of warning from behind, "This is the path. Walk along it and turn neither to the right nor to the left" ' (Is 30:20–21). And so it will happen that not only the whole thrust and thought of your heart, but even all the wanderings and the straying of your thoughts will turn into a holy and unending meditation on the Law of God.

14

"But, as we have said already, it is impossible either to know or to teach that of which one has no experience. For how can someone pass on what he is incapable of perceiving? And if he is presumptuous enough to teach, his words will come to the ears of those listening to him as being worthless and useless. He will not reach their hearts. He will be betrayed by his lack of practical experience and by his own fruitless vanity. For his words come not from the treasury of a good conscience but from the emptiness of his arrogance.

"The fact is that it is impossible for an unclean soul to acquire spiritual knowledge, no matter how hard it labors at the reading of the Scriptures. No one pours some rare ointment or the best honey or a precious liquid into a foul and filthy container. A jar once shot through by evil smells will more easily contaminate the most fragrant myrrh than receive from it some sweetness or capacity to please. Purity is corrupted more speedily than corruption is made pure. So it goes with the container which is our heart. If it has not first been cleansed of all the foulest contagion of sin it will not deserve to receive that perfume of benediction about which the prophet speaks, 'Like the oil poured over the head, comes down on to the beard of Aaron, comes down on to edges of his clothing' (Ps 132:2). He will not keep unpolluted possession of that spiritual knowledge and scriptural lore which are 'sweeter by far than all honey' (Ps 18:11). 'What share does justice have in iniquity? What companionship has the light with the shadows? What agreement can there be between Christ and Belial?' (2 Cor 6:14–15)."

15

Germanus: "This assertion does not look to us to be founded upon truth or supported by plausibility. Those who withhold faith in Christ or who corrupt it by the unholy perversity of their ideas are quite clearly unclean of heart. Yet how is it that there are many Jews and heretics—and even Catholics—who are sinners in many ways and who nevertheless, have a perfect knowledge of Scripture and who can boast about the extent of their knowledge of things spiritual? And on the other hand there is a countless mass of saints with hearts entirely cleared of sin who are satisified with a faith that is simple and that is unaware of the mysteries characteristic of a more profound knowledge. What, therefore, will be the force of that idea of yours which attributes spiritual knowledge solely to purity of heart?"

16

Nesteros: "Someone who does not carefully examine all the words of a proferred opinion is not really examining the aptness of a particular definition. I have said already that people of this sort have a certain articulateness and style but that they cannot enter either the heart of Scripture or the hidden depths of spiritual meanings. True knowledge is found only among those genuinely worshiping God, and of these other kinds of people it is said, 'Listen, foolish people. You have no heart. You have eyes and do not see. You have ears and do not hear' (Jer 5:21). Or again: 'Since you have rejected true knowledge I will reject you and will not have you function in my priesthood' (Hos 4:6). Since 'all the treasures of wisdom and true knowledge are hidden in Christ' (Col 2:3) how can one believe that he who refuses to find Christ or who, having found Him, blasphemes with sacrilegious tongue, or who dishonors the Catholic faith by unclean works—how can one believe that such a one has arrived at true knowledge? 'For the spirit of God flees from cunning nor does it dwell in a heart enslaved by sin' (Wis 1:4–5).

"To attain spiritual knowledge there is no other route except the following, which has been so aptly described by one of the prophets: 'Sow integrity for yourselves, reap a harvest of the hope of life, light up within you the light of knowledge' (Hos 10:12). First, then, we must sow integrity for ourselves, that is, we must propagate real perfection in us with the works of justice. Second, we must reap the hope of life. In other words, the fruits of spiritual virtue must be gathered by way of the expulsion of the sins of the flesh and in this way it will be possible for us to turn on the light of knowledge within us.

"The psalmist also declares that this is the sequence we must follow. He says: 'Blessed are those who are unsullied upon their journey, who walk in the Law of the Lord. Blessed are those who pay heed to His witness' (Ps 118:1–2). He does not first say, 'Blessed are those who pay heed to His witness,' followed by 'blessed are those who are unsullied upon their journey.' He starts by saying 'blessed are those who are unsullied upon their journey.' In this way he shows clearly that no one can manage to engage in the correct scrutiny of God's Word unless in his daily life he proceeds unstained along the road of Christ.

"Therefore those you have mentioned cannot possess this knowledge if they are unclean. What they have is a false so-called lore, the kind about which the apostle had this to say: 'O Timothy, guard what has been given to you. In all that you say avoid profane novelties and the claims of a falsely named knowledge' (1 Tm 6:20).

"As for those who seem to have some semblance of knowledge and those who do not abandon the sins of the flesh even when they apply themselves diligently to the reading and the memorizing of Scripture, Proverbs has the following well-put statement: 'The beauty of a woman of evil ways is like a golden ring in the snout of a pig' (Prv 11:22). What use is it for a man to possess the jewel of heaven's words and to give himself over to that most precious loveliness of Scripture if he himself is stuck fast in muddied works and thoughts? It is as if he were taming a most unclean earth by smashing it up into little pieces or polluting it with the filthy wallowings of his own passions. Normally this is an adornment for those who make right use of it. But people of this kind will not only fail to be enhanced but they will be covered by even greater defilement. 'There is no beauty in the praise coming from the mouth of a sinner' (Ps 15:9). And God Himself says to him through the words of the prophet: 'Why are you reciting my commands and why does your mouth speak of my covenant?' (Ps 40:16). In Proverbs one reads the following quite appropriate words about souls which do not have a sufficiently adequate fear of the Lord: 'Fear of the Lord is a discipline and a wisdom' (Prv 15:33). Yet such people persist in their meditation in order to enter into the meaning of Scripture. 'What is the value of riches for a fool? The stupid man will not lay hold of wisdom' (Prv 17:16).

"True knowledge is far removed from that worldly lore which is polluted by the gross sins of the flesh. Indeed, this true knowledge has sometimes flourished miraculously among men who were inarticulate and often illiterate. This is clearly shown among many of the apostles and saints. Such men were not like trees which are thickly covered with useless leaves. Rather, they were bent down by the real fruits of spiritual knowledge and it was about them that the following was written in the Acts of the Apostles: 'Seeing the assurance of Peter and of John and knowing that they were illiterate and lowly men they were amazed' (Acts 4:13).

"So then if you are anxious to win the incorruptible fragrance of Scripture, begin by turning your effort to winning the cleanness of chastity from the Lord. No man who is still under the sway of fleshly passion and, especially, of fornication will be able to possess spiritual knowledge. 'Wisdom comes to rest in a good heart' (Prv 14:33). 'He who fears the Lord will find knowledge as well as justice' (Eccl 32:20). The blessed apostle also teaches us the sequence I have mentioned, if we are to arrive at knowledge. He wanted to put together a list of all his virtues and also to show the source and sequence of each of them. Then, after a bit, this is what he says: '. . . in sleeplessness, in fasting, in chastity, in knowledge, in patience, in kindness, in a spirit of holiness, in genuine love' (2 Cor 6:5–6). This way of linking the virtues is clearly designed to teach us that one passes from sleeplessness and fasting to chastity, from chastity to knowledge, from knowledge to patience, from patience to kindness, from kindness to a spirit of holiness, and from a spirit of holiness to the rewards of genuine love. When, therefore, you too reach spiritual knowledge by way of this discipline and this sequence I have no doubt that, as I have said already, you will possess a lore which is neither sterile nor dead but living and bearing fruit. The seed of your saving words, which you have planted in the hearts of your audience, will be made fruitful by the generous waterings of the Holy Spirit. As was promised to the prophet, 'Rainwater will be given to your seed wherever you have sown in the earth and the bread coming from the fruits of your land will be very rich and nourishing' (Is 30:23).

17

"But be careful. You will be teaching something acquired not so much by reading as by the sweat of experience. Your greater age will incline you to teach. But do not be seduced by a love of vainglory to scatter what you know among men who are unclean. You may risk what the very wise Solomon proscribed: 'Do not bind the unholy man in the pastures of the just and do not be deceived by satiety' (Prv 24:15). 'Delicacies are useless to a fool' (Prv 19:10) and 'there is no need for wisdom when common sense is lacking. Folly will be all the more easily led on' (Prv 18:2). 'The obstinate servant will not be cured by words, and even if he were to have understanding he will not obey' (Prv 29:19). 'Say nothing in the hearing of an imprudent man in case he laughs at the wisdom of your words' (Prv 23:9). 'Do not give what is holy to the dogs and do not scatter your pearls before swine in case they stamp on them and turn around to tear you apart' (Mt 7:6). The mysteries of spiritual meanings must be hidden from such men so that you may rightly sing, 'I have kept your words hidden in my heart in order not to sin against you' (Ps 118:11).

"Perhaps you may ask to whom the mysteries of the divine Scriptures are to be granted. The very wise Solomon has instructions for you. 'Give strong drink to those who are in gloom and wine to those who are sad so that they may forget their poverty and be reminded no more of their grief' (Prv 31:6–7). What he means is this. To those filled with bitter regret and sadness over their earlier lives give abundantly the joy of spiritual knowledge like 'a wine which gladdens the heart of a man' (Ps 103:5). Warm them with the headiness of saving words lest they sink into gloom and deadly despair and, 'being the kind they are, they are sucked into a greater misery' (2 Cor 2:7).

"As for those who are lukewarm and careless, who are gnawed by no heartfelt remorse, this is what is said: 'He who is soft and without pain will be in want' (Prv 14:23).

"So take the greatest possible care not to be puffed up by a love of vainglory in case you cannot be a colleague of that man whom the prophet praises 'who has not given his money for interest' (Ps 14:5). Now 'the words of the Lord are chaste words, coinage tested in the fire, pure from the earth, refined seven times' (Ps 11:7). And every man who hands out the words of the Lord because of love for human praise is giving his wealth out for interest. For this he will not only deserve no praise but will earn punishment. He chose to waste his Lord's wealth so as to gain worldly reward for himself, instead of acting like the Lord, of whom it is written: 'Coming He will receive back what is His own and with interest' (Mt 25:27).

18

"Clearly, there are two reasons why spiritual lore does not work. Either the teacher has no experience of what he is talking about, so that all his effort to instruct the listener is simply the empty sound of words, or else the listener is loaded down with sin and his hardened heart is closed to the saving and holy teaching of a spiritual man. About such people the prophet has this to say: 'The heart of this people is blinded and their ears barely hear and their eyes are closed so that they may not see anything with their eyes or hear anything with their ears or have understanding in their hearts or be converted or have me heal them' (Is 6:10).

19

"Still there is the providence of our God, 'who wants all men to be saved and to come to the recognition of the truth' (1 Tm 2:4). With splendid generosity this providence sometimes allows someone who has not earned the right to preach the gospel by a blameless mode of life to receive, nevertheless, the grace of spiritual knowledge for the salvation of the multitude.

"This brings us now to the discussion of the various ways in which the Lord bestows the charisma of healing so that demons may be driven out. But we must rise now and go to take a meal. We will leave the examination of that problem until this evening. Anyhow, the mind can better understand what is presented to it bit by bit and without too much strain on the body."

Conference Fifteen

THE GIFTS OF GOD

1

After the evening meal we sat on the mats, as monks do, and we waited for the discussion which had been promised us. Out of deference to the old man we remained silent for a while. Then he interrupted our respectful silence with the following words.

"The direction taken by our earlier discussion has brought us now to the need to state the nature of spiritual gifts, and the tradition of our elders, as we know, tells us that this takes a threefold form.

"The first cause of the gift of healing is the merit earned by holiness. The grace of working miracles is to be found among specially chosen and just men. It is quite evident that the apostles and many saints worked miracles and wonders. This was in accordance with what the Lord Himself had commanded when He said, 'Heal the sick, raise the dead, cleanse the lepers, expel the demons. You have freely received. Give freely.' (Mt 10:8)

"Second, for the edification of the church or of those who bring forward their own patients or of those who have to be healed, the virtue of healing comes even from sinners and from the unworthy. Of such people the Savior had this to say in the gospel: 'They will say to me on that day: Lord, Lord, did we not prophesy in your name, and did we not drive out devils in your name, and did we not do many wonders in your name? And I will say out loud to them, I do not know you. Leave me, you workers of iniquity' (Mt 7:22–23). But by contrast, if faith is lacking in those who bring forward the sick, then it will not be permitted, even to those with the gift of healing, to work a cure. The evangelist Luke had this to say: 'And Jesus could not work miracles among them because of their unbelief' (Mk 6:5–6 [this is *not* in Luke]). It was

174

at this time that the Lord said: 'There were many lepers in Israel in the days of Elisaeus the prophet and no one of them was cured except Neman the Syrian' (Lk 4:27).

"The third kind of healing is a trick and deception worked by demons. A man caught up in obvious wrongdoing is an object of admiration because of the wonders worked by him. He acquires the reputation of being a holy man and a servant of God and he becomes, for evil spirits, the means of enticing others to imitate him even to the extent of doing wrong like him. The way is now open for scandal and even the sanctity of religion is maligned. And it is quite certainly the case that this man who credits himself with the gift of healing is brought crashing down all the harder because of the pride in his heart.

"The demons have also the following trick. They cry out the names of those whom they know to have none of the merits of holiness and to possess none of the fruits of the spirit. They pretend to be burnt up by the merits of such people and to take flight from the bodies of the possessed. Deuteronomy has this to say about such persons: 'If a prophet should arise among you or a man claiming visionary dreams, and if he foretells a sign and a portent, and if what he says should actually happen, and if he should say to you, "Let us go and follow strange gods who are unknown to you and let us serve them," do not listen to the words of that prophet or dreamer. For the Lord your God is putting you to the test, bringing out into the open whether or not you love him with all your heart and with all your soul' (Dt 13:1–3). And in the gospel he says this: 'Fake Christs and fake prophets will rise up and they will perform great signs and wonders so that if possible even the chosen will be led into error' (Mt 24:24).

2

"Therefore we must never be admirers of those who pretend to do such things out of virtuousness. We must note, instead, whether they have become perfect as a result of driving out their sins and because of the improvement of their way of life. This is something that is certainly not achieved through the act of faith of someone else or for reasons that are obscure to us. It happens because of a man's own zeal and the divine gift of grace.

"Such, then, is the practical knowledge which is otherwise called 'charity' by the apostle and which, on his apostolic authority, is to be preferred to all the speech of men and angels, to the full faith which can even move mountains, to all knowledge and prophetic power, to the utter abandonment of the things of the world, and, finally, even to glorious martyrdom. He listed all the types of charismatic gifts and had this to say: 'To one man the Spirit grants wisdom in preaching, to another knowledgeable discourse, to another faith, to another the gift of healing. to another the working of cures' (1 Cor 12:8–10) and all the rest. But he will go on to speak of love, and notice how he put this before all the charisms: 'I will show you a way that is better than any of them' (1 Cor 12:31).

"In this way it is clearly shown that the high point of perfection and blessedness does not lie in the working of those miracles but rather in the purity of love. And not without good reason. The former have to vanish and to be done away with. But love will endure forever. Hence we never see the Fathers caught up in these wonderworkings. By the grace of the Holy Spirit they were possessors of such capacities but they never wanted to use them unless they were coerced by utter, unavoidable necessity.

3

"Such was the situation when, as I remember it, abba Macarius, the first of those dwelling in Scete, raised someone from the dead.

"There was a certain heretic who was a follower of the Eunomian deception and who tried by means of dialectical skills to undermine the purity of the Catholic faith. He deceived a great number of men, so that many Catholics, who were deeply upset by the extent of the disaster, asked the blessed Macarius to rescue the simple faith of the whole of Egypt from the shipwreck of infidelity. He came. He was set upon by the dialectical skill of the heretic who tried to draw him unknowingly onto the thorns of Aristotle. But with the brevity of an apostle, the blessed Macarius brought the long-drawn-out talk to an end: ' "The kingdom of God does not lie in talk but in virtuous activity" (1 Cor 4:20). Let us go to where the dead are buried and let us utter the name of the Lord over the very first corpse we find and, as it is written, let us show our faith by what we do. Here will be the clearest evidence of true faith. Empty argument will not manifest the truth but rather the miraculous power and decision of the One who cannot be deceived.'

"When the heretic heard this he was embarrassed in front of the whole crowd and therefore he pretended to agree with the proposed plan. He promised to be there 'tomorrow.' And on the next day everyone was waiting. They poured out toward the agreed place and they were full of eagerness for the sight that would be seen. But, knowing his own lack of faith, the heretic was frightened. He fled and immediately left Egypt.

"Macarius waited for him amid the crowd until the ninth hour and then saw that the other man, stricken with a bad conscience, had avoided the event, and so he took command of the crowd which had been corrupted by the heretic, and he led the way to the graves which had been chosen.

"Now in Egypt the overflow of the river Nile sweeps along in such a way that for no little part of the year the land is covered along its entire length by the invasion of the waters and it is like a huge sea. No one can get about except by traveling on small, fast-moving boats, and the bodies of the dead, preserved in sweet-smelling ointments, are kept in small cells on higher ground. The earth, because it is continually dampened, hinders the task of burial. If it were dug to receive corpses it would be forced to disgorge them because of the excesses of the flooding.

"Blessed Macarius came to a halt beside a very old corpse, and this is what he said to him: 'O man, if that son of perdition, that heretic, had come along here with me, and if I called upon the name of Christ my God, tell me if you would have risen before all these people who were close to being undermined by his deceit.' Then the dead man rose up and answered that he would most certainly have arisen. Abba Macarius asked him what he had been in the past when he had tasted this life, what era of man he had belonged to, and whether in those days he had known the name of Christ. The other replied that he had lived in the oldest period of the kings and that at that time he had never heard the name of Christ. And abba Macarius said to him, 'Sleep in peace until the final day, when you and those of your class will be raised up by Christ.'

"So far as he was concerned, this power and this grace would probably have always been hidden if the urgent need of a whole endangered province and if his own abundant devotion to Christ and his real love had not driven him to work this miracle. He certainly did not do it out of vain ostentation. What dragged it out of him was his love of Christ and the need of all the people.

"A reading of the Book of Kings shows that blessed Elias did the same. He called fire from heaven down onto the sacrificial victims on the pyre so that he might set free the faith of an entire people, a faith endangered by the deceits of fake prophets.

4

"Do I need to remind you of the accomplishments of abba Abraham? Abraham the Innocent they called him, because of the artlessness of his character and his simplicity.

"At the season of Pentecost he emerged from the desert and went to Egypt to do some farming. A woman tearfully begged him for help. She carried her little child in her arms. The child was wasted away and half dead because she had no milk. Abba Abraham gave her a glass of water to drink, one on which he had made the sign of the cross. As soon as she had finished her drink, her dried breasts filled up with milk and flowed abundantly.

5

"The same man went to a town, and was surrounded by a crowd of people who made fun of him. As they heaped ridicule upon him, they pointed out to him a man with a constricted knee who, for many years, had been unable to walk and who slunk around with his old malady. They tried to tempt him. 'Prove to us, abba Abraham, that you are a servant of God. Restore this man to his former healthy state so that we may come to believe that this name of Christ, whom you worship, is not an empty one.' Immediately he called upon the name of Christ and he bent over, took hold of the dry foot of the man, and pulled. At the moment of his touch, the dry and twisted knee was straightened. The man recovered the use of his limbs, which his long malady had consigned to oblivion, and he joyfully went away.

6

"These men did not make selfish use of the power to work such miracles. They proclaimed that these had been done not through any merit of their own but by the Lord's mercy. Faced with the awe evoked by these wonders they resorted to the words of the apostles in order to ward off glory among men: 'Men, brothers, why are you amazed at this? Or why do you keep looking at us, as if it were our power and our piety which caused this man to walk?' (Acts 3:12). They believed that no one should draw praise upon himself because of the gifts and the miracles of God. Instead, praise should be given for the fruits of a man's virtue since these came into being from the zeal of a mind and the excellence of achievements.

"But as was already said, it often happens that men of corrupt disposition and spurious faith can drive out demons in God's name and work the very greatest miracles. The apostle once complained about the like: 'Master, we saw a man driving out demons in your name. We told him not to do so, because he does not go around with us' (Lk 9:49). Christ was immediately able to say to them: 'Do not stop him. Anyone who is not against us is on our side' (Lk 9:50). However there are those who at the end of time will say, 'Lord, Lord, did we not prophesy in your name, did we not work great wonders in your name?' (Mt 7:22). And He says that this is what He will say in reply: 'I never knew you. Go away from me, you workers of evil' (Mt 7:23). In this way He gives a warning to those to whom, as a reward for holiness, He had given this glory of working signs and miracles: 'Do not be exultant because demons have submitted to you. Rather be delighted because your names are written in heaven' (Lk 10:20).

7

"Then the Author of all signs and miracles called upon His disciples to be guided by His teaching. He made abundantly clear what His true and very special followers should learn from Him. 'Come,' he said, 'and learn from me' (Mt 11:28–29) not to drive out demons by means of heavenly power, not to cleanse lepers, not to give light to the blind, not to raise the dead. I do all this through the agency of certain of my servants. Humankind cannot be included in the praises which belong to God. The agent and the servant cannot take a portion of the glory belonging solely to God. This, He said, is something for you, to 'learn from me because I am meek and humble of heart' (Mt 11:29).

"This is something which is capable of being learned and practiced by all. The working of signs and miracles is not always necessary nor useful to everyone nor granted to everyone. Humility, therefore, is the teacher of all the virtues. It is the surest foundation for a heavenly building. It is the personal and splendid gift of the Savior. It achieves all the miracles which Christ worked and does so without risk of vanity. It is a disciple of the gentle Lord by virtue not of astounding miracles but by the power of its patience and lowliness. A man may wish to control unclean spirits or to grant the gift of health to the sick or to do some astounding deed before the populace, and in his display he may call upon the name of Christ, and yet he is a stranger to Christ because his proud heart is no follower of the teacher of humility.

"When He was about to return to the Father, Christ left His disciples something of a testament. 'I give you a new command,' He said, 'to love one another as I have loved you' (Jn 13:34). And straightaway he added: 'Everyone will know that you are my disciples if you have love for one another' (Jn 13:35). He did not say 'if you work signs and wonders like me' but rather 'if you have love for one another,' something which can quite definitely not be done except by the meek and the humble.

"For this reason our predecessors always held that monks were neither good nor free of vainglory if they proclaimed before men that they were exorcists and if, filled with assertive pride, they proclaimed to admiring crowds that they had this gift, which they had either earned or had grabbed. All of this would be empty, 'The man who depends on lies feeds the winds. He runs after birds which fly away' (Prv 10:4). And without doubt there will happen to him what is affirmed in Proverbs: 'Just as the winds and the clouds and the rainfall are plain to see, so too are those who make boasts about a false gift' (Prv 25:14).

"So, then, if someone works one of these wonders in our presence he should be praised by us not because of our amazement at his miracles but because of the goodness of his life. What we have to ask is not whether demons yield to him but whether he possesses the elements of love described by the apostle (cf. 1 Cor 13:4ff).

8

"Actually, the greater miracle is to root out the tinder of luxury from one's flesh rather than to drive unclean spirits from the bodies of others. A more resplendent wonder is the restraint exercised over the wild stirrings of anger by the virtue of patience, rather than the capacity to hold sway over the creatures of the air. Much more important is the exclusion of ravening gloom from one's heart than the ability to drive out the sicknesses and the bodily fevers of someone else. Lastly, it is in many ways more remarkable and more sublime virtue to be able to heal the weaknesses of one's own soul rather than the failings of another's body. The more exalted the soul is by comparison with the body, the more its salvation is to be preferred; the more valuable and excellent its substance, the graver and more deadly its ruin.

9

"This is what is said to the most blessed apostles concerning bodily cures: 'Do not rejoice because demons submit to you' (Lk 10:20). It was the invoked name which achieved this and not the power of the apostles. Therefore they are warned not to dare to lay claim to blessedness or glory because of what is done through the power and the virtue of God, but rather to make such a claim because the deep purity of their lives and hearts has earned them the right to have their names written in heaven.

10

"I must prove what I have been saying by means of the witness of the ancients and the oracles of God.

"Here is what the blessed Paphnutius thought about the amazement evoked by signs or about the grace of purity. (And, in particular, there was the knowledge he had acquired by an angel's revelation.) These were his words and his experiences.

"For many years he lived in great austerity and he came to believe that he was completely free of the snares of cupidity. He had fought for a long time against all the open attacks of the demons and he felt that he had risen above their onslaughts. Some holy men came along. While he was making a dish of lentils for them—the lentils called *athera*—a flame from the oven burned his hand. He was greatly upset by what happened. He began to think as follows: 'Why,' he said, 'is the fire not at peace with me? Have I not won more serious battles, those with the demons? On the day of judgment when the inexhaustible fire, which tests the merits of everyone, shall enter into me, will it not burn me up if even this worldly and small fire will not spare me?'

"Tossed about by these unhappy thoughts, he was suddenly overcome by sleep, and an angel of the Lord appeared to him. 'Why are you sad, Paphnutius,' he said. 'Is it because this earthly fire is not at peace with you? There still linger in your body the urgings of the flesh. They have not yet been cleared out, and as long as their roots remain alive in your marrow they will not allow this worldly flame to be at peace with you. You will not cease to be open to its onslaught until the day when, by the very sign it gives you, you will find that all the urges within you are dead. Go. Find a young girl who is naked and very beautiful. Take hold of her, and if you find that your peace of heart remains untroubled and that the surges of the flesh remain calm, then indeed will the touch of this visible flame be gentle and unharming, as happened to the three children in the Babylonian furnace.'

"The old man was deeply affected by this revelation and he had no wish to try the experiment suggested to him by God. Instead he scrutinized his own conscience. He examined the purity of his heart, and he came to the conclusion that his chastity was not yet strong enough for such a test. 'It is no wonder,' he said, 'that when I saw the unclean spirits falling back before me I was not alert to the hostile burning fire which I had thought of as being much less terrible than the cruel onslaughts of the demons. It is a higher virtue and a more sublime grace to extinguish the cupidity within one's own flesh than, with the sign of the Cross and by the power of the Most High, to subjugate evil spirits whose attack comes from outside and to drive the devils from the bodies of the possessed by calling upon the name of God.' "

Here abba Nesteros ended his discussion of the true working of miracles. And all the time that he was teaching us he escorted us to the cell of the old man Joseph, a distance of some six miles.

Conference Eighteen

THE THREE KINDS
OF MONK

1

Having seen and talked to the three elderly men, whose discourses I wrote down at the behest of our brother Eucherios, we found ourselves with a more burning zeal to visit the remoter districts of Egypt where the number of holy men was greater and more practiced in perfection.

We reached the village of Diolcos, lying on one of the seven mouths of the Nile, and we came there not because of any requirements of travel but because we were urged on by the wish to see the holy men who were living there. We were rather like extremely zealous purchasers of goods, and we had heard that the most famous monasteries had been established there by the oldest of the fathers. So we undertook a voyage of discovery with hopes all the greater for ever more gain.

Traveling very far we raised our eager eyes to those high mounttains with their crown of virtue and we saw, first of all, abba Piamun. He was the oldest of all the anchorites living there and he was also their priest. He was like a very high beacon. He was like the city on a high mountain referred to in the gospel and he immediately shone in our sight.

I think I must silently pass over his virtues and those miraculous acts which by God's grace were revealed to our gaze as a witness to his merits. I would simply go too far beyond my plan here and beyond the limits of this book. What I have promised to hand on are not the miracles worked by God but, so far as my memory goes, the teachings and the practices of the saints. The object is to provide light for the life of perfection rather than food for the empty curiosity of my readers, food which would in no way serve to correct their faults.

The blessed Piamun welcomed us with a lively show of gladness. He also gave us the refreshment which we needed, and seeing that we were not from this area he was very interested to know where we came from and why we had come to Egypt. When he discovered that we had traveled from a Syriac monastery because of our longing for perfection he began to speak to us as follows.

2

"My sons, when a man wishes to acquire the skills of a particular art he needs to devote all his possible care and attention to the activities characteristic of his chosen profession. He must observe the precepts and, indeed, the advice of the most successful practitioners of this work or of this way of knowledge. Otherwise he is dealing in empty dreams. One does not come to resemble those whose hard work and whose zeal one declines to imitate.

"I have known some people who came here from where you live and who traveled around to the monasteries of the brethren, and all for the sake of acquiring knowledge. But it never occurred to them to practice the rules or the customs which were the objective of their travels. Nor would they withdraw into a cell where they could try to practice what they had seen and heard. They stuck to their old habits and practices, just as they had learned them, and the criticism was made of them that they had left their own provinces not for the sake of their own progress but to avoid the presence of poverty. Not only were they unable to acquire any learning but they could not even stay around here because of the sheer stubbornness of their disposition. They would make no changes in their habits of fasting, in the order in which they followed the psalms, or even in what they wore. What else could we believe except that they had come here solely for the purpose of getting fed?

3

"Now I believe that it is for the sake of God that you have come here to get to know us. You must therefore abandon all those teachings which marked your own beginnings as monks. You must take to yourselves, completely and quite humbly, all the practices and teachings of our old masters. It may be that a moment will come when you fail to grasp the deep meaning of a certain statement or of a mode of conduct.

Do not be put off, and do not fail to conform. Those seeking profit only, and struggling to imitate faithfully what they have seen their masters doing and saying, and have not argued about them, these will receive a knowledge of everything even while they are still undergoing the experience. But the man who teaches himself by engaging in arguments will never reach the truth. The Enemy will note that he relies more on his own judgment than upon that of the fathers and he will easily bring him to the point where he considers even the most useful and saving matters to be unnecessary or dangerous. The Master of deceit will take advantage of his presumptuousness and the man will hold so stubbornly to his unreasonable opinions that he will reach the stage of being convinced that the only thing that is holy is that which his own blind obstinacy deems to be right and just.

4

"What you have to learn first, therefore, is the appropriate sequence and the first steps of our profession. You must know about how they came into being and where they came from. Then it will be possible for a man to pursue more effectively the discipline of the art to which one is committed. One will be moved to practice it more eagerly when one has recognized the worth of those who originated it and established it.

"In Egypt there are three types of monk. Two of them are quite excellent. The third is a lukewarm type and is to be avoided in every way.

"The first type is that of the cenobites, those who live together in one community under the authority of an elder. Most of the Egyptian monks are of this kind.

"The second type is that of the anchorites, men who are first trained in monasteries, have achieved perfection in their way of life and who have chosen the hidden life of solitude. And our wish is to belong to this profession.

"The third type—and one to be deplored—is that of the sarabites.

"To all of those, one by one, we will devote a fuller discussion.

"The founders of these three professions are those whom, as I have said, you must first get to know. Out of this will arise the detestation of the profession to be avoided and a longing for that which ought to be followed, for it is necessarily the case that each route will take its follower to the end reached by the one who established it and founded it.

5

"The cenobitic life came into being at the time of the apostolic preaching. It was all there in that crowd of believers at Jerusalem, as described in the Acts of the Apostles. 'There was one heart and one mind among the crowd of believers, nor did anyone claim as his own whatever it was that he possessed, but all things were held in common among them' (Acts 4:32). 'They sold their possessions and their goods, and they divided the money for these among everyone, in accordance with need' (Acts 2:45). 'No one among them lacked anything. Owners of land and of houses sold them, brought the prices of what they had sold and laid them at the feet of the apostles. And this was divided among individuals in accordance with need' (Acts 2:34–35).

"As I say, that was how the whole Church was then, and very few like them can be found today in the monasteries. After the death of the apostles, however, the mass of believers began to turn lukewarm. This was especially true of those who had come from among foreign and different peoples to faith in Christ. Their belief was rudimentary and their pagan habits were deeply ingrained, and so the apostles demanded no more of them than that they abstain from 'food sacrificed to idols, from fornication, from strangled animals, and from blood' (Acts 15:29). This freedom granted to pagans because of the weakness of their elementary belief began, little by little, to contaminate the Church in Jerusalem. Every day the numbers of Jews and outsiders grew, and the zeal of that first faith began to grow cool. Not only those who came to faith in Christ but even Church leaders relaxed the original austerity. There were even quite a few who came to believe that the concessions which they saw granted to the pagans were also allowed in their own case and they did not think there was any danger in following and confessing faith in Christ side by side with ownership of goods and wealth.

"But as for those in whom there was still the zeal of the apostolic days, these remembered the old perfection and they went away from their own communities and from the company of those who believed that it was quite lawful for themselves or for the Church of God to display the neglectfulness of a more relaxed way of life. They settled in the neighborhood of cities and in more remote places and, individually and in their own way, they began to put into practice those rules which, as they remembered, had been laid down by the apostles for the whole body of the Church. And so there came into being that organized life which, as I have said, was characteristic of those disciples who had withdrawn from the contagion of the multitude.

"Gradually, with the passing of time, they were cut off from the mass of believers. Because they avoided marriage and because they kept themselves away from their parents and from the life of this world they were called monks or solitaries because of this life of solitude separated from their families. As a result of this living together on their part they were called cenobites and their cells and their quarters were called monasteries.

"This, then, was the only type of monk in the earliest days. They were first not only in time but in grace and they endured safely through all the years until the era of abba Paul and abba Antony. And we see traces of them still continuing in the monasteries where austerity is practiced.

6

"From this number of perfect men and, if I may put it so, from this most fertile root there came subsequently those flowers and those fruits, namely, the holy anchorites. As I have already said a little while ago, Saint Paul and Saint Antony were the originators of this profession. Unlike the case of some, it was not petty-mindedness nor the scourge of impatience which moved them to look for the secrets of solitude. Rather, it was the desire for greater perfection and a more contemplative route. This is so despite what is said regarding Paul, that the treachery of his own kin compelled him to flee to the desert at the time of persecution.

"And so it was that, as I have said, there arose out of the discipline of the early days another way of seeking perfection. Adherents of this are rightly called anchorites, that is, people who go aside into a retreat. It is not enough for them to have successfully trampled down the snares of the devil among men. They long to join in open combat and in clear battle against the demons. They are not afraid to push into the great hiding places of the desert. They are surely the imitators of John the Baptist, who remained in the desert throughout the whole of his life. They do like Elias and like Elisaeus, about whom the apostle had this to say: 'They wandered about dressed in the skins of sheep or goats. They were persecuted and poor—they of whom the world was unworthy. They went to live in lonely places, on mountains, in caves, in the hollows of the earth' (Heb 11:37–38). The Lord, using figurative language, had this to say about them to Job: 'Who was it that set the donkey free and loosened his chains? I have given him the desert for a home and the salt plains as his place of dwelling. He laughs at the city mob. He does not hear the complaint of a taskmaster. He will look to the mountains for his pasture and afterward he will seek all things green' (Jb 39:5–8). Furthermore, there is this in the psalms: 'Let those rescued by the Lord speak out, those whom he has bought back from the land of the enemy' (Ps 100:2). Later on there is this: 'They wandered about in a waterless solitude. They did not find the road to a city where they might live. They were hungry and thirsty. The spirit within them grew weak. In their misery they cried out to the Lord and He freed them from their needs' (Ps 100:4–6). These are the men described by Jeremiah: 'Lucky the man who bore the yoke from the days of his youth. He will sit alone and will be silent because he has taken this yoke upon himself' (Lam 3:27–28). These are the men who in their love and in their work sing, with the psalmist, 'I have become like the pelican in the desert. I have kept watch. I have become like the lonely sparrow on the roof-top' (Ps 101:7–8).

7

"The Christian religion rejoiced in these two monastic professions. But a gradual decline began to set into this scene. A very bad and unfaithful band of monks emerged subsequently. Back to life and growing once again came that dangerous plant which, at the beginning of the Church, had grown because of Ananias and Sapphira and which had been cut down by the severity of Peter. For a long time it was looked upon by monks as something detestable, something accursed, and the frightening memory of a sentence so terrible had kept it from appearing among anyone. Those first guilty of it were given no chance at all by the blessed apostle either to repent or make recompense. A speedy death had cut out the very deadly germ.

"Yet, little by little, prolonged carelessness and the passage of time ensured that many forgot the example of severe punishment set by the apostle in regard to Ananias and Sapphira. And it was then that there appeared that band of sarabites. The name *sarabites* is Coptic and they are so called because they cut themselves off from the monastic communities and take care of their own needs. They are descendants of that crowd I mentioned who prefer to put on the show of evangelic perfection rather than to take it up for what it really is. Their incentive to act in this way is envy, as well as the praises heaped upon those who prefer the utter poverty of Christ to all the riches of the world.

"These men of puny spirit concern themselves with something requiring the highest virtue or else there was some compulsion upon them to approach this profession. They hurried to bear the name of being monks, though they lacked all urge to be really like them. They have no interest in monastic discipline. They do not submit to the direction of elders and they do not learn their instructions in how to overcome their own desires. They do not accept any of the correct and formative rules deriving from sensible guidance. Their withdrawal from the world is for the sake of public show and is something done before men's eyes. Or else they remain in their own houses, enjoy the name of being monks, and continue to do what they always did. Or else they build cells for themselves, give them the title of monasteries, and then freely live in them as they choose. They never fall in with the gospel commands not to be concerned about one's daily bread and not to be taken up with worldly affairs. This is something done, without any of the doubtings of lack of faith, by those who have liberated themselves from all the wealth of this world and who have submitted themselves to monastic rules to the extent that they do not admit to having any authority over themselves. But these others, as I have said, run from monastic austerity. They live two or three to a cell. The last thing they want is to be guided by the concern and the authority of a father-superior. Their special concern is to be free of the yoke of elders, to be free to do what they themselves wish, to travel out, to wander wherever they please, to do what takes their fancy. In their activities they do more by day and by night than those who live in monasteries, though not from the same kind of faith and for the same purpose. They do this not with the intention of handing over the fruit of their work to be disposed of as their mentor thinks fit but to collect and to save money.

"Observe the great difference between both kinds of monk.

"Cenobites think nothing of the morrow. They present the fruit of their sweated labor as an offering that is most agreeable to God. But the others push the selfish concerns of their faithless souls not only into the coming day but over the length of many years. They think of God as being a liar or as one without resources, as someone unable and unwilling to live up to His promise of adequate food and clothing.

"The ceaseless plea of the cenobites is to be bereft of everything and always to be poor. The others wish for an abundance of all goods.

"The cenobites strive in their daily work to go beyond what is required of them so that whatever remains over and beyond the needs of the monastery can, at the abbot's discretion, be given to prisons or hostels, to hospitals or to the poor. The others work so that anything left after the satisfaction of daily greed can be available to their profligate wishes or saved to gratify avarice.

"Finally I wish that the sarabites would make better use of the money which, with their bad objectives, they had accumulated for themselves. They come nowhere near the virtue or the perfection of the cenobites, who earn so much money for their monasteries, hand it over each day, continue to persevere in their utterly humble submissiveness; who stand away from deciding themselves what to do with what they have earned by the sweat of their brow and who, in this daily renunciation of what they have earned, manage to renew ceaselessly the zeal of their first act of renunciation. But these others are puffed up by the fact of giving something to the poor, and every day they slide headlong to disaster.

"The cenobites continue to show the patience and the discipline with which they persevere in this profession which they once adopted. They never do what they themselves wish. Every day they are crucified to this world and are living martyrs, whereas, in the case of the others, their lukewarm spirit plunges them into damnation.

"The numbers of both sorts of monk—cenobites and anchorites— are roughly equal in this province. As for the other provinces through which I had to travel because of matters connected with the Catholic faith, I discovered that this third kind—the sarabites—flourished and indeed was almost the only kind to exist. In the days of Lucius, who was bishop of the Arian perfidy—this was in the reign of Valens—I brought help to our brothers, from Egypt and the Thebaid, who had been condemned to the mines of Pontus and of Armenia because of their loyalty to the Catholic faith. In a few towns I saw very little monastic discipline and I could not find out if the name of anchorite had ever been heard among them.

8

"Now there is a fourth type which we have seen emerging lately, men who flatter themselves with seeming to look like anchorites. At the beginning of their career such is their zeal for a short while that they seem to be in active pursuit of monastic perfection. They then turn very lukewarm. They neglect to cut out their old bad habits and faults. They are no longer satisfied to endure the yoke of humility and patience. They disdain to be ruled by elders. They look for remote cells and they wish to live alone so that with no one to bother them they can have the name among men of being patient, gentle, or humble. But this way of life and this lack of warmth prevent those once infected from ever achieving perfection. Indeed, not only do they fall short of this perfection but their faults grow much worse when there is no one there to challenge them. It is like a deadly poison within. The more it is hidden the more deeply does it generate incurable disease in a sick man. Out of reverence for the monk's cell no one dares to give open evidence of the sins of a man living alone, sins which he himself preferred to ignore rather than to cure. But the fact is that virtues are brought into being not by the concealment of sins but rather by their expulsion."

9

Germanus: "Is there any difference between a house of cenobites and a monastery, or is one thing covered by the two names?"

10

Piamun: "Many people are accustomed to use without any differentiation the terms monastery and house of cenobites.

" 'Monastery' is the name of the residence and does not imply more than the place where the monks live. 'House of cenobites' points to the character and the way of life of the profession.

"The residence of a simple monk can be called a monastery. But a place cannot be termed a house of cenobites unless one means a community of many people living together. And those places where bands of sarabites dwell are called monasteries.

11

"But I note that you belonged to an excellent group of monks before you sought out the principles of our profession. I mean that you came from the praiseworthy arena of a cenobitic house in order to push on to the high peaks of anchoritic discipline. With sincere hearts you are in search of that virtue of humility and patience which, no doubt, you learned there in the house of cenobites. And I see that you are not content simply to put on appearances, pretending humility as you speak and displaying politeness by means of affected and exaggerated gestures.

"Abba Sarapion once made elegant fun of fake humility. Someone came to him displaying the utmost self-objection by means of what he wore and what he said. In accordance with custom the old man invited him to offer up a prayer. But the other vigorously refused all his pleas, claiming to be wallowing in sinfulness to such an extent that he did not deserve even a portion of the common air. He would not sit upon his mat of reeds, choosing the ground instead. And when it came to the washing of the feet he was even less accommodating.

"When the meal was over, abba Sarapion, taking advantage of the custom of holding discussions, began to give him good and gentle advice. He told him that since he was young and strong he ought not to be lazy or footloose, that he should not be frivolously rushing in all directions. Instead, he ought to remain in his cell, as the teaching of the elders demanded, and he should choose to support himself by his own efforts rather than through the generosity of someone else, a situation which the apostle Paul took care to avoid. For laboring as he did for the sake of the gospel he could have claimed hospitality as a right. However, he preferred to work day and night to earn bread for himself and for those who were ministering along with him and who could not work with their own hands.

"Hearing these words, the young man was so filled with sadness and grief that his expression could not hide the bitterness which had arisen in his heart.

" 'My son,' said the old man, 'up to now you were loading yourself with the weight of your wrongdoing. You had no fear that in confessing such awful crimes you would be much remarked upon. I have just now given you a little bit of simple advice, which of itself implies no criticism of you and is prompted by the wish to edify and to show care. Yet, I ask you, how is it that I see you stirred by such anger that your expression has not been able to hide it nor have you been capable of putting on a pretense of being serene? Did you imagine that while you were displaying your humility you would hear from me the words "at the beginning of his discourse the just man accuses himself?" (Prv 18:7).'

"What you must cling to is genuine lowliness of heart, which comes not from show and from words but rather from the central humility of the spirit. When you give the clearest proof of patience, then your humility will shine splendidly. It will shine not when someone boasts of wrongdoing which nobody believes but rather when a man is indifferent to arrogant accusations made against him and when he endures, with peacefully gentle spirit, the wrongs done to him."

12

Germanus: "We would like to know how this tranquility may be acquired and kept. It is one thing for us to have silence laid upon us, to keep our mouths shut, to restrain all loose speech. But gentleness of heart must also be preserved by us. It can sometimes happen that while one restrains one's words one loses the peacefulness within—hence our belief that someone can only preserve the virtue of gentleness by living alone in a cell that is far away."

13

Piamun: "True patience and humility can only be acquired and kept when the innermost heart is humble. Coming from such a source it will have no need of the help provided by a cell nor of the refuge characteristic of living alone. It does not need the protection of something exterior since it is supported within by the virtue of humility, its mother and custodian.

"If we become upset by some provocation, then clearly the foundations of humility are not solidly established in us and the edifice we have raised is struck down into disastrous ruin by the onset of even a minor storm. Indeed, patience is neither praiseworthy nor admirable if its condition of tranquility remains unassailed by any hostile attacks. But it is outstanding and splendid when it remains immovable during the raging storms of temptation. The notion is there that it will be harassed and wrecked by adversity. In fact it is made all the stronger and it becomes more sharply real in a situation when there is the conviction that it will be battered. Everyone knows that passion and forebearance underlie patience, and obviously no one may be called patient except the man who has endured without rancor all the suffering heaped upon him. This is the man so rightly praised by Solomon: 'Better a patient man than a strong one, better the man who restrains his anger than the one who captures a city' (Prv 16:32). And again: 'The equable man is very rich in prudence, and the puny-minded man is certainly foolish' (Prv 14:29).

"When someone is the victim of an injury and is then consumed by the flame of anger it must not be thought that the bitterness of the affront done to him is the cause of his sin. Rather, here is evidence of a hidden infirmity, evidence that accords with the parable told by our Lord and Savior concerning the two houses, the one founded on a rock, the other built on sand. The onslaught of rains and rivers and storms was the same for both, he said. But the one built on the solidity of rock suffered no damage from such a violent battering. The one built on the unstable shifting sands collapsed at once, and the reason for the immediate ruin was quite obvious. It was not because of the beating of rains and torrents but because it had been built stupidly on sand.

"The holy man does not differ from the sinner in the fact of not being similarly tempted, but rather to the extent that the former is not overcome by some great onslaught, whereas the latter is defeated by even a minor temptation. And, as I have said, the brave endurance of some just man would not be worthy of praise if his victory were unaccompanied by temptation, for it is surely true that there can be no place for a victory where the clash of a contest is missing. 'Blessed indeed is the man who endures temptation because after passing the test he will receive the crown of life which the Lord has promised to those who love him' (Jas 1:12). According to Paul the apostle the virtue of a man is brought to perfection not amid idleness and pleasure but in infirmity. And then this saying: 'Today I have set you up into a fortified city, into a pillar of iron and a wall of bronze over all the land, over the kings and leaders of Judah, over its priests and over all the people of the earth. And they shall make war against you, and they shall not be victorious because I am with you, says the Lord, so that I may protect you' (Jer 1:18–19).

14

"I want to give you at least two examples of this patience.

"The first has to do with a woman in religious life. She was so enthralled by the virtue of patience that not only did she not turn away at the onset of temptation but she even sought out occasions of challenge before whose constant onslaughts she would not falter. She lived in Alexandria and came of well-to-do parents. She served the Lord religiously in the house which her parents had left to her.

"She came to bishop Athanasius, of happy memory, and she asked him to give over to her care of one of the widows who was being kept at the expense of the church. Let me tell you the words of her request. 'Give me one of the sisters to look after,' she said. The pontiff, seeing that she was so very eager to perform the work of mercy, gave praise to the woman's project. He gave instructions that a widow be chosen who surpassed all others in goodness of character, seriousness, and discipline. This was in order to ensure that the woman's urge to be generous would not be overcome by some drawback, that in looking for the reward due to someone helping the poor she might not experience a loss of faith on account of another woman's debased morals. The woman brought the widow to her house and lavished attention on her. The widow found her to be all modesty and gentleness.

"A few days later the woman came back to the pontiff mentioned above. 'I asked you to give me a widow whom I could help and serve in all her needs,' she said. Now he still did not grasp what it was that the woman wanted or wished. He thought that her request had been neglected by the person in charge, and so he made urgent inquiries about the reasons for this delay. When he learned that a widow superior to all the others had been chosen for this woman he quietly arranged that there be sent to the lady the worst of all the women, someone who surpassed all others in being irritable, quarrelsome, boozy, and garrulous. Such a one was easier to locate and she was handed over to the lady, who took her home and looked after her with the same attentiveness, indeed with more zeal, than had been lavished on the first one. As sole thanks for these services all she got was to have continuous outrages inflicted on her, to be persistently criticized and denounced. The woman insultingly claimed that the lady had asked for her from the bishop not in order to provide protection but to annoy and to insult her. She had taken her away from being at peace to being bothered, instead of the opposite. From continuously complaining to her this violent woman carried on to the extent that she could not refrain from doing physical violence. The lady, seeking to be ever more humble, redoubled her efforts. She learned to overcome the raging woman not so much by her own restraint as by her ever more humble submissiveness.

"The victim of every kind of indignity, she softened, through her humane gentleness, the wildness of that rowdy female. Deeply strengthened by this task she attained the longed-for and perfect virtue of patience. And she returned to the pontiff to thank him both for the wisdom he showed in the choice he had made and also for the profit which the exercise had brought to her. In accordance with her wishes, he had found her a good teacher of patience whose ceaseless insults had strengthened her every day, like the oil that toughens athletes. As a result she had been able to attain the utmost patience of soul. 'You gave me someone I could really help,' she said. 'The first woman honored me and soothed me with her own good manners.'

"Enough now about a woman. We are not simply edified by a story of this sort. We are put to shame, we who cannot preserve our patience unless, like wild animals, we go to ground in the very depths of our cells.

15

"Let me now give you the example of abba Paphnutius. He is now the priest in that desert of Scete which is renowned and which ought to be famous everywhere.

"Now Paphnutius has displayed such a love of the hidden life that the other anchorites have nicknamed him Bubalus. They have called him the Wild Ox because of this innate longing he has for solitude, because of the joy he has in always living alone.

"Even as a very young man he was preeminent in virtue and grace. The most celebrated and skilled fathers of that time admired his seriousness and his unshakable constancy. Despite his youthfulness they regarded him as equal in virtue to the elders and they chose to include him in their own ranks.

"But that malice which in the old days turned the minds of his brothers against Joseph set off the consuming fire of jealousy in one of the brethren and he was filled with the wish to sully the other man's beauty with some tarnish or stain. So he thought up the following evil plan. One Sunday he took advantage of the time when Paphnutius had gone to church from his cell. He crept in and hid his book among the weavings which the other man was accustomed to make out of palm leaves. Then, sure of the success of his trick, he went to church himself, like a man of pure and simple good conscience. When the whole solemn rite had been celebrated in the usual fashion he made complaint, in the presence of all the brethren, to Saint Isidore who at that time was the predecessor of Paphnutius as priest in the desert. He claimed that his book had been stolen from his cell. His complaint so moved the hearts of all the brethren, and especially of their priest, that at first they did not know what to think or what to do. Everyone was astounded by such an unheard-of crime. No one could remember any such thing happening before in the desert there nor what could follow such a deed. The man who made the accusation urged that everyone should remain in the church and that some people should be sent around to search all the cells of the brethren one by one.

"The task was given by the priest to three of the older men. These searched all the cells. Finally they came to the cell of Paphnutius and they found the book hidden where the culprit had concealed it among palm leaves which had been woven into *sirae*, that is to say, cords. The searchers hastened back to the church and produced the book before everyone.

"Now Paphnutius was certain of his own clear conscience. But he acted as though he acknowledged the theft. He agreed to render full satisfaction and he humbly asked to be allowed to do penance. In his modesty and humility he realized that if he tried to claim innocence of the theft, there would be added to the situation the fact that a lie had been told, since no one would suspect that matters were anything other than what had been found. So he went out of the church. He was not so much downhearted as full of trust in the judgment of God. He poured out tearful prayers continuously to God. He tripled his fast. He prostrated himself with complete humility in the sight of men.

"For nearly two weeks he submitted in this way. He was full of contrition in flesh and spirit, and on Saturday and Sunday he hastened in the morning not to receive holy communion but to prostrate himself at the church door and to ask pardon.

"He who knows the deepest secrets did not allow him to remain for long the victim of his own penance and of the disgust of the others. For the man who thought up the crime, the shameless thief of what had belonged to himself, the sly purloiner of another's good name—he it was who revealed what he had done unknown to the others. He did so at the instigation of the devil who had driven him to his own act of mischief. He was possessed by one of the cruelest of demons and he openly described all the trickery involved in his hidden crime. The designer of these fraudulent charges was the very one to uncover them. He was plagued grievously and for long by the unclean spirit. No deliverance came of the prayer of the holy men living round about, men who had received the divine gift of conquering evil spirits. Not even the outstanding grace lavished on the priest Isidore was able to drive out from the man the power that tormented him, and Isidore was someone to whom the Lord's generosity had given so great a power that any victim of possession was cured before he was brought even to the threshold of his cell. The glory of success was reserved by Christ for the young Paphnutius. His prayers alone were able to cleanse the man guilty of working against him. The man now called upon the name of the very one whose reputation he had in jealous hostility sought to take away, and it was from him that he received pardon for his sin and the end of present woe.

"Thus it was that from his youngest years Paphnutius gave clear indications of the sort of man he would be in the future. In the years when he was still a boy he showed the signs of that perfection which would come to such growth in the time of his maturity. And if we wish to arrive at the summit of a virtue such as his then we too must establish our first steps along the same path.

16

"I have told you this story for two reasons.

"First let us note the unshakable calm and constancy of this man. Now we are the victims of much less hostile attack and, hence, we should adopt a much greater stance of tranquility and patience.

"Second, let us be quite clear about the fact that we can never be fully confident in the face of the storms of temptation and the on-slaughts of the devil if the only protection of our patience and all our trust lie not in the strength of the inner man but in the closed doors of a cell, in the escape to solitude, in the company of holy men or in some other external source of defense. If He who in the gospel said, 'The kingdom of God is within you' (Lk 17:21)—if He does not give us strength of soul through His protective virtue, then it is for nothing that we seek to defeat the hostile attacks of the creatures of the air or try to avoid them in far-off places or strive to bar their approach through the protection of a dwelling place. For none of these things were lacking in the case of the holy Paphnutius and still the tempter was able to find a way to get at him. Neither the enclosing walls nor the loneliness of the desert nor the superabundant merits of that group of holy men drove off that foulest of spirits. Yet because the holy servant of God had placed his heart's hope not in externals but in that Judge of all things hidden he could not be overcome by the devices of so great an on-slaught.

"By contrast, there was the man whom jealousy drove headlong into so great a crime. Did he not have the advantage of solitude, the protection of a far-off cell, Isidore for director and priest, and the company of other holy men? And still the devil's tempest found he had built on sand and not only did it batter him but it brought his dwelling place tumbling down.

"So let us not look for peace outside ourselves and let us not count upon another's patience to rescue us from our sins of impatience. For just as the kingdom of God is within us so too is it the case that 'the enemies of a man are of his own household' (Mt 10:36). No one fights against me more than my own heart, which is surely close to me in my own household. If we are careful, however, we can suffer the minimum harm from the enemies within. When the enemies in our own household are not at war with us, then, in the tranquility of the spirit, the kingdom of God becomes a possession. To put the matter quite clearly to you, I cannot be harmed by the malice of any man if my own unquiet heart does not set me against myself. If I suffer harm it is not from the attack of an outsider but because of the snare of my own impatience. Strong and solid food is good for someone healthy and harmful to someone who is sick. It cannot be harmful unless the weakness of the person taking it is such as to reinforce its capacity for injury.

"Therefore, if it should ever happen that a like temptation should arise among brethren, we should not be driven off the path of tranquility and we should shut out the blasphemies and the violent words of the world. Furthermore, we should not be astonished by the fact that perverse and detestable men can hide in the company of saints, for as long as we tread upon and wear down the dry land of this world it will inevitably happen that the chaff destined for everlasting fire will be mixed in with the choicest fruits of the harvest. Indeed, let us remember that a Satan was found among the angels, a Judas among the apostles, and a Nicholas, author of the most depraved heresy, was in the choice company of the deacons. So it will not be surprising that the very worst of men are found in the ranks of the saints. (It is true that some people maintain that this Nicholas is not the one chosen by the apostles for the work of ministry. They cannot deny, however, that he was not one of the disciples who was of outstanding perfection, one of the very perfect whose like we rarely see in the monasteries of today.)

"But let us not linger over the ruin of that brother mentioned above who fell with such painful misfortune in that desert. Let us not think, either, of the ghastly stain which he later washed away with the great tears of repentance. Rather, let us contemplate the example of the blessed Paphnutius. We ought not to be pulled down by the fall of a man who, pretending to be a monk, gave a head to the old sin of envy. No. We should imitate completely the humility of the other man. The quiet of the desert did not suddenly produce it in him. It was acquired in the company of men. It developed and reached its peak in solitude.

"One needs to know that the disease of envy is harder to cure than any other. I would say that someone striken by its poison is almost beyond healing. This is the pestilence described figuratively by the prophet: 'See, I will send you serpents against which there are no incantations and they will bite you' (Jer 8:17). The bites of envy are quite rightly compared by the prophet to the lethal poison of the basilisk. For it was because of this that the very first to perish and to fall was the one who is the source of everything deadly. He brought about his own downfall long before he poured the virus of death over man, of whom he was jealous. 'Death came into the world because of the devil's envy. So let his own kind go on to imitate him' (Wis 2:24–25).

"The devil was first to be ruined by this scourge, and he kept at bay the cure of penance and the warmth of healing medicine. And in similar fashion those who have allowed themselves to be gnawed in the same poisonous way have barred all the efforts of the holy exorcist, for they are tormented not by the faults of the one they envy but rather by his good fortune. They are too embarrassed to admit the truth and so they look outside for extra, stupid reasons for their bad humor. And since these reasons are completely spurious and since they do not wish to publicize the deadly virus lying within their very marrow, all the work of healing them is useless. A very wise man had this very apt word to say about them: 'If the serpent bites without a hiss, there is no success for the exorcist' (Eccl 10:11). These silent bites are alone in fending off the medicine of wise men. This deadly menace is so utterly incurable that it is worsened by soothings, inflamed by serious treatment, and irritated by gifts. For 'jealousy can endure nothing,' as Solomon said (Prv 27:4). The more a neighbor advances in submissive humility, in outstanding patience, in glorious generosity, the more the jealous man is moved by the greater goads of envy and all he wants is the ruin or the death of the one he envies. Nothing of the humility of their innocent brother could soften the jealousy of those eleven patriarchs. This is how Scripture tells the story about them: 'His brothers were jealous of him because his father loved him and they could speak no peaceful word to him' (Gn 37:4). It revealed the point that their jealousy could accept no friendly gestures from their humble and obedient brother. They wanted him dead and they were barely satisfied by the crime of selling their own brother into slavery.

"So it is that of all sins envy is the most dangerous and the hardest to cure. It is stimulated by the very remedies for all the others. Thus, for instance, a person grieved by some loss is healed by a generous compensation. Someone angered by an injury done to him is mollified by a humble gesture of satisfaction. But what can you do with a man who, the humbler and kindlier you are, feels increasingly angry with you? If his anger were kindled by cupidity he could be made gentle by a gift. If he were fired by a sense of grievance or by a love of vengeance he could be overcome by soothing gestures of deference. But, in fact, what stirs his wrath is the good fortune of someone else. And is there anyone who for the sake of appeasing a jealous man would choose to abandon happiness, give up prosperity, give in to some calamity?

"This is the reason why to escape one of the lethal bites of the basilisk, to keep everything alive in us, to have ourselves, so to speak, under the living sway of the Holy Spirit Himself, we must ceaselessly beg for the help of the God to whom nothing is impossible. As regards the poisonous bites of other snakes—and here I mean the sins and the vices of the flesh—human frailty, despite the speed with which it falls into them, is just as readily purged of them. The wounds that they cause leave their own evident marks on the flesh. And although the earthly body swells up most dangerously because of them, yet some very skilled declaimer of the divine words of Scripture can provide an antidote or saving cure of those words and the rampant poison will not bring everlasting death to the soul. But like the poison spurted out by the snake, the bane of envy shuts out the very life of religion and of faith before the wound can ever be diagnosed in the body. For the fact is that a blasphemer rises up not against a man but against God. He launches his complaints against nothing other than the good fortune of his brother. He criticizes not so much the fault of a man as the judgment of God. Here surely is that 'root of bitterness cropping up' (Heb 12:15), raising itself up on high to hurl spite against the One who bestows all that is good upon man.

"Now let no one be upset when God threatens to send serpents to bite those at whose wrongdoing He is angry. For God is certainly not the author of envy. Good things are given to the humble and withheld from the proud and the reproved, and it is surely right, surely appropriate, to God's judgment that jealousy should appear as a scourge from His hand and that it should strike and consume those who, as the apostle says, are left to their own deplorable doings. As the saying has it: 'They have roused me to jealousy with what is no God and I will rouse them to jealousy with what is no people' (Dt 32:21)."

"We had longed to rise from the first lessons of the monastery to the higher grade of anchorite, and with these words of his, blessed Pianum inspired us with ever greater eagerness. It was he who taught us the first essential steps of the solitary life, the knowledge of which we were later to acquire more fully at Scete."

Index to Introduction

INDEX

Germanus, 7
God: contemplation of, 33; favor of, 1; grace of, 26; light of, 33; mercy of, 26; resistance to, 26; as sovereign, 12; as Three-in-One, 4; unity with, 21, 33; will of, 1; Word of, 23
Gregory the Great, St., 32–33

Hesychast, 13
Holy anarchy, 21, 27, 30
Holy Spirit, 14

Idleness, 20
Intercession, 11
Ireland, 32

Jerome, St., 28
"Jesus prayer," 18
John the Scot, 35

Light-mysticism, 15
Literature, 25
Luther, Martin, 26

Macarius of Egypt, 18, 21
Mary, St., 35
Meditation, 22–23
Meditations and Prayers of Anselm, The, 35
Middle Ages, 19, 21, 26, 33
Miracle-hunting, 21
Miracles, 20–21
Monasticism, 2, 9, 28, 29–30, 34
Monotony, 20
Moral growth, 3
Motives, 9–10
Mysticism, 30, 35

Nestorius the Patriarch, 2

Obedience, 28
Oneness, 3, 21
Ordinations, 30
Origenist school, 4
Origen of Alexandria, 4

Passion, 4, 25
Passionlessness, 4
Paul the Apostle, St., 36
Penitence, 11, 13, 31–32
Perfection, 8–10, 25
Plato, 3, 4

Prayer: and anxiety, 20; Cassian on, 11–14, 19; corporate, 16–17; and fanaticism, 21; life of, 14; and meditation on Scripture, 22; private, 16–17, 27; pure, 4, 15, 35; unceasing, 15, 17–18
Priesthood, 31
Provence, 5
Providence, 12
Psalms, Book of, 13
Psalter, 13
Pseudo-Dionysius the Areopagite, 35–36
Purity of heart, 4, 11, 25–26

Reformation, 26, 31
Repetition, 14
Resolution, 11
Roman Empire, 1, 31
Romania, 32
Rome, 32
Rosaries, 13
Rufinus, 28
Rule of Saint Benedict, 36
Rule of the Egyptian Saint Pachomius, 28

Sacraments, 22, 31
Scholarship, 24
Self-discipline, 28
Sexuality, 5
Sigismund, King, 17, 18
Silvanus, Abba, 9
Simplicity, 19
Sin, 11
Sinlessness, 10
"Sleepless, the," 18
Spain, 18
Syria, 1

Thankfulness, 12
Theonas, Abba, 10
Traherne, Thomas, 21
Treves, 32
Truth, 3, 6

Union of mind, 4

Vogue, Adalbert de, 10

Way of a Pilgrim, The (French), 13
"White lie," 6
Work, 19

Index to Texts

INDEX

Daniel, Book of, 48, 162
David, 86
Death, 48
Demons, 105, 135, 173, 175
Despair, 72–74
Detachment, 61
Deuteronomy, Book of: 6:4, 161; 6:7, 136; 7:1–3, 97; 13:1–3, 175; 32:7, 76; 32:21, 201; 32:32, 104; 32:33, 104
Devil: deception from, 55–56, 64–66; delays answers to prayer, 122; Hero and, 64–65; and jealousy, 200; is kept underfoot, 136; kingdom of, 46–48; thoughts from, 53; mentioned, 66, 76, 95, 98, 199
Dioclos, 183
Discernment: Antony and, 64; benefit of, 60; gift of, 61; goodness of, 60; grace of, 64, 67, 76, 80; is "the guide," 63, 64; and humility, 67–70; kinds of, 57–58; lack of, 62–65; is "the lamp of the body," 62, 63; is mother, guardian, and guide of all virtues, 64; processes of, 63; is source and root of all virtues, 67; is "the sun," 63; true, 67–70; use of, 60–79
Drunkenness, 103–04

Ecclesiastes: 5:3, 108; 5:4, 109; 8:11, 69; 10:4, 53; 10:11, 69, 200; 32:20, 171
Ecclesiasticus, 86
Egypt, 87, 141, 177, 183–84, 190
Elderly, 67–71, 74–75
Elias, 129, 157, 177, 187
Elisaeus, 157, 187
Enoch, 87
Envy, 196–201
Ephesians, Letter to the, 63, 86
Eternal life, 40
Eucherios, 183
Eunomian deception, 176
Exodus, Book of: 16:3, 88; 22:21, 121; 22:27, 121; 32:31–32, 112; 33:20, 51
Ezechiel, the Prophet, 97
Ezekiel (Ezechiel), Book of, 86, 97

Faith, 144
False modesty, 70

Fasting, 42, 61–62, 64, 76
Fear: degrees of, 152; of earthly law, 143; of hell, 143–44; of the Lord, 143, 149, 151; love and, 151; servile, 153
Forgiveness, 115
Fornication, 72, 171
Free will, 52, 92, 96–100, 150

Galatians, Letter to the: 1:1, 123; 1:4, 123; 2:2, 75; 4:4–5, 161; 4:10, 166; 4:22–27, 160; 5:17, 44; 6:2, 149
Genesis, Book of: 1:26, 126; 5:24, 87; 12:1, 83, 85, 92; 37:4, 200
Gergashites, 97
Germanus, 37, 67, 92
Gifts, spiritual, 174
Gluttony, 76
God: arranges everything, 113; as Author of human salvation, 95; to cling to, 42, 45–46, 131; contemplation of, 43, 46, 50, 102, 111, 113; and free will, 92–93, 96–100; grace of, 72, 74, 93, 98, 117, 134; journey to, 158; kingdom of, 38–39, 46–49, 113; knowledge of, 45, 50–51; of the living, 48; love for, 45, 145; loves us, 129–30, 145; mercy of, 72, 96, 114; of peace, 96; permission of, 98; providence of, 98–99, 173; and temptation, 72, 96; things of, 43; and our thoughts, 52–53; union with, 129–30; vocation from, 83, will of, 98, 113. See also Holy Spirit, Jesus Christ
Good deeds, 44–45
Greed, 68–69

Hagar, 160
Healing, 173–74
Heart, purity of, 39, 40–41, 45, 61, 80, 170, 181
Hebrews, Letter to the: 4:12, 64; 5:14, 64; 9:4–5, 164; ch. 11, 49; 11:5, 87; 11:24–26, 149; 11:37–38, 187; 12:9, 50; 12:15, 201; 12:22–23, 50; 13:20–21, 97
Hell, 47, 48
Hero, 64
Hittites, 97
Hivites, 97

INDEX

Holy Spirit, 47, 53, 60, 112, 135, 163, 176, 201
Hope, 144, 151
Hopelessness, 71
Hosea, Book of: 4:6, 170; 4:12, 166; 7:9, 71; 10:12,162, 170; 14:9, 94
Humility, 134, 164, 179, 191–93, 196–200

Innocence, 134, 137
Isaiah, Book of: 6:10, 173; 11:2, 153; 29:9, 105; 30:20–21, 168; 30:23, 172; 33:6, 152; 35:10, 47; 46:10, 114; 47:13, 165; 49:6, 150; 51:3, 47; 53:7, 123; 58:6, 121; 58:9, 121; 58:11–12, 168; 60:17–20, 47; 65:2, 99; 65:17–18, 47; 66:23, 47
Iscariot, Judas, 53, 85, 199
Iscariot, Simon, 5
Isidore, St., 196
Israel, 97

James, Letter of: 1:12, 115, 194; 1:17, 96; 1:19, 163; 2:13, 115
James the Apostle, St., 129
Jealousy, 196–201
Jebusites, 97
Jeremiah, Book of: 1:10, 156; 1:18–19, 194; 2:11, 128; 3:6, 165; 5:21, 170; 8:17, 199; 8:22, 90; 9:1, 119; 10:23, 94; 32:39–40, 97
Jeremiah, the Prophet, 97, 119
Jerusalem, 119
Jesus Christ: cross of, 58; as the fullness of purity, 129; and Martha and Mary, 42–43; prayed, 110–11, 123; and prayer, 128–29; presence of, 50; and riches, 91; simplicity of, 166; suffering for, 95; temptation of, 55; union with, 129–30; mentioned, 49, 98, 161, 164
Job, Book of, 74, 188
Joel, Book of, 104
John, the Abbot, 56, 158–59
John, Gospel of: 2:19, 123; 3:13, 49; 3:16, 123; 7:18, 112; 7:26, 129; 8:35, 152; 8:44, 86; 10:18, 123; 11:26, 87; 11:41–42, 111; 12:26, 48; 13:2, 53; 13:27, 53; 13:34–35, 180; 14:2, 151; 15:4, 96; 15:5, 96; 15:13, 151; 15:14, 152; 15:14–15, 151; 15:19, 87; 16:15, 145; 16:20,

47; 17:4, 111; 17:16, 87; 17:19, 111, 17:21, 129; 17:22–23, 130; 17:24, 111, 130
John the Apostle, St., 129, 171
John the Baptist, St., 187
1 John: 1:8, 148; 1:10, 148; 3:9, 148; 4:1, 54; 4:10, 129; 4:17, 148; 4:18, 150, 152; 4:18–19, 145; 5:14, 122; 5:16, 148; 5:18, 148
Joseph, 116, 196
Joseph the anchorite, 142, 182–201
Judaism, 66
Judas Iscariot, 53, 85, 199
Judith, Book of, 84

1 Kings, 74
3 Kings, 53
Knowledge: and contemplation, 156; and humility, 164; kinds of, 155; practical, 155–56, 162, 175; of Scripture, 169; spiritual, 155–63, 167–70; true, 171; and worship, 169–70

Lamentations, Book of, 118, 188
Lazarus, 49
Laziness, 71, 76
Leviticus, 164
Literature, 166–67
Lord's Prayer, 112–16
Lot, 157
Love: expels fear, 145, 150; Godlike, 89, 129, 144–47; of goodness, 145; is higher than all charisms, 151; perfect, 145, 150, 153–54; will never cease, 45, 151; and zeal, 144, 146
Lucius, 190
Luke, Gospel of: 4:27, 175; 6:24, 90; 6:25, 47; 9:49, 179; 9:50, 179; 10:20, 179, 180; 10:40, 43; 10:41–42, 43; 11:3, 114; 11:8, 121; 11:9–10, 121; 12:47, 147; 14:26, 83; 15:17–19, 145; 16:21, 91; 17:5, 95; 17:10, 144; 17:20–21, 46, 198; 19:17–19, 47; 21:34, 103; 22:31–32, 95; 23:24, 111, 149

Macarius, 157, 176–77
Malachi, Book of, 147, 152
Mardochaeus, 53
Mark, Gospel of, 96, 120, 174
Martha, 42–43

INDEX